CERTAIN TRUMPETS

The Call of Leaders

—

Garry Wills

Simon & Schuster
New York London Toronto
Sydney Tokyo Singapore

SIMON & SCHUSTER
Rockefeller Center
1230 Avenue of the Americas
New York, New York 10020

Designed by Levavi & Levavi

Manufactured in the United States of America

1   3   5   7   9   10   8   6   4   2

Library of Congress Cataloging-in-Publication Data

Wills, Garry, date.
    Certain trumpets: the call of leaders/Garry Wills.
        p.   cm.
    Includes bibliographical references and index.
    1. Leadership—Case studies.   2. Power (Social sciences)—Case
studies.   3. Social participation—Case studies.   I. Title.
HM141.W525   1994   94–6526
303.3′4—dc20   CIP

ISBN: 0-671-65702-X

A leatherbound signed first edition of this book has been published by
The Easton Press.

To Natalie
my leader

For if the trumpet give an
uncertain sound, who shall
prepare himself to the battle?
—I Corinthians 14.8

Contents

—◆—

Introduction

I had just turned seventeen, did not know Los Angeles, had never even driven in a big city. I had certainly never backed a swivel trailer up to a loading dock. But my father gave me a map, marked a warehouse's location, and told me to deliver a refrigerator there. I would have to get someone to help me unload it when I arrived. It was very clever of him. I knew what he was doing. But I complied anyway.

I had a chip on my shoulder, since my father had left my mother to marry a (much younger) Hollywood model. While I was in California for a high school contest, he asked me to work at his nascent business for the rest of the summer. But for that offer, I would not have stayed—I needed a job in any event. He knew that the way to recruit a resisting son-employee was to give me independence—not only in things like deliveries, but in sales and purchasing of household equipment. If I failed, that might break down my resistance. If I didn't, pride in the work might renew a bond that had been broken. Paradoxically, by giving me independence he got me to do his will. That is the way leadership works, reciprocally engaging two wills, one leading (often in disguised ways), the other following (often while resisting). Leadership is always a struggle, often a feud.

Why, after all, should one person do another person's will? The answer that used to be given is simple: the leader is a superior person, to whom inferiors should submit. But modern democracies are as little sympathetic to this scheme as I was to the authority of my father. Patriarchal society, it is true, was rooted in a radical inequality between leaders and followers. Even ancient Athens, the first western democracy, submitted to "the best man," according to Thucydides:

> [Pericles], a man clearly above corruption, was enabled, by the respect others had for him and his own wise policy, to hold the multitude in a voluntary restraint. He led them, not they him; and since he did not win his power on compromising terms, he could say not only what pleased others but what displeased them, relying on their respect.[1]

Some still subscribe to that notion of leadership. How often have we heard that we lack great leaders now, the clearly virtuous kind, men like George Washington and Abraham Lincoln? The implication is that we could become great again with a great man to guide us. We would not mind submitting to anyone *that* good. (Of others we continue to be wary.)

I shall be arguing in this book that the Periclean type of leadership occurs rarely in history, if at all. Scholars have questioned Thucydides' description of Pericles' position—Athenians seemed quicker than most to *ostracize* leaders who thought themselves above the people.[2] Why *should* people immolate their own needs and desires to the vision of some superior being? That has happened in some theocratic societies—but then people were obeying *God* in his representative; and it was their own belief in God's will that constrained them.

In a democracy, supposedly, the leader does not pronounce God's will *to* the people but carries out what is decided *by* the people. Some might object that the leader is, in that case, mainly a follower—he or she does what the community says when it "speaks" through elections, through polls, through constituent pressure. Such leaders are not, like the Pericles of Thucydides, able to displease their followers. They compromise their principles. They are bribed, if not with money, then with acceptance, or office, or ego satisfaction.

We seem stuck, then, between two unacceptable alternatives—the leader who dictates to others, or the one who truckles to them. If leaders *dictate*, by what authority do they take away people's right to direct their own lives? If, on the contrary, they truckle, who needs or respects such weathervanes?

Most of the how-to manuals on leadership assume one or other of these models—or, inconsistently, both. The superior-person model says the leader must become *worthy* of being followed—more disciplined than others, more committed, better organized. This sends aspiring leaders to the mirror, to strike firm-jawed poses, to cultivate self-confidence and a refusal to hedge.

Or the leader is taught to be ingratiating. This is the salesmanship or Dale Carnegie approach—how to win friends and influence people. It treats followers as customers who "buy" the leader's views after these have been consumer-tested and tailored to maximum acceptance.

The *followers* are, in this literature, a hazy and not very estimable lot—people to be dominated or served, mesmerized or flattered. We have thousands of books on leadership, none on followership. I have heard college presidents tell their students that schools are meant to train leaders. I have never heard anyone profess to train followers. The ideal seems to be a world in which everyone is a leader—but who would be left for them to be leading?

Talk about the nobility of leaders, the need for them, our reliance on them, raises the clear suspicion that followers are *not* so noble, not needed—that there is something demeaning about being a follower. In that view, leaders only rise by sinking others to subordinate roles. Leaders have a vision. Followers respond to it. Leaders organize a plan. Followers get sorted out to fit the plan. Leaders have willpower. Followers let that will replace their own.

We have long lists of the leader's requisites—he or she needs determination, focus, a clear goal, a sense of priorities, and so on. We easily forget the first and all-encompassing need. The leader most needs followers. When those are lacking, the best ideas, the strongest will, the most wonderful smile have no effect. When Shakespeare's Welsh seer, Owen Glendower, boasts that "I can call spirits from the vasty deep," Hotspur deflates him with the commonsense answer: "Why, so can I, or so can anyone. But will they come when you do call them?"[3] It is not the noblest call that gets answered, but the *answerable* call.

Abraham Lincoln did not have the highest vision of human equality in his day. Many abolitionists went farther than he did in recognizing the moral claims of slaves to instant freedom and something approaching a recognition of their human dignity. Lincoln had limited political goals, and he was willing to compromise even those. He knew that no one could be elected in or from Illinois if he espoused full equality for blacks—so he unequivocally renounced that position:

I am not, nor ever have been, in favor of bringing about, in any way, the social and political equality of the white and black races . . . I am not, nor ever have been, in favor of making voters or jurors of negroes, nor of qualifying them to hold office, nor of intermarrying with white people; and I will say, in addition to this, that there is a physical difference between the white and black races which I believe will forever forbid the two races living together on terms of political and social equality. And inasmuch as they cannot so live, while they do remain together, there must be the position of superior and inferior; and I, as much as any other man, am in favor of having the superior position assigned to the white race.[4]

But for that pledge, Lincoln had no hope of winning office. The followers were setting the terms of acceptance for their leader. He could not issue calls they were unprepared to hear. (He *could* do it, of course—as Owen Glendower can shout summonses down into the deep. But it would be a waste of time.)

This Lincoln has disappointed people who think followers should submit to a leader's superior vision, those who want the leader to be active, the followers passive. Lincoln's career shows response from both sides of the process. His leadership was a matter of *mutually* determinative activity, on the part of the leader *and* the followers. Followers "have a say" in what they are being led to. A leader who neglects that fact soon finds himself without followers. To sound a certain trumpet does not mean just trumpeting one's own certitudes. It means sounding a specific call to specific people capable of response.

Does this remove or reduce the heroic note from Lincoln's leadership—as if he were only *allowed* to lead, by followers who could withhold their response? Well, what is the alternative—people who cannot refuse to follow? If that were the case, the leader would be marshaling automatons, not voluntary respondents.

It is odd that resentment should be felt toward the demands of followers when the limiting power of *circumstance* is so readily accepted. Even the most ardent hero worshipers of Winston Churchill admit that he needed an occasion for the exercise of his skills. But for World War II, we would never have known what he could do in the way of rallying English spirit. Yet the followers are even more intimate in their cooperation with the leader than are external circumstances. The leader can have the skill for his or her role, the occasion for its use, and still lack followers who will respond to the person or the moment.

So much for the idea that a leader's skills can be applied to all occasions, that they can be taught outside a historical context, learned as a "secret" of control in every situation. A leader whose qualities do not match those of potential followers is simply irrelevant. The world is not playing his or her game. My favorite example of this is the leadership of Syrian holy men in the fifth century of the Common Era.[5] Those men, who made policy for whole communities, were revered for their self ravaging austerity. The man who had starved himself most spectacularly was thought the best equipped to advise pious consultants. So delegations went to consult Simeon the "Stylite" (Pillar Man), perched in his midair hermitage. Leadership was entirely conditioned by the attitudes of contemporary followership. Who would now write a manual called *The Leadership Secrets of Simeon Stylites*, telling people to starve and whip and torture themselves into command positions?

Closer to our time, Thomas Jefferson thought the French Revolution had been less successful than the American one, not because the French lacked leaders but because they lacked discerning followers. A corrupt people is not responsive to virtuous leadership. The French spirit had been sapped, he claimed, by superstition (Catholicism) and despotism (monarchy). Napoleon, to retain the people's allegiance, had to revert to both, calling on the pope to crown him emperor.[6]

It may seem that the Lincoln example has moved us too far from the Periclean "best man" toward the Dale Carnegie accommodator. If the leader is just an expediter of what other people want, a "resource" for their use, the people are not being led but serviced.

But Lincoln had no clear expression of popular will to implement. He had to *elicit* the program he wanted to serve, and that always involves *affecting* the views one is consulting. Even pollsters, seeking to understand what is on the minds of people, affect the outcome by their mode of questioning. In Lincoln's constituency were some abolitionists, many defenders of slavery, many more who wanted to avoid facing the issue of slavery. Unlike the abolitionists, who were leaders of a small elite putting pressure on the government from outside, Lincoln had to forge a combination of voters who would join him in at least minimal disapproval of slavery. He had to convince some people that it was in their own interest not to let the problem fester—he told them they could not *afford* to take Stephen Douglas's "hands-off" attitude.

Many voters resisted Lincoln—as I did my father in the summer of 1951. Lincoln deferred to some of their prejudices—left them independent in that sense—in order to win agreement on a policy of (at least) some hope for ultimate manumission. He argued in terms of his listeners' own commitment. They celebrated the Declaration of Independence, with its claim that all men are created equal. How could they stay true to their political identity, based on the Declaration, if they did not at some level oppose slavery? By keeping this option open for gradual approximation, Lincoln was able to move at a later period for more direct action on the problem. In that sense, he temporized not to evade the problem but to *prevent* its evasion. G. K. Chesterton perfectly captured the delicacy of his operation:

> He loved to repeat that slavery was intolerable while he tolerated it, and to prove that something ought to be done while it was impossible to do it. . . . But, for all that, this inconsistency beat the politicians at their own game, and this abstracted logic proved most practical after all. For, when the chance did come to do something, there was no doubt about the thing to be done. The thunderbolt fell from the clear heights of heaven.[7]

In order to know just how far he could go at any moment, Lincoln had to understand the mix of motives in his fellow citizens, the counterbalancing intensities with which the different positions were held, and in what directions they were changing, moment by moment. The leader needs to understand followers far more than they need to understand him. This is the time-consuming aspect of leadership. It explains why great thinkers and artists are rarely the leaders of others (as opposed to influences on them). The scientist absorbed in the solution of his problems does not have the energy or patience to understand the needs of a number of other people who might be marshaled to deal with the problem. That is something the popularizer of the great man's thought usually does. More important, the pure scientist does not *tailor* his view of, say, the atom to whatever audience he hopes to influence, as Lincoln trimmed and hedged on slavery in order to make people take small steps in the direction of facing the problem.

My father was a natural leader who acted in small arenas. Even as a child, I thought it childish of him to want to get his way all the time. I did not notice then that he got his way by entering into the minds of others and finding something there that would respond to his attentions— as, on a vastly different scale, Lincoln found a grudging acceptance of the Declaration's pledge on which to build his strategy of emancipation. My father's tactics were different with me, with my sister, with the golfing friends I observed him with while caddying. There is something selfless in the very selfishness of leaders—they must see things as the followers see them in order to recruit those followers.

If the followers get marshaled toward action by a leader, the leader need not be loved or admired (though that can help). I had no great admiration for my father when I found myself responding to his initiatives. Conversely, one can admire or love people who are not, by virtue of that love, leaders.

Imagine a meeting called to consider a course of action—let us say, to mount a protest against an employer whose hiring and promotion practices discriminate against women. A speaker rises who is stunningly eloquent. Listener A knows and admires the speaker, would go anywhere to hear her speak, hopes to emulate her eloquence in his own way; but he does not care about the issue, and the speech does not bring him any closer to caring. Listener B, on the contrary, has never met the speaker, does not particularly like her, is disposed to resent the employer but had no hope of finding allies to resist him, and is now heartened to act in conjunction with others responding to the speaker. Who is the follower here? If, as seems certain, it is Listener B, then admiration, imitation, and affection are not necessary to followership. Agreement on a *goal* is necessary.

So far I have been discussing just two things—leaders and followers. That is better at least, than treatments dealing with only one thing—leaders. But the discussion cannot get far without a third thing—the goal. This is not something *added on* to the other two. It is the reason for the other two's existence. It is also the equalizer between leader and followers. The followers do not submit to the person of the leader. They *join* him or her in pursuit of the goal. My father and I were working together for the success of his new business. Of course, he had separate motives for wanting me there, and I had motives for not wanting to be there. We could not share *those* motives, unique to our own situation. It was the thing we *could* share that created the possibility of leadership.

It is time for a definition: the leader is one who mobilizes others toward a goal shared by leader and followers. In that brief definition, all three elements are present, and indispensable. Most literature on leadership is unitarian. But life is trinitarian. One-legged and two-legged chairs do not, of themselves, stand. A third leg is needed. Leaders, followers, and goals make up the three equally necessary supports for leadership.

The goal must be *shared*, no matter how many other motives are present that are not shared. Go back to the meeting that called for a protest at employer discrimination. The speaker may have had many ancillary motives for speaking—to show off her rhetorical style, to impress a sexual partner in the audience, to launch a larger political career. Her listeners surely would have many motives—some to improve their prospects with the employer, or their regard among fellow workers. But the followers *become* followers only insofar as they agree with the speaker on a plan of action against the employer.

This plan is cast in terms of justice, though it is easy to think this is only a rationale for the mix of various motives, some shared, some not. Each is in this to get something different. David Hume, the eighteenth-century philosopher, said people obey others for their *own* advantage, and this writhing of various wormlike urges for advantage is far from the picture of idealistic leaders and docile followers.

Yet Hume, perceptive as he was, knew that people follow most reliably when they are convinced that what they are doing is right. He knew the *utility* of that belief.[8] If, at the meeting to discuss discrimination, only those who would benefit directly by the protest were to join the speaker, that would limit the followership from the outset. And that small number would always be fraying away. The boss could buy off dissent by special favors to a few of the activists, or threats to the weak-hearted. Once one person got what *she* wanted, there would be no future motive for supporting her sisters. Private advantage shifts constantly, and is a poor basis for public action. That is why Lincoln based his policy on the *moral* claim of the Declaration of Independence. Some thought he did not go far enough, others that he went too far; but the moral ground of the Declaration was both broad and narrow enough to accommodate many positions while remaining fixed itself.

Lincoln had to persuade voters. He could not force them. Where coercion exists, to the extent of its existence, leadership becomes unnecessary or impossible. Loose uses of the word "lead" can mislead. We talk of a policeman leading his prisoner to jail. But the captor is not a leader in our sense—he is a captor. Though he is mobilizing another toward a goal, it is not a goal they share in their intentions. The prisoner's goal is to get as far away from the prison as possible.

A slave master buying labor can "lead" slaves to his plantation, but that does not make him their leader. He is their owner. If I had worked for my father only because I needed the money and could get it nowhere else, I would not have been a follower, just an employee. Coercion is not leadership, any more than is mesmerism. Followers cannot be automatons. The totalitarian jailer who drugs a prisoner into confession of a crime has not *led* him to some shared view of reality.[9]

James MacGregor Burns's well-known definition of leadership, though it tries to cover all bases, is inadequate precisely because it leaves out this note of a goal *shared* by leader and followers:

> Leadership over other human beings is exercised when persons with certain motives and purposes mobilize, in competition or conflict with others, institutional, political, psychological, and other resources so as to arouse, engage, and satisfy the motives of followers.[10]

Any person who *affects* others is a leader, by this definition. Hitler's enormities, let us say, arouse hatred in me, mobilize me, and that hatred is satisfying to me—am I, then, a follower of Hitler? Not when the goals of our action are so different. My aim is to destroy Hitler. That is not his aim. Hitler's followers shared, at some level, his goals—vindication of German complaints about the Versailles treaty, the restoration of discipline in society, the glorification of the German nation (and, to varying degrees, the German race) at the expense of others.

Burns's definition would cover all kinds of influence on others—a musician's arousing of pleasure in the audience, a celebrity's gratification of curiosity. A person does not become a "follower" of Bach by being aroused and satisfied. A reader of the *National Enquirer* "follows" reports on Cher or Michael Jackson, but is not a follower of them toward some shared goal. A thinker may be influenced by the philosophy of Ludwig Wittgenstein, but their wills were never consciously engaged in cooperative movement toward a goal. (On Wittgenstein's influence, see chapter 10.) A fan of Madonna is not like a soldier in Joan of Arc's army. Influence is not, of itself, leadership. The weather influences us. So do earthquakes, or background music in public places.

The leader does not just vaguely affect others. He or she takes others toward the object of their joint quest. That object defines the *kind* of leadership at issue. Different types of leaders should be distinguished more by their goals than by the personality of the leader (the most common practice). The crisis of mere subsistence on a life raft calls for one type of leader. Democratic stability for another. Revolutionary activity for still a third. The compromise and flexibility of Lincoln were appropriate for his kind of leadership. But in his own time other leaders had to be quite different in their methods. General Grant could not sound out his military "constituents." William Lloyd Garrison could not temporize on principle when leading the abolitionists. Harriet Tubman, organizing raids to rescue slaves in the South, could not lead by discussion-group methods.

It is one of the major disservices of the "superman" school of leadership that it suggests a leader can command *all* situations with the same basic gifts. Businessmen study the leadership style of General Patton. People assume that Napoleon would make a good CEO—which is like assuming that he would make a good Simeon Stylites. General Grant proved that a great military commander is not necessarily, by reason of his martial success, a good political leader in an electoral democracy—as Lyndon Johnson proved that a superb Senate leader can make a poor president.

Since leadership must differ from situation to situation, it will not be treated in the book as a single thing. I have considered sixteen different *kinds* of leadership—and, of course, there are subdivisions within those. (The norms for choosing the types are discussed in the Appendix—where I encourage readers to join the intellectual game of improving on my choices.) Those chosen are not the "greatest" leaders, but the ones who seemed to exemplify the distinctive type. Skills overlap from type to type, without obscuring the fact that the military leader's goal is quite different from the social reformer's. A Napoleon's leadership resembles only very distantly an Eleanor Roosevelt's. It is the goal that, in the first place, sets the type. The tactics will be affected, also, by the followers available.

It is easier to see the type when the exemplar is large in scale. Yet not every military leader can be (or should be) a Napoleon, not every politician an FDR, not every intellectual leader a Socrates. What is said about the outsize figure can be applied, *mutatis mutandis*, to leaders in a smaller sphere. The military adjutant has something to ponder in the career of Napoleon, or the precinct worker in Roosevelt's techniques. Templates from the past can be laid over living leaders around us.

I try further to define each person I study by considering an *antitype* to him or her, one who exemplifies the same characteristics by contrast. Roger Smith shows how Perot succeeded by the way he (Smith) failed. The marketing leadership Perot had is made clearer by considering its lack in Smith. For both types and the antitypes I do not offer brief biographies. Only the aspects of their careers that exemplify the stated kind of leadership (or its lack) will be emphasized. Thus Napoleon's military career is considered apart from his legislative and imperial politics.

Most important, I hope that readers will keep in mind the different types of *followers* appropriate to historically conditioned goals. Not many of us will be leaders; and even those who are leaders must also be followers much of the time. This is the crucial role. Followers judge leaders. Only if the leaders pass that test do they have any impact. The potential followers, if their judgment is poor, have judged themselves. If the leader takes his or her followers to the goal, to great achievements, it is because the followers were capable of that kind of response. Jefferson said the American people responded to revolution in a way that led to a free republic, while the French responded to their revolution in a way that led to an imperial dictatorship. The followers were as much to blame for the latter development as was Napoleon. In the same way, the German people were jointly responsible for Hitler's atrocities. He was powerless to act without followers.

Show me your leader, and you have bared your soul. You respond only to one who has set certain goals. You are responsible for that activity, for motion toward those goals. If leadership is mysterious and often scary, so is followership. That is why some would prefer not to follow at all. At the dawn of the ancient Greek achievement, Hesiod had already identified the problem with people who will neither lead nor follow:

> The best is he who calls men to the best.
> And those who heed the call are likewise blessed.
> But worthless who call not, heed not, but rest.[11]

Some people lament a current lack of leaders, implying that they would become wonderful followers if only some leader worthy of them came along. But perhaps they have not been looking very hard. Others think that if the president is not a leader to their liking, the whole national scene is empty. But, throughout our history, the great leaders have not been only or mainly in the White House. Except in time of war or other crisis, a democratic leader is usually a reconciler of voting blocs rather than a leader of embattled causes. Resisted change has been accomplished by abolitionists, suffragists, labor organizers, civil rights defenders, antiwar activists.

In our own day, vast changes have been taking place, with strong leaders on both sides of each issue. Dr. King led the integration struggle, and George Wallace opposed it, with great skill. No social change has been more vast than that of women's place in society. Leaders on one side, like Gloria Steinem and Faye Wattleton, have been met and resisted by a Phyllis Schlafly or a Beverly LaHaye. The environmental movement, the consumer movement, the gay rights movement have had devoted leaders, and devoted opposition. Randall Terry and his followers have been inventive and determined in their opposition to abortion. A Ralph Nader on the left faces a leader on the right like William F. Buckley. We do not lack leaders. Various trumpets are always being sounded. Take your pick. We lack sufficient followers. That is always the real problem with leadership. Calls are always going down into the vasty deep; but what spirits will respond?

1.

ELECTORAL LEADER

Franklin Roosevelt

S ome believed, in the past, that leadership was at odds with democracy. They thought it contradictory for leaders to depend on followers. Thucydides, after claiming that Pericles told the Athenians what to do, not vice versa, went on to draw this conclusion: "What was called a democracy was, in fact, the rule of one man."[1] If Pericles had been ruled by the people, only then would Athens have been a democracy.

Even when democratic leaders are wooing voters, they claim to be taking lonely stands on principle, not acting from "expediency." Senator John F. Kennedy, when he wrote (in a way) a book about other senators, *Profiles in Courage*, found courage only in those who defied their constituents—with the result, sometimes, that they lost the constituents' support. Kennedy praised them at the very point where they *ceased* to be leaders, to have followers. He quotes with approval Daniel Webster's boast that he was able "to push my skiff from the shore alone."[2] That may be a proper credential for the lonely genius, the martyr to a truth, the austere intellect—people who forge their own souls in fierce independence. But what have such heroes to do with leading other people? Einstein was a great man, but he would have made a poor congressman. The politician's skills may not be the highest, but they are distinct and necessary, and no popular leader can dispense with them.

Praise of the political leader *as a compromiser* is so rare that, when we find an example of it, it sounds more like satire than sincere praise. Here, for instance, is a tribute to the nineteenth-century British statesman, Sir Robert Peel, from the brilliant journalist Walter Bagehot:

> From a certain peculiarity of intellect and fortune, he was never in advance of his time. Of almost all the great measures with which his name is associated, he attained great eminence as an opponent before he attained even greater eminence as their advocate. On the Corn-Laws, on the currency, on the amelioration of the universal code, on Catholic emancipation, he was not one of the earliest laborers or quickest converts. He did not bear the burden and heat of the day; other men labored, and he entered into their labors. As long as these questions remained the property of first-class intellects, as long as they were confined to philanthropists or speculators, as long as they were only advocated by austere intangible Whigs, Sir Robert Peel was against them. As soon as these pressures, by the progress of time, the striving of understanding, the conversion of receptive minds, became the property of second-hand intellects, Sir Robert Peel became possessed of them also. He was converted at the conversion of the average man. His creed was, as it ever had been, ordinary; but his extraordinary abilities never showed themselves so much. He forthwith wrote his name on each of those questions; so that it will be remembered as long as they are remembered.[3]

Some would think this very grudging praise, or even a form of indirect attack. But everything said here of Peel could also have been said about Lincoln. He, too, renounced the high ideals of the abolitionists until key portions of the people would accept some *parts* of them.

There is a tendency to downplay the degree to which great political leaders are responsive to demands made on them by the electorate. We like to believe that in some golden age there were leaders of such recognized integrity that the American people simply accepted their determinations, issued from on high. But even Washington, in the deferential eighteenth century, was solicitous enough of public opinion to be called cowardly by some of his critics.

In the twentieth century, only one president has been consistently rated among the top three or four chief executives of our history—Franklin Delano Roosevelt. He has been taken as a model of leadership by many authors, notably Richard Neustadt, who wrote the most influential modern book on presidential power:

No President in this century has had a sharper sense of personal power, a sense of what it is and where it comes from; none has had more hunger for it, few have had more use for it, and only one or two could match his faith in his own competence to use it. Perception and desire and self-confidence, combined, produced their own reward. No modern President has been more nearly the master in the White House.[4]

The emphasis is all on the leader's internal qualities—mainly his confidence, ambition, and determination: "Roosevelt had a love affair with power. . . . Roosevelt's methods were the product of his insights, his incentives, and his confidence."[5] Neustadt describing Roosevelt sounds like Thucydides describing Pericles—here, at last, is a ruler who can, by sheer mastery, impose his views on the multitude.

But another school of historians—including the eminent Richard Hofstadter—has described Roosevelt as one who veered with shifting popular responses. "He was content in large measure to follow public opinion."[6] Because he was "a public instrument of the most delicate receptivity," Roosevelt proved that "flexibility was both his strength and his weakness." The result was great energy employed in "harum-scarum" ways: "Hoover had lacked motion, Roosevelt lacked direction."[7]

Some more recent treatments of Roosevelt—notably Kenneth Davis's multivolume biography—have been more hostile than Hofstadter in describing Roosevelt's subservience to public opinion. And, in fact, FDR's record seems hard to reconcile with the Neustadt picture of firm control. In New York politics, Roosevelt first opposed, then cooperated with, the Tammany political machine. He supported, then opposed, Al Smith; promoted, then abandoned, the League of Nations—"the first Democratic candidate [for president] who explicitly repudiated the League."[8] He fluttered back and forth on Prohibition. As president, he reversed himself on the balanced budget, on business consolidation, on farm subsidies, on labor protection, on aid to Europe. Friends as well as foes, from both the right and the left, noticed that the probusiness "First New Deal" of 1932 was profoundly at odds with the prolabor "Second New Deal" of 1935—and many ascribed the change to Roosevelt's fear that the populist Huey Long was taking away some of his support on the left.

Which is it to be—the masterful Roosevelt of Neustadt, or the scrambler after popular acceptance of Hofstadter? Can the two be reconciled? Not if we keep as our ideal the Periclean man, above the need for popular acceptance. If Roosevelt had power, it came precisely from his responsiveness to public opinion. And that came, indirectly, from the crushing blow that took from him, at the age of thirty-nine, all future use of his legs.

Students of Roosevelt are agreed that the polio attack of 1921 profoundly changed him. He might have become president without having to surmount that obstacle, but it is unlikely that he would have been a great (or even a good) president. Before he was crippled, Roosevelt had been a genial glad-hander, an acceptable politician considered lightweight by the pros (men like Al Smith), too anxious to please, clumsily ingratiating. Even in pictures from that time, he seems a dithery Bertie Wooster in his straw boater. His caustic cousin, Alice Roosevelt Longworth, called him a sissy and a "mama's boy." As the sole child of the frostily patrician Sara Delano Roosevelt, he had been sheltered from hardship, cushioned in privilege.

At the least, then, the struggle to walk again—always defeated, but never quite given up—toughened Roosevelt. His legs withered away; but, from the waist up, the willowy youth became a barrel-chested man able to swing the useless parts of his body around to give an artful impression of overall strength. Some say that the suffering imposed on him deepened his sympathy with others who were afflicted—and that was certainly true among his fellow "polios" (their favored term) at Warm Springs, the Georgia clinic Roosevelt established for his and others' use. He had a comradeship in that setting he never experienced elsewhere. With its patients he shared his otherwise lonely fight to achieve mobility.

While granting all this, we should resist the sentimentalism that creeps into much of the discussion about Roosevelt's polio. Some talk as if polio sealed him with a *redemptive* mark of suffering. They use language of the romantic school, as if he were a doomed artist—a *poète maudit* or *monstre sacré*. The Byronic hero is marked by deformity or defect in a way that drives him from the comforts of the prosaic world, into the enforced solitude where genius creates an entirely new human vision, brilliant even if one-sided. The artist suffers, but gains from his suffering, because it severs him from "the herd."

Roosevelt's polio did not separate him from others but drove him out toward them—and not to crave sympathy. He would accept no pity. The shrewdest judges of polio's impact on Roosevelt are two authors who themselves underwent the polio experience—Geoffrey Ward and Hugh Gregory Gallagher. There is no sentimentality in these men's views of

Roosevelt. They both see that what polio did was make him preternaturally aware of others' perceptions of *him*. This increased his determination to control those perceptions. People were made uncomfortable by his discomfort. He needed to distract them, direct their attention to subjects he preferred; keep them amused, impressed, entertained. That meant he had to perfect a deceptive ease, a casual aplomb, in the midst of acute distress. He became a consummate actor.

For Roosevelt to "walk" in public, he had to balance on his locked braces and pretend to be using his legs while he was actually shifting back and forth from one cane to the man (often one of his sons) whose arm he gripped on the other side. The strain always left his suit soaked with sweat, the hand on the cane shaking violently from the effort, the son's arm bruised where his fingers had dug in. And all this while he would be smiling, keeping up pleasant banter, pretending to enjoy himself. It was an excruciating ordeal turned into a pleasant stroll.

The danger was always there. His sticklike legs in their metal binding could snap easily at a blow. If he fell, it was almost impossible to raise him, with his heavy braces to lock the legs in an unbending position, without the help of several strong men. When he fell in the lobby of his law-office building, his chauffeur could not pull him up off the slippery floor and had to recruit two other men in the lobby to help him. The surprised men dragooned into this rescue effort were the recipients of a flow of jokes and chatter, Roosevelt treating this episode as a particularly funny game. When they got him propped up again, "still smiling and laughing, but with knuckles white on the handles of his crutches and his legs alarmingly splayed for balance, he said 'Let's go,' and started for the elevators once more."[9] He could never let a fall keep him from what he had set out to do.

Roosevelt rarely fell in public—partly because he gave up the attempt at public "walking" as the years went by. But each time he did fall, it was a searing crisis to those few who understood how truly helpless he was in that situation. He fell going to the podium to accept the 1936 presidential nomination in Philadelphia. He had leaned sideways to say hello to the poet Edwin Markham. Despite the efforts of his son James, "FDR began to twist off center. As he swiveled past a certain point, his hip joints buckled. Under the pressure, a knee lock on his brace snapped."[10] James, who had been carrying the pages of his speech, dropped them and they fluttered around on the platform. Two of Roosevelt's bodyguards, prepared for such an emergency, pulled him up while others clustered around to hide what was happening. Roosevelt remembered telling his son to help the agent with his unlocked brace: "To hell with the speech. Fix the God-damned brace. If it can't be fixed, there won't be any speech."[11] Luckily, the restored brace held. At the podium, calmly reshuffling pages as he recomposed himself and beamed at the crowd, Roosevelt gave one of his most memorable speeches, the one denouncing "economic royalists."

The iron control of his own reactions, necessary for handling a crisis of that sort, was something Roosevelt had achieved by the time he ran for president. While he was sitting in an open car in Miami, in 1933, a would-be assassin, standing within twelve yards of the president, fired at him five times. Roosevelt stared at the man, unflinching, while Mayor Anton Cermak of Chicago, who had been standing next to the car, fell, mortally wounded. The Secret Service tried to move the car away, but Roosevelt stopped it and had Cermak put into the seat with him. He ordered the car to the hospital, and tried to revive the dying Cermak on the way. FDR's calm command of the situation came from over a decade of sitting in judgment on the passing scene, ready to make the proper moves to keep people from panicking at the sight of his helplessness. Franklin Roosevelt had always wanted to imitate his admired cousin Theodore, and had usually failed—at Harvard, as a warrior, as a writer. But that day he displayed the same *sangfroid* Teddy had when an assailant wounded him in the 1912 campaign and he gave his scheduled speech anyway, though blood was oozing from his shirt.

In less dramatic daily ordeals, Franklin kept control of others' reactions when he was lifted in or out of cars, carried up stairs, or straightened up again when he tilted over in a seat without arms. He did this by teasing others, making them think of their own vulnerability, or telling jokes, or locking their eyes to his—some polios call this "walking on your tongue."[12]

When he had no one to carry him upstairs, he sat on the bottom step, reached backward to the higher step, and pulled his body up with his powerful arms, engaging in distracting talk as if he were not doing anything extraordinary. Someone had to be with him always; he was uneasy when no one could respond to a sudden threat—an accident, the need for help to the bathroom. He was especially worried at the thought of a fire in his house or on his boat.[13] Despite this extreme dependence on those around him—he was carried to and from bed, lifted in and out of his bath, clothed by others—Roosevelt kept up a tiring regime of *public* activity, where he looked only slightly inconvenienced. This "splendid deception" involved careful stage management of all his appearances, ruthless suppression of any camera in his vicinity until he had settled into the pose he wanted to strike, and carefully constructed ramps, bathrooms, and rails wherever he was going to appear. This regime of deception reached its climax in the 1944 campaign, when the terminally ill Roosevelt tried to show his strength in an open-car ride through New York City, where he was pelted by a driving rain. The Secret Service occupied key garages along the way and prepared "pit-stop" procedures to revive and protect the president—he was stripped, wrapped in a blanket, given a rubdown and a shot of brandy, then dressed in warm clothes.[14]

It is a tribute to Roosevelt's ambition and courage that he went out as much as he could to meet the public and be seen, risking humiliation and accidents. He was determined not to let his condition cut him off from the voters. He set the tone of his presidency as soon as he was nominated, defying convention by flying to Chicago to accept the honor in person.[15]

When he could not get out, he drew others in around him, maintaining a crowded schedule of interviews, entertainments, meetings with members of Congress, with the press, with celebrities. His press conferences were frequent, two a week or more, well staged to seem informal. The reporters clustered around Roosevelt's desk, so he did not have to move. They could not quote him directly, but that made the banter on both sides freer and more revealing. Roosevelt probed and learned from them while showing his dexterity in avoiding their attempts to learn anything he was not ready to say. His aides marveled at the bits of information he had managed to acquire. He liked to keep some mystery about his sources. It was another way of demonstrating that he was in touch.

To avoid podiums where he might fall, Roosevelt invented the "fireside chat." Again he could sit at his desk while the world came to him. For people used to seeing political oratory on newsreels, or hearing speeches broadcast from auditoriums, where the acoustics and the size of the audience made for slow and pompous delivery, Roosevelt's seated-in-the-same-room-with-you style gave a shock of intimacy. This was a new thing in people's relation to their president. Cousin Theodore had been a tub-thumper. Woodrow Wilson was mellifluous but exalted. Herbert Hoover was pinched and pedantic. People felt that Roosevelt, unlike his predecessors, was confiding in them, consulting them. The man who seemed immobilized had ghosted himself into their front rooms.

His delivery was superb. He had studied people's reactions to his every move. He used theatrical props to rivet attention on his upper body. His pince-nez, his long cigarette holder, the cock of his head, his expansive gestures, his navy cape, his crumpled hats—all were calculated for effect. (The cape was useful because he did not need help to put it on or take it off, as with a sleeved coat.)

Some might think it an insult to call a president an actor. It was certainly intended that way when Ronald Reagan was dismissed as "just an actor." But all politicians need some of an actor's abilities. They must feign a welcome to unwanted constituents' attentions, cooperate with despised party allies, wax indignant at politically chosen targets. This is not the work of inferior politicians, but of the masters. The three presidents normally at the top of historians' lists—Lincoln, Washington, and Roosevelt—all had strong histrionic instincts. Roosevelt could not go to the theater—or to church, for that matter—because of his logistical problems; but Washington and Lincoln were both avid theatergoers. Washington's favorite literature was Joseph Addison's play, *Cato*. Lincoln's was *Macbeth*. Lincoln read aloud the speeches of Shakespeare to anyone who would listen to him.

Washington was a master of the theatrically telling gesture. Even his Christmas Eve assault on Trenton was more a *coup de théâtre* than a strategically meaningful step. His various resignations from office were choreographed. When he could not count on a response from his audience, he hesitated to act.[16] Lincoln knew the impact of his haunting features, and loved to pose for photographers. A great storyteller, he could milk a line for laughs as surely as Roosevelt did in his speech on "Fala"— the one where he feigned shock that enemies would think his Scottish terrier a wastrel.

An actor is not, as such, a leader. The appreciation of an audience is not motion toward some goal shared with the actor. Fans are not followers. But a popular leader must use some tricks from the actor's stock. Above all, the leader must be sensitive to the followers' reactions, must know when he or she is "losing the audience." It was so rare for Roosevelt to offend (where he did not intend to) that people were flabbergasted when he persevered in his unpopular attempt to expand (his enemies said to "pack") the Supreme Court in 1935.[17]

A good leader must know what is appealing to followers, and what risks that appeal. Roosevelt had that sensitivity to others' reactions, developed to an almost morbid degree, because of his awareness of their attention to his physical condition. He had to know, to a centimeter, the line that divides pity from compassion, condescension from cooperation, mere sympathy from real support. The French philosopher Denis Diderot said that the best actor sits inside his own performance as a cool spectator of the effects he is creating in an audience.[18] Such actors will sense it if an audience thinks they are playing a scene too "broad," and will rein in the effects. The actor is working at several different levels of awareness—fiery in the character's emotions, icy in the adjustment of those emotions to the intended results in onlookers. Feigned tears must be used to elicit real tears.

Roosevelt's manipulation of others' reactions to the manipulatings of his own body perfectly prepared him to be an actor in Diderot's sense. He could change pity into admiration. He could keep intruders into his privacy off guard with a teasing challenge, which made them look to their own defenses, too flustered to advert to Roosevelt's problem. He could put people at their ease, or deliberately cause discomfort. He controlled people by the use of nicknames (a familiarity not to be reciprocated).[19] According to his son James, he could play with people's emotions with a teasing that verged on the cruel.[20]

Roosevelt was so confident that he could affect others' attitudes that he called himself "Dr. Roosevelt," for his ability to improve the health of patients at his Warm Springs clinic, where he was more in charge than were the attendant physicians. Roosevelt knew what demons haunted polio-stricken people in those days—families hid their blighted children, who were treated as if they had insulted others when they tried to get about in public. Cures were contradictory and ineffectual; they soon broke the spirits of those who tried or trusted them. Roosevelt had been through all that, was still going through it—chasing every vain hope, tiring himself in exercises that hurt as much as they helped (which was not much in either case).

What made Warm Springs different was Roosevelt's refusal to let society dictate the terms on which polios would live. "From the first, Roosevelt seemed to understand that rehabilitation of the polio patient was a social problem with medical aspects. It was not a medical problem with social aspects, as previous American treatment efforts had assumed."[21] Roosevelt, so assured, lifted others on the strength of his assurance. The man who went to extraordinary lengths to hide the extent of his damage in all other contexts, revealed his shared weaknesses to those at Warm Springs—exercised with them, observed the same schedule, entered into their self-mocking expressions of humorous frustration. He was sensitive to their need for sexual expression. He challenged and consoled as the occasion required; and he knew, with uncanny acuity, when the occasion required. There was only one other place where he threw away pretense to make the effect called for—during World War II, when he visited wounded soldiers in their hospitals, he got into a wheelchair and rolled it himself from bed to bed.[22] Doctor Roosevelt indeed.

As president, Roosevelt came to minister to a sick nation. Economic cures were being proposed on all sides, and Roosevelt was ready to try any of them, often in bewildering succession. He was criticized as an ignoramus because he hesitated between competing promises of cure. But he knew that the soul needed healing first, and the confidence he had instilled in the patients of Warm Springs was the most measurable gift Roosevelt gave to the nation during the Depression. He understood the importance of psychology—that people have to have the courage to keep seeking a cure, no matter what the cure is. America had lost its *will* to recover, and Roosevelt was certain that regaining it was the first order of business.

In 1932–33, the long interregnum between election and a March inauguration was still constitutionally mandated. Poor Herbert Hoover had to lead the country as a lame duck for a third of a year. He tried to recruit Roosevelt's support for measures that FDR was in fact considering and would finally take himself—bank regulation, manipulation of farm prices, monetary control. But Roosevelt would not be drawn into these plans, sound as they might have been. He realized that the nation needed a clean break, a slap in the face, a sense that the past had been strongly repudiated. It took cool nerves to watch the country slide farther into trouble, knowing he would have to pick up the pieces. But he was confident to the point of foolhardiness in all his ways, and that was what was called for in this desperate situation. When he took office, he closed the banks, imposed regulations far-reaching enough to be called (in time) unconstitutional, and filled the nation with a bustle of make-work, real work, fake work. The patient was resuscitated, up off the bed, moving about. The perception of control, of direction, returned to a nation that had felt itself drifting slowly in a windless sea.

From then on, Roosevelt would make many deals with the devil in order to keep his hold on those who might respond to his call. Since Congress was controlled by southern chairmen of the indispensable committees, he paid a price for their support—sabotaging antilynch planks in the Democratic platforms, putting off civil rights action (except for inclusion in the public works programs). The right wing yelled the loudest at him, but the left may have been more deeply disappointed. Social Security was a boon to the worker, but in a regressive form, making the poor pay disproportionally to get what the government was also giving (as a payoff) to the better-off. When Franco took over Spain in a right-wing coup, Roosevelt gave the legitimate government no help for fear of losing the Catholic component in his Democratic coalition. When dictators came to power in Europe, Roosevelt placated isolationists, not to win their support but to neutralize them for a while. First things first. The audience had to be worked with many thousands of strings, and the strings must be kept from tangling.

Those who wanted ideological consistency, or even policy coherence, were rightly exasperated with Roosevelt. He switched economic plans as often as he changed treatments for his polio, and often with as little improvement in results. Many of his early "brain trust" advisors went off in disgust at his unwillingness to stick by their advice when the polls turned adverse. The Depression was not really overcome by the New Deal. Its effects were ameliorated, its burdens shifted, its ravages cloaked over. But that kept people going until the world itself was changed drastically by war. The president could not do everything. But Roosevelt stiffened people's spines to face hardship, even when the hardship did not go away. He knew a good deal about spines. When he wheeled himself up to a war casualty who had cut himself free of wreckage by amputating his own leg, Roosevelt said: "I understand you are something of a surgeon. I'm not a bad orthopedist, myself."[23] Legs spoke to legs. The public did not know the whole extent of Roosevelt's impairment; but it knew enough to feel that if he could go on as he did, gaily despite loss, so might they.

So—to go back to the alternative posed by Neustadt and Hofstadter— which is it to be? The dominating figure, or the accommodating one? I am not sure that choice would have made sense to the patients of Warm Springs. They were certainly dominated by Roosevelt; but they seem to have felt his domination as their own liberation. He did not prevail by ignoring their demands. If anything, he anticipated those demands, tailored whatever he said or did to acknowledge and respect and further them. The demands were not all consistent, or sensible, or even constructive in the long run. But Roosevelt was quick to respond to them, ruling none out as below his notice or contrary to his program. He prevailed by service to them.

Which does not mean, by a long shot, that he was humble. Mother Teresa never had a potential rival in him. He wanted his own way. But he knew that the way to get it was not to *impose* it. And by the time he got his way, it turned out to be the way of many other followers as well. He could only win by letting them win. Great leadership is not a zero-sum game. What is given to the leader is not taken from the follower. Both get by giving. That is the mystery of great popular leaders like Washington, Lincoln, and Roosevelt.

The final mystery is that this physically impaired man made his physical characteristics so comforting to the nation facing hardship and war. People drew strength from the very cock of his head, the angle of his cigarette holder, the trademark grin that was a semaphore of hope.

Franklin D. Roosevelt
AP/Wide World Photos

ANTITYPE

Adlai Stevenson

In 1952, liberals who grew up admiring Franklin Roosevelt thought they had found his rightful successor in Adlai Stevenson. They hoped he would go to Washington from the governor's mansion in Springfield as Roosevelt had gone from the governor's mansion in Albany. Stevenson came from families as socially prominent in Illinois as the Delanos and Roosevelts were in New York. Roosevelt had grown up with the example of his cousin Theodore always vivid in his mind.[1] Stevenson's grandfather was a model just as inspiring to him—Adlai E. Stevenson, for whom he was named, had been Grover Cleveland's vice president. Stevenson's father served in Washington with Secretary of the Navy Josephus Daniels, to whom FDR was the under secretary.

The similarities between Roosevelt and Stevenson are eerie—though not all of them were known during Stevenson's lifetime. Both men were raised by domineering mothers who followed their pampered sons to college. Sara Delano Roosevelt moved to Boston during the winters when Franklin was a junior and senior at Harvard. Helen Davis Stevenson rented a home in Princeton, near where Adlai was going to classes. Both Roosevelt and Stevenson were poor students who had trouble getting through law school—Roosevelt never got his degree at Columbia and Stevenson flunked out of Harvard Law.

Both men wed socially proper wives from whom they were estranged by the time they had national careers—the Roosevelts ceased having conjugal relations after Eleanor discovered Franklin's love affair with Lucy Mercer, and the Stevensons were divorced. Each man depended on the ministrations of a devout female acolyte—Missy LeHand was Roosevelt's indispensable social secretary–nurse–companion as he made his comeback from polio, and Dorothy Fosdick of the State Department was the assembler of Stevenson's foreign-policy brain trust for the 1952 presidential campaign.[2]

Though neither was much of a reader or writer, Roosevelt and Stevenson enjoyed the company of people who were, and delivered the speeches written for them with great style. Neither was an ideologue, but they were progressive enough to be praised and damned as left-liberals. They were moderate reformers in their terms as governor, though both had been elected with the help of their strong state machines—Tammany Hall in New York and Jacob Arvey's Chicago organization in Illinois. (Arvey ordered Stevenson to run for governor after Stevenson had decided to run for senator.)[3]

The liberals of 1952 were *almost* right—they almost got another Roosevelt. Stevenson was Roosevelt without the polio—and that made all the difference. Adlai remained the dilettante and ladies' man all his life.[4] Franklin was a mama's boy who was forced to grow up. Stevenson had noble ideas—as did the young Franklin for that matter. But Stevenson felt that the way to implement them was to present himself as a thoughtful idealist and wait for the world to flock to him. He considered it below him, or wrong, to scramble out among the people and ask what *they* wanted. Roosevelt grappled voters to him. Stevenson shied off from them. Some thought him too pure to desire power, though he showed ambition when it mattered. Arthur Schlesinger, Jr., who wrote speeches for Stevenson and worked for him in the 1952 and 1956 campaigns, thought he might feel guilty about wielding power because he had accidentally killed a playmate when he wielded the power of a gun in his boyhood.[5]

Stevenson believed in the "Periclean" ideal of leadership—that a man should be above the pressures of the multitude, telling people uncomfortable truths. His admiring brain trust found this charming at first, but concluded that he overdid it. As Schlesinger said: "It was a brilliant device to establish Stevenson's identity. As a permanent device, it was an error."[6] Stevenson kept some distance from the crowd by indulging "inside" comments that played to the intellectuals. This, too, got on the nerves of his entourage. Carl McGowan, the head of Stevenson's staff, had these rueful memories: "His wit was not as great as it was popularly assumed to be, but it was not as damaging as was believed, either. He always had a risky sense of humor—some of it was not funny at all."[7]

Liberal intellectuals stayed true to Stevenson in the 1950s despite misgivings, because they were horrified at what they took to be the anti-intellectual alternative of Dwight D. Eisenhower. It was literally inconceivable to these people that a rational electorate would prefer Ike to Adlai—which shows how far out of touch they were with the American people, and just how far Stevenson was from Roosevelt.[8] Louis Howe, Roosevelt's great admirer-manager, would have had no trouble understanding Ike's appeal.[9]

Not only did Stevenson think voters should come to him, instead of he to them; but, once in office, he thought the power of the office was self-enacting. He did not realize that it is only what one *makes of* the office that creates real followers. Installed as the United States representative at the United Nations, he clung to that position, with the perks he relished (parties every night, a delightful "harem" of adoring ladies), though his liberal friends repeatedly urged him to resign rather than keep on defending American actions in Cuba, Latin America, and Indochina.

When Stevenson found that he had presented false information to the world in the aftermath of his government's invasion of Cuba (at the Bay of Pigs) he was indignant that his own president had lied to him. He went to the New York apartment of his friend Alistair Cooke, the British journalist, and poured out his trouble over a drink. Cooke tried to comfort him with the thought that men who resigned from intolerable situations have made their contribution to history. Stevenson was shocked at the mere suggestion that he would resign. "That would be burning my boats," he said. Even then he did not grasp his real position with President Kennedy, who treated him as a patsy because he considered him one.[10]

Later, while the left broke from President Johnson's foreign policy, Stevenson doggedly defended it. The journalist Murray Kempton, writing in the name of former Stevenson supporters, sent a private letter to Adlai begging him to resign. The government was telling lies: "The need now is for commoners, for men *out* of office. . . . I know that I am asking you to do one more messy and exhausting thing; but would you come out here and lead us?"[11] But Stevenson was having too much fun on the embassy party rounds. His doctor warned him that his sybaritic life was a form of suicide.[12] Friends were telling him the same thing.[13] He died after a diplomats' lunch in London, age sixty-five.

Roosevelt, too, drove himself to an early death (sixty-three), but that was in his grueling fourth term as president during World War II. His talents had been put to maximum use because he could find common ground with those he sought to lead. He succeeded by *not* being a Pericles (as Thucydides presents Pericles), by being what some of Pericles' defenders called a "demagogue" (the word means, etymologically, "people leader").[14]

2.
RADICAL LEADER

Harriet Tubman

F ranklin Roosevelt, as an elected leader, had to be as
inclusive as possible in moving a whole society forward,
first against the Depression, then against the Axis. But
other leaders must forswear inclusiveness to accomplish
their quite different objectives. Narrowness and focus are called for. The
number of followers will necessarily be smaller, but they will be more
intense.

Single-minded leaders are prophets to their admirers, fanatics to their
critics. These radicals refuse to be distracted by other issues, no matter
how worthy, while fighting the injustice that mobilizes their followers.
Mother Jones, the Irish-American labor organizer of the late nineteenth
and early twentieth centuries, had little patience for more leisurely activities, like voting for reform laws or supporting women's suffrage.[1] She
wanted the exploitation of miners to stop *now*, and she organized strikes,
marches, and resistance to achieve her goals. Often in jail, she was loved
by her constituents and became a legend to radicals of many stripes.

Impatience with the electoral process is a mark of inspired trouble-
makers like Mother Jones. Voters give part of a day (every few years) to
expressing themselves, and then abide by the outcome, even if it goes
against their sense of justice. Slavery will continue if the voters say it
must. Segregation will continue. War will. Persecution will. Thoreau
spoke for those who do not submit to this:

All voting is a sort of gaming, like chequers or backgammon, with a slight moral tinge to it, playing with right and wrong, with moral questions. . . . The character of the voter is not staked. I cast my vote, perchance, as I think right; but I am not vitally concerned that that right should prevail. I am willing to leave it to the majority. Its obligation, therefore, never exceeds that of expediency. Even voting for the right is *doing* nothing for it. It is only expressing to men feebly your desire that it should prevail. . . . Cast your whole vote, not a strip of paper merely, but your whole influence.[2]

Not many people will vote with their whole lives—give their days and nights, their money and influence, to a single cause. But those who do have a disproportionate impact on society, as one would expect from their investment of energy and conviction, as compared with the lukewarm or diffident commitment of others. That is why intense minorities often prevail over lackadaisical majorities in a democracy. This does not happen, in the first place, at the ballot box, where the indifferent can outvote the passionate. Protest, dramatization, civil disobedience, imprisonment, and fines precede the great *resisted* changes in our society—abolition, women's suffrage, union recognition, racial integration. The "fanatics" of yesterday, detained in a society's jails, become the prophets and martyrs of the future. Dr. King was only one of the great American radicals who made a good pulpit of his jail cell. Alice Paul and her suffragists took a detour through jail toward their goal of female emancipation. Thoreau's words have inspired later radicals to look on prison as a test of principle:

Under a government which imprisons any unjustly, the true place for a just man is also a prison. The proper place today, the only place which Massachusetts has provided for her freer and less desponding spirits, is in her prisons, to be put out and locked out of the State by her own act, as they have already put themselves out by their principles. It is there that the fugitive slave, and the Mexican [War] prisoner on parole, and the Indian come to plead the wrongs of his race, shall find them; on that separate, but more free and honorable ground where the State places those who are not *with* her but *against* her—the only house in a slave state in which a free man can abide with honor.[3]

Followers who are asked to risk their freedom, and sometimes their lives, obviously need leaders of great devotion and self-sacrifice. Harriet

Tubman was such a leader. She did not have to go to jail for principle, but to break out of jail. She was born (c. 1825) in the social imprisonment of slavery. By ingenuity and determination, she escaped north from her native Maryland; then, defying the odds, she went back again and again to rescue other slaves. Her first followers were those with the courage to go north with her. But as word of her deeds spread, of her preternatural elusiveness, her repeated defiance of an alerted slavocracy, she became a kind of Sable Pimpernel, instilling hope in slaves who never saw her and winning converts in the North to the view that African-Americans were capable of conducting their own affairs. The illiterate Tubman had outwitted posse after posse of slave hunters who claimed that blacks were too undisciplined to manage their own lives.

Tubman gave the name Harriet to herself, in honor of her mother. Her owners had called her Amarintha (shortened to "Minty" in daily use)—the South liked to give its slaves names from the classical past, to remind themselves and others of the long heritage of owning other people.

Harriet's master rented out child slaves to neighbors for day labor, but Harriet did not get along with the women to whom she was sent to do housework. She preferred harder labor outdoors—she liked far horizons when she lifted her eyes from the wood she was chopping. The surprising strength she developed in the fields served her well in later years. As a teenager, she tried to stop the beating of a fellow worker and was felled with a two-pound weight snatched up from a store counter. The blow left a dent where it broke the skull, and Harriet lingered near death for weeks afterward.

This was the turning point in her life, as Tubman described it in the only extensive interviews that survive—those given to the writer Sarah Bradford.[4] Harriet lay ill, after the blow, reciting feverish prayers for her master's conversion to loving ways. She would suffer the rest of her life from catatonic spells she connected with the long semiconsciousness of her convalescence. The experience also liberated her, in ways that others have described—Rousseau knocked unconscious by a dog and easing back into consciousness freed of all worldly concerns, as if born again; Dostoyevsky giving Prince Myshkin his own deliciously liminal states as he veered toward epileptic seizure. The blow that cracked Tubman's skull struck off her psychic chains. She had already died once; she had nothing to lose.

It is not stretching things, I believe, to connect this experience with a funeral ceremony she described having seen later. A natural mimic, she appreciatively re-created the midnight ceremony for Sarah Bradford, taking the part of an impressive minister who pronounced the man lying before him *"dead-a-dead-a."* (Bradford copied her dialect clumsily.)[5]

> Who ob all dis congregation is gwine next to lie *dead-a-dead-*a? You can't go nowheres, my frens and bredren, but Def will fin' you. You can't dig no hole so deep an' bury yourself dar, but God A'mighty's far-seein' eye'll fin' you, an' Def will come arter you. You can't go into that big fort [pointing to Hilton Head] an' shut yourself up dar—dat fort dat Sesh Buckra said the debil couldn't take—but Def will fin' you dar.[6] All your frens may forget you, but Def will nebber forget you. Now, my bredren, prepare to lie *dead-a-dead-*a.

The sermon led to a dance Tubman called a "spiritual shuffle," where every member of the congregation shook hands with every other, using each other's name in song:

> My sis'r Mary's boun' to go.
> My sis'r Nanny's boun' to go.
> My brudder Tony's boun' to go.
> My brudder Julie's boun' to go.

When they circulated past Tubman, not knowing her name, they sang "Eberybody's boun' to go."

This liberating acceptance of death, the inclusion of the departed in a community of the departing, impressed Tubman because she knew something of that feeling from the dreamy state after her concussion, when she had accepted her own death. Of her escape north—a daring move from which her brothers drew back—she said to Sarah Bradford:

> I had reasoned dis out in my mind: there was one of two things I had a *right* to, liberty or death. If I could not have one, I would have de oder, for no man should take me alive. I should fight for my liberty as my strength lasted, and when de time came for me to go, de Lord would let dem take me.[7]

That passage reveals the combination of qualities that made Tubman so formidable—her mystical resignation to the form of liberation God would grant her, the certitude that she *would* be liberated in any case, and the ferocious reliance on her own strength to make *one* of the two forms happen here and now. When she made sure she had crossed into free territory, her reaction was blissful, as if waking from her concussion:

> I looked at my hands to see if I was de same person now I was free. Dere was such a glory ober eberything, de sun came like gold through de trees and ober de fields, and I felt like I was in heaven. . . . I had crossed de line.[8]

This may seem to be making too much of Tubman's concussion and the "spells" (as people called them) consequent on it. But there is evidence that these spells were at least partially within her control. They did not interfere, for instance, with the strenuous and alert labors involved in her missions back to rescue other slaves. And the best-attested single spell shows that she turned to it when she was resigning herself to providence. When, after several rescue raids, a divine signal convinced her it was time to bring her parents out, she needed twenty dollars to take with her on the mission. She went to an abolitionist's business office and asked for it. He asked what made her come to him. "De Lord tole me, sir." The man answered, "I guess the Lord's mistaken this time." She was undeterrable: "De Lord's neber mistaken. Anyhow, I'm gwine to sit here till I get it." She sat down and went off into one of her spells. The day passed, with her coming out of the trance and lapsing back into it at intervals. Her story was told around her as visitors came and went; and when she woke she found sixty dollars had been accumulated for her.[9] The Lord was never mistaken; but she knew how to help the Lord's work along.

Her spells, her dreams and divine promptings, the spirituals she sang about death and freedom, all merged in Tubman's life because she had a religious experience during her convalescence—not an unusual occurrence in the history of people starting their lives over in the aftermath of a close brush with death. St. Francis of Assisi and St. Ignatius are famous examples. Life henceforth was a matter of staying true to the liberated feelings of recovery. When friends tried to keep Tubman from journeying back to the South, she answered:

> "John saw the city, didn't he?" [She refers to the vision of John at Rev. 21.12–13.] "Yes, John saw the city." "Well, what did he see? He saw twelve gates, didn't he? Three of dose gates was on de north; three of 'em was on de east; an' three of 'em was on de west; but dere was three more, an' dem was on de *south*; an' I reckon if dey kill me down dere, I'll git into one of dem gates, don't you?"[10]

Bradford's account is condescending to this form of "spiritual geography," but it shows how well the illiterate Tubman had mastered, through sermons and spirituals, the language of freedom that made all of life a form of biblical parable. This was not only a language of submission, as Nat Turner's use of it proved during his slave rebellion. Tubman was called "Moses" because she used the songs of escape from Egypt as part of her signal system in conducting her rescues.[11] Her own singing was her trademark, and she seized any opportunity to improve it. She was excited to come across new songs and new styles of singing in the deeper South. She told Bradford:

> I wish you could hear 'em sing, Missus. Der voices is so sweet, and dey can sing eberything we sing, an' dey can sing a great many hymns we can't neber catch at all.[12]

The mystical side of Tubman did not interfere with her practical approach to tasks. A hard worker, she financed most of her efforts by earning money for them, and then she ran her raids into the South with quiet efficiency. Quakers in the Underground Railroad could help her in the North, but she was on her own as she went secretly gathering the slaves who would take risks with her. It was dangerous for everyone involved, even those who did not follow her but knew of her activities. It is a mark of the slave ethos of solidarity that she was not betrayed, even inadvertently. Not only was she never caught, but none of her escape groups lost a single member.

Her discipline shows in the treatment of her family. When she returned south, at first to bring out her husband (who had remarried and would not go), she did not inform her parents of her comings and goings, lest they inadvertently betray her. Even when she went to pick up her brothers, her mother was kept in the dark, and her father insisted that they blindfold him so he could say with conviction that he had not seen her.[13] The spirit of the enterprise infected those who joined her with the seriousness of her secret.

She ran the operation with military rigor, learning the pass systems, the allowable excuses for blacks to be seen abroad, the secret routes through areas where no excuse would serve. She carried a gun to use on anyone who tried to recapture her fleeing charges; and she was ready to turn it against the unruly in her own band. When she had made her own first journey into the unknown, with nothing but the North Star to guide her during her night travel, hiding by day, her brothers turned back out of fear. This jeopardized her escape, but there was nothing she could do about it. Later, she would brook no such departure from the ranks. When one man wanted to turn back, she pulled her gun on him and said, "Dead niggers tell no tales; you go on or die!"[14]

Tubman, it is clear, did not confine her social agitation to nonviolent civil disobedience. She had lived among violent men, like the one who cracked her skull, and she did not expect to steal their human property from them in polite ways. She admired Nat Turner, John Brown, and James Montgomery, men who had decided to free slaves by force. As her fame grew, Brown and Montgomery sought her out. Brown, going to Canada in 1858 to get information on recruits and resources in the South, met Tubman and called her "the General," admiring her "masculine" toughness of mind: "He-Harriet is the most of a *man* naturally that I ever met with."[15]

Brown got little concrete aid from Tubman. He claimed at the time to be recruiting help for rescue raids like hers, but on a grander scale. She could give him little information about routes, since she read no maps. She knew only the visual markers in areas she was familiar with. Besides, her contacts would trust her, but not a stranger. Nonetheless, Brown was wise to get her blessing, since her raids, however exaggerated later in their numbers, were a symbol of black initiative, the very thing Brown said he would rely on after he freed the slaves.[16] Abolitionists were divided in their view of the African-American's capacity for self-governance after liberation.[17] Even an ardent abolitionist like Theodore Parker, who was certain that all people should be free, doubted the black's capacity for self-management. Tubman's exploits were read, rightly, as decisive evidence of slave ingenuity, discipline, and self-help. Only this can explain the use made of her in the Civil War.

Testimonials written in Tubman's old age, to win her a government pension for war service, claimed that she had been a scout and a spy for the Union army. But Tubman's own words to Sarah Bradford show that her field of effort in the war—South Carolina around Hilton Head—was so new to her that she could barely if at all understand the local black dialect. Obviously, her raids had been to familiar country, on the Eastern Shore of Maryland. (Her owner's habit of sending her out to jobs around the countryside had equipped her in ways he could not have anticipated.) She would have been useless as a guide, or even as an intermediary, with local African-Americans elsewhere. When the abolitionist Thomas

Wentworth Higginson, who had known her before the war, saw her again in South Carolina, he said only that she was "a sort of nurse and general care taker."[18] Then what purpose did she serve—aside from the nursing by which she earned her keep with the army?

The answer lies in the officer who requested her services, a man she had praised when he worked with John Brown—James Montgomery. Actually, Montgomery and Brown had been rival "jayhawkers" in the Kansas violence of the late 1850s, differing on the tactics for freeing slaves, though both men were religiously devoted to the effort.[19] Montgomery was as theologically superheated as Brown, though more cautious in his resort to arms. He had been a revivalist minister before the war and he became a First-Day Adventist preacher after it. During the war, he was authorized to raise a regiment of African-Americans in South Carolina, and it was to this effort that he recruited Tubman. She was a challenge to white prejudice and an inspiration to black soldiers because of her famous exploits and her humble service to the cause. She was uncritical of Montgomery's cruel treatment of southern whites, which blocked his rise to higher rank in the army.[20] She could work with nonviolent Quakers like Thomas Garrett in Delaware, with moderate abolitionists like Gerrit Smith in New York, or with radical abolitionists like Thomas Wentworth Higginson in Massachusetts. She wanted to free her people. She had no theories about why they should be free. She was willing to cooperate with anyone who took practical steps toward their liberation— though she communicated most easily with those who saw their rescue in religious terms, whether the pacific Thomas Garrett or the choleric James Montgomery.

Tubman did little talking. She acted—precipitately, but not foolishly. Her intrepidity went with a sense of danger that she related to her divine signs, warning her off or urging her on. We have few testimonies to her quick reactions while working underground in the South, but we can imagine them from a well-authenticated episode that occurred in the North, in Troy, New York, on April 26, 1860.

Charles Nalle, a fugitive slave, had been arrested in Troy, an Underground Railroad town, and the hearing on his status was scheduled for April 26. Abolitionists had differed on the proper response to make when the government "kidnapped" escaped slaves for return (called "rendition") under the Fugitive Slave Act. A famous attempt to block such action had fizzled in Boston, in 1854: Anthony Brown was "rendered back" while the abolitionists' attempt to kidnap the kidnapped man fell victim to their own conflicts.[21] Opposition to the law had then grown bolder, for a while, but the capture of John Brown in the fall of 1859 threw the abolitionists on the defensive. The "Secret Six" who had supported Brown in New England were accused of conspiring at treason— Frederick Douglass fled to Canada; Theodore Parker was already out of the country; Gerrit Smith suffered or feigned a mental breakdown. The rest, except for Thomas Wentworth Higginson, were hesitant about risking violence to save a slave taken in this period of hysteria.[22]

But Tubman, who was passing through Troy when the hearing occurred, had little to do with strategic arguments about "this stage of the struggle." She simply saw a fellow African-American—one of those she had risked her life again and again to get *out* of the South—on the verge of being returned to the South. When Charles Nalle, condemned to be rendered, came out of his hearing onto the street, she scuttled over to him, threw her powerful arms around him, making herself a hostage, and shouted to the crowd, "Drag us out! Drag him to the river! Drown him, but don't let them have him."[23] The guards, unable to pry Tubman loose from their prisoner, rained blows on her, which just inspired the crowd to tug her more energetically toward the river, where Nalle was put on a boat, leaving the guards stymied. Tubman found another boat and crossed the river—but by the time she arrived, Nalle had been captured again and imprisoned in a nearby building. The mob stormed the building. Some were shot at the door, but Tubman dashed over their bodies and reached Nalle, who was stunned and helpless by now. Tubman carried him downstairs in her arms, and the crowd commandeered a wagon to drive him off into the countryside. He escaped, leaving Tubman a perfect record—she never lost a slave she took into her care. By the time officials tried to arrest her, she was gone as well. Nalle's lawyer wrote: "How she came to be in Troy that day is entirely unknown to our citizens; and where she hid herself after the rescue is equally a mystery."[24]

The South had set a high price on her head, but that did not stop her from returning to the area where she was known by sight. She relied on her skills as a mimic—posing as a feeble old woman, creating distractions, driving her escapees on. When slaves unable to swim refused to ford a river, she preceded them, though she was barely five feet tall, to show they could cross.[25] She was never at a loss for the expedient of the moment. John Brown was wiser than he knew when he called her the General.

Though she was ready to use violence against violent captors, she had no relish for it, as Brown and Montgomery did. She prayed for her enemies, and did not take sides with any of her squabbling allies. She continued to labor for her own upkeep, doing housework, cooking, nursing. After the war, she set up a home in New York for homeless blacks. She had a mission to her people, and nothing could come between her and that mission. She had the singleness of purpose that social agitators can indulge, released from responsibility to many competing interests.

This is the paradox of the radical leader, that his or her very narrowness becomes a release from the general immobility induced by "balanced" leaders. A fierce concentration on one point causes a general loosening and liberation. Common sense resists "single-issue politics." But the leader who sees infinite suffering in a single individual arrives at a higher sanity by way of "unbalanced" concentration on specific injustices.

Tubman's feats are wrapped in a haze, because of her necessary secrecy, because of her admirers' exaggerations, because she could not communicate in writing. But it is easy to imagine the rumors of hope that followed her invisible movements through slave country. Even those she did not physically carry to freedom were freed, in spirit, just knowing that she was defying the masters, time and again, and giving to others what she had earned herself in that first terrifying trip with nothing to guide her but the North Star.

Jacob Lawrence, in a brilliant series of tempera panels painted in her honor (1939–40), captures the meaning of the woman, especially in Panel 19. While white slave hunters puzzle over a letter she had a friend write to mislead them, she spirits others off behind their backs. She has thrown her cloak over those being rescued, and while she moves ahead, the hand gesturing behind her shows the way for those still to come.[26]

Harriet Tubman Series No. 19—*Jacob Lawrence*
Hampton University Museum, Hampton, Virginia

ANTITYPE
Stephen A. Douglas

T he opposite of a bracing narrowness is flaccid inclusion. There is nothing wrong with inclusion as a goal—just as there is nothing good about narrowness considered in itself. The relevance of such terms to leadership depends on personal and historical context. Stephen A. Douglas, Lincoln's rival, is an example of a misguided inclusiveness that, by trying to combine everything, makes everything fall apart.

Compromise is the essence of the political art, and especially of American politics. This was never truer than in the mid nineteenth century, when attempts to hold together a fissiparous country led to repeated compromise on the status of slaves in the new territories of the West. Henry Clay and Daniel Webster forged the compromises of 1820 and 1850 that were meant to avert secession, though they only postponed it. Douglas saw himself as the heir to those giants of the Senate, each of whom aspired to the presidency. In many ways Douglas was a typical politician of his period—hard-drinking, large-gesturing, continually orating. His short stature just made his outsize head and matching energies more prominent. Descriptions of him tended to the leonine—shaggy mane, arresting head, thick chest, dwindling hindquarters.

The uselessness of compromise as a palliative for America's deep troubles was becoming clear as the century came to its midpoint. The only politicians who could hold North and South together were modeled after John Bunyon's Mr. Facing-Both-Ways. James Buchanan, elected president in 1856, was called by a great journalist of the time "the personification of evasion, the embodiment of an inducement to dodge."[1] Douglas, though a better politician than Buchanan, merely went more nimbly down the discredited road of compromise, making the same journalist call him, in 1856, "an exposed political empiric [quack]."[2]

Though Douglas and Lincoln made a Mutt-and-Jeff study in contrast during their 1858 debates for the Illinois Senate seat—the short and irascible versus the lank and ironic—the early stages of their careers were remarkably similar. Both largely self-educated, they rose from menial jobs to a law practice. Each invoked the memory of Clay and promoted western expansion, a position that allied them with the railroad interests. Though Lincoln was four years older than Douglas, the "Little Giant" had risen faster and filled more posts. He was an active contender for the presidential nomination in three Democratic conventions (1852, 1856, and 1860). Though Lincoln began as an anti-Jackson Whig, and Douglas as a Jacksonian Democrat, they competed for the allegiance of similar groups—and of backers like the newspaper editor Horace Greeley.

But all that ended in 1854, when Douglas pushed the Kansas-Nebraska Bill through Congress. In order to promote the development of that territory, Douglas broke the Missouri Compromise (1820), which barred slavery there. Invoking popular sovereignty, he said it was up to the settlers to choose what form of society they wanted. He claimed he was not supporting slavery, only the right of the people themselves to choose. Three years after the bill's passage, in a statement Lincoln would hammer back at him again and again, Douglas declared: "It is none of my business which way the slavery clause is decided. I do not care whether it is voted down or voted up."[3]

Although he knew his stand would make him more acceptable to the South, which had up to that point blocked his rise to the presidency, Douglas sincerely believed in the democratic system as the solution to all problems. If a matter could not be resolved by a vote—preferably a vote on a compromise—then it could never, in his eyes, be settled at all. Thoreau's description of people who accept the outcome of democratic process, no matter what that outcome may be, might have been written with Douglas in mind:

> They hesitate, and they regret, and sometimes they petition, but they do nothing in earnest and with effect. They will wait, well disposed, for others to remedy the evil, that they may no longer have it to regret. At most, they give only a cheap vote, and a feeble countenance and God-speed, to the right as it goes by them.[4]

In normal times, a politician must trust and support the system that gives him his authority. In America, a large and heterogeneous society, the need for compromise has shaped our nonideological electoral framework of two vague parties in shadow combat over minor issues. But the genius of politics, as opposed to the mere practitioner—the Lincoln, not the Douglas—knows when compromise can go no further without becoming incoherence. Douglas tried to hold together incompatible things, as when he supported the Dred Scott decision (imposing the right to slaveholding in the territories) and simultaneously preached his own "Freeport Doctrine" (which said de facto exclusion of slaves could result from local police enforcement of popular sovereignty). At this stage, Douglas was asking people to believe more impossible things before breakfast than Alice's Red Queen ever dreamed of.

The worst nightmare of the congenital compromiser, who tries to please everyone, is to find that he has, in fact, angered everyone. That realization hit a stunned Douglas after Congress passed the Kansas-Nebraska Bill; he found he could "travel from Boston to Chicago by the light of my own effigy. . . . All along the Western Reserve of Ohio I could find my effigy upon every tree we passed."[5] The believer in the system and nothing but the system is a pragmatist with no practical effect. Even fanatics accomplish more.

3.
REFORM LEADER

Eleanor Roosevelt

Although J. Edgar Hoover, the director of the FBI, thought Eleanor Roosevelt might be a Communist, there was nothing radical about her, either in temperament or principle. She would not join in civil rights activities if they included civil disobedience. She was law-abiding to the tips of her well-cared-for fingernails. She was like Harriet Tubman in one respect—she carried a gun. But that was a concession to the Secret Service when her husband was president. She refused to let Secret Service agents accompany her when she was driving her own car. To still their protests, she agreed to carry a gun and learn on the shooting range how to use it. But then she put it, unloaded, in her locked glove compartment.[1] Even if it had been loaded, and on the seat beside her, she would never have used it on a human being. She was not the same kind of leader Harriet Tubman was.

What kind of leader was she? The kind who could say, "I doubt if 'lighting into' people ever does much good."[2] Imagine the contemptuous snort that would have brought from Mother Jones. Mrs. Roosevelt was exactly the type of genteel and gradual reformer for whom Mother Jones had no patience. And this attitude is widely shared. The conservative writer Tom Wolfe could join the fiery leftist in making fun of rich folks playing at reform. Wolfe called it "radical chic." Marxists, at the other end of the spectrum from Wolfe, hold that the rich act in bad faith when they do favors to the poor (thus buying off protest). Only the poor themselves are allowed to mount "authentic" protest.

But, in many cases, the poor have the least resources for helping the poor. It would have been a cruel friend of the poor who told a northern abolitionist to let slaves in the South free themselves, since they alone had a right to voice their plight. The belief that only self-interest can motivate people reduces the range of human possibilities when it claims that radiantly good people (like Eleanor Roosevelt) are too good to be true.

The moderate reformers, the philanthropists, have few defenders. Only the rare spirit, someone like George Bernard Shaw, sees how admirable can be the Working Rich, as he called them, who are to be distinguished both from the Idle Rich and from those who work to make themselves richer.

> Florence Nightingale organized the hospital work of the Crimean war, including the knocking of some sense into the heads of the army medical staff, and much disgusting drudgery in the wards, when she had the means to live comfortably at home doing nothing. John Ruskin published accounts of how he had spent his comfortable income and what work he had done, to show that he, at least, was an honest worker and a faithful administrator of the part of the national income that had fallen to his lot.[3]

Ruskin, the art lecturer turned social critic, was so effective that he influenced more liberal politicians in turn-of-the-century England than did Marx.[4]

Eleanor Roosevelt ranks with great philanthropists like Nightingale and Ruskin. She did not renounce wealth or position, but *used* both to good purpose. She realized that being the president's wife gave her increased opportunities to go places and accomplish things. That made her an "unauthentic" feminist to people who say that women should not hitch themselves to their husband's success—another form of the argument that a person should not use social advantage to help the socially disadvantaged.[5]

Eleanor Roosevelt first experienced her social advantages as disabling. Only later was she able to turn them to her own and other's improvement. She was the prisoner of a Victorian lady's "proper" upbringing. Sometimes the constraint was literal—she was forced to wear an iron brace, as a girl, to achieve a "ladylike" posture. She could not go anywhere without a chaperone. Once, when no family member was available to accompany her to school in England, she had to hire a chaperone from an agency (and then never saw her on board the ship). No wonder, then, that she later refused Secret Service "chaperoning." She drove herself in an open car. She was not going back to the dread days of her childhood, when supervisors surrounded and cowed her.

The coldness of her mother and grandmother damaged her early days; but the greatest hurt was caused by love, by devotion to her father. Elliott Roosevelt grew up in the shadow of his vigorous younger brother, Theodore. In competition with that beaming ogre of a sibling, Elliott made desperate bids for his father's love, writing him as a fifteen-year-old:

> Dear old Govenor—for I *will* call you that not in publick but in private for it does seem to suit you, you splendid Man just my ideal, made to govern & doing it so lightly & affectionately that I can call you by the name as a pet one. . . . Oh. Father will you ever think *me* a "noble boy" [what the father had called Theodore], you are right about Tede he is one & no mistake a boy I would give a good deal to be like in many respects. If you ever see me not stand by Thee [Theodore] you may know I am entirely changed.[6]

Elliott was the healthy and athletic older brother at the outset. But grimly his younger sibling acquired strength and began to beat Elliott at the games they both played so passionately. They were almost suicidally competitive on the polo field. As Elliott receded into the dust behind Theodore, he relied on his charm, on mistresses, on alcohol to bolster his self-esteem—and on the adoring love of his daughter.

After a brief time as the handsome young husband of the most glamorous debutante of her season, Anna Hall, Elliott began coming apart. When Eleanor was seven, the family was retrieving him from his escapades and committing him to a series of asylums and alcoholic-treatment centers. Theodore stiffened the family resolve to keep him in line—he was worried about the effect of Elliott's scandalous behavior on his wife (who was herself sickly) and on his daughter (toward whom Theodore felt especially protective in later years). Anna, in fact, died in 1892, leaving Eleanor to be brought up in her grandmother's home, where she lived on hopes of reunion with her mysteriously distant father. (He was kept away from her, and she was not even allowed to go to his 1894 burial.)

Her father died when Eleanor was ten years old. He had written her fond letters, which she memorized, addressed to "Little Nell." As a boy, he had himself borne the nickname Nell—his kindly nature made his family compare him to the little girl, solicitous for her elders, in Dickens's *Old Curiosity Shop*. When his daughter was born, she was given both parents' names—Anna Eleanor (feminine for Elliott).

The mother's name was dropped, the father's retained. Elliott read his young daughter the Dickens novel and passed on to her his own childhood nickname. When he was still living with the family, he encouraged little Eleanor to take care of him, lecture him, act like his mother—just as the Dickens character mothers her own father. Eleanor's own favorite picture from her childhood shows her shaking a finger to "scold" her father (Little Nell, as it were, admonishing Big Nell).[7]

In his letters and rare visits after their separation, Elliott promised his daughter a home over which she should preside. She wrote in her autobiography: "Some day I would make a home for him again. . . . Somehow it was always just he and I. I did not understand whether my brothers were to be our children or whether they would be at school. . . ."[8] She did not use her nickname again until she felt the promise of her own home was about to be realized at last. Her love letters to Franklin, her fiancé, were signed "Little Nell."

Eleanor later told her own daughter, Anna, that sex is a duty for women, not a pleasure.[9] This view is usually attributed to Eleanor's Victorian upbringing, with some justice. She was prudish for most of her life. She imprisoned her baby daughter's hands in metal cages to prevent her from masturbating. When her daughter asked her about this after she had become an adult, Eleanor was still prudish. In Anna's words, "The indication was that I had a bad habit which had to be cured and about which one did not talk."[10] When Eleanor was teaching high school girls at New York City's Todhunter School (and her husband was governor), a fellow teacher lent her André Gide's *The Counterfeiters*: "She read it in terms of a forbidden subject. She couldn't bring herself even to consider homosexuality."[11]

But even apart from her Victorian upbringing, setting up house as Franklin's "Little Nell" would inhibit her sexuality. The approximation of the situation to earlier fantasies of an ideal life with her father must have triggered the incest taboo at some level of refusal to sexual surrender. She seems to have accepted the fact that her husband would seek sexual pleasure elsewhere—as she was forgiving to her father's mistresses after she learned about them—and only threatened to break up the marriage when she learned (in 1918) that Franklin *loved* Lucy Mercer. Though she was cruelly wounded by this infidelity of the heart (as opposed to mere physical indulgence), there was undoubtedly some sense of liberation in her agreement to live with him without sex. She would care for him as for her father—a task that became even more fulfilling after he contracted polio (in 1921) and she helped him defy his mother, who tried to use this illness to reclaim him as *her* boy.

The Lucy Mercer affair liberated her in several ways. For one thing, she was spared any further pregnancies. Though she loved children—her favorite hours as a single person had been spent teaching poor children of the Benington Street School—she felt uneasy with her own five children, and counted herself a failure as a mother.[12] This was because her mother-in-law appropriated the children begotten in part out of a dynastic imperative. A woman, Alice Sohier, whom Franklin courted before he wooed Eleanor, had broken off their courtship in horror at the number of children he wanted to sire. She "did not wish to be a cow."[13] As soon as children were born to Eleanor and Franklin, Sara Delano Roosevelt descended upon them, insisting on the same disciplines and indulgences (which tended to cancel each other out) that she had lavished on Franklin, her only child. When Eleanor tried, periodically, to rebel, Sara used the children against her, saying she was trying to deny *their* joys. Eleanor felt that her children had been taken away from her the minute they were born, turned over to nurses chosen by Sara, nurses Eleanor could not discipline, even when she thought they were treating the children badly.[14]

When Eleanor disapproved of Franklin's conduct as a father, she had to hold her tongue for fear of Sara's retaliation. She went into a "Patient Griselda" silence which, she later realized, was unhealthy for her and unpleasant to others. One friend finally told her that her martyred silences were "the most maddening things in the world."[15] Wrongs endured were turned to wrongs inflicted. It took tragedy to cure this situation by inverting it. Before Franklin's polio, the Roosevelt couple had seemed effortlessly successful on the surface, but only because Eleanor submitted to Sara's bullying. Afterward, their life seemed a powerful struggle from the outside; but, under the surface, the couple reached a new accord and mutual support.

That is because Franklin had finally declared his independence, too. Against his mother's campaign to use the polio as a reason for withdrawing her son from politics (which she had always considered a pursuit too vulgar for her boy), Franklin kept up his brave battle to walk again, with the hope of a political future. Since he could no longer go to his political advisor, Louis Howe moved into the Roosevelts' home. This disgusted Sara, who always considered Howe an "ugly little man," perpetually disheveled, chain-smoking, covered with ashes. Since Howe had been put in her grandchild Anna's room, Sara mobilized the children against him.[16] But Franklin was fighting for his life now, and he stood up for Howe as he had never stood up for Eleanor.

Eleanor, who had at first shared Sara's distaste for the gnomelike Howe, now joined him in a close alliance to rescue Franklin and fend off Sara. For the first time, she had under her roof a person *she* could use against the woman who had used all its prior inhabitants against her.

Franklin, at his doctor's suggestion, moved out of the house when family tensions became too great for him to concentrate on his therapy.[17] Eventually, he found in Warm Springs a place Sara disliked too much to follow him there. Building up a treatment center others could come to, Franklin for the first time in his life served the needs of others, discovering a satisfaction that Eleanor had always experienced. Some have expressed surprise that two people could work so well together for the rest of their lives, after the deep betrayal Eleanor had experienced. But the Roosevelts grew in respect for each other as they recognized how similar in some way their lives had been. Both had been emotionally handicapped by a difficult parent. Both freed themselves from the confines of their upbringing after a sharp blow from fate. They forged a new life after that. Eleanor purchased the Todhunter School, where she could teach and serve others. Franklin created the Warm Springs therapeutic center. Eleanor built a separate cottage at Hyde Park, the ancestral Roosevelt home, where she could be the mistress of her own space. He built a similar "getaway" above it on a hill. Both threw themselves into politics, Eleanor becoming a public speaker (an activity she had previously abhorred), just as he was learning to face crowds despite the humiliation of being carried around and propped up. They became models, to each other, of strength and dedication. The marriage came right only after everything had gone wrong.

In the 1920s, the intelligence, energy, and compassion of Eleanor Roosevelt were at last released. Baffled in their natural outlets at home, these now turned toward the problems of others. With Howe's help,

Eleanor became active in Democratic politics. She also became an advocate of women's causes. Since her one period of brief liberty as a teenager had been at the all-girls school in England where she became a model achiever, she formed overlapping circles of supportive female comradeship.[18] With Nancy Cook, she opened a furniture factory connected with her Hyde Park cottage. With Marion Dickerman, she bought, and taught in, the Todhunter School for girls. With Esther Lape and Elizabeth Read, she took up feminist causes. With Caroline O'Day she promoted world peace. When she became the president's wife, she gave regular press conferences (a bold departure), but only women journalists were admitted, and several reporters—most notably Lorena Hickok of the Associated Press—became her close friends.[19]

The 1920s had seen an explosion of occupations for Eleanor. At first, her husband needed her, not only for support in his fight against polio but to keep up the political round of appearances, duty calls, and political-reconnaissance trips that he could no longer undertake. But as he moved onto the national scene, with an expanding male team of advisors, she became less important to him. By 1928, when Franklin moved into the governor's mansion in Albany, he was once again in charge of his own political network.

By that time Eleanor had several careers of her own, which placed increasing demands on her. She commuted from Albany twice a week to teach at the Todhunter School—she did not like leaving Missy LeHand, Franklin's secretary, to preside over entertainment in her absence, but she could not give up her rewarding tasks at the school. By the end of the decade, she was writing and speaking in many forums, had contracted for her own radio show, and was editing one of the flamboyant Bernarr MacFadden's magazines—in this case *Babies, Just Babies*.

All this flurry of activity seemed destined to come to an end when Franklin won the presidency. She must give up her days at the school. She said she would maintain the radio show and the magazine—but she was at last persuaded that this would be impossible. In time she resumed the radio show and substituted a daily newspaper column for her teaching schedule; but she could not foresee that liberation as the prison walls of the White House began to close around her.

No wonder Lorena Hickok, sensitive to women's moods, noticed that a gloom was descending on Eleanor during her preparation for the move to Washington. Presidents were not inaugurated at that time until

March—over a third of a year after the election. In those four and a half months, Eleanor, facing the breakup of her old female support system in New York, turned to her new friend, Hickok, to tell her about the demands of Washington. It was Hickok who sought out new avenues for her activity, beginning with the White House press conferences. Hickok would later suggest the newspaper column, too. Her own journalistic success encouraged Eleanor.

On the day before Franklin was inaugurated, Eleanor, stranded and alone amid all the bustle, let Hickok into the secret of her sadness. Together they went out, by cab, to the grave of Henry Adams's wife in the Rock Creek Park cemetery, a grave for which Augustus Saint-Gaudens had created his larger-than-life hooded figure of grief. This is where Eleanor had come, as the wife of the secretary of the navy, after she learned of the Lucy Mercer affair, to brood and to brace her soul.

During her first days in the White House, Eleanor clung to "Hick," as everyone called her, as to a safety blanket. This strained Hick's journalistic ethics, so she went off to New York to write a book; then, when that proved a dead end, she traveled for Harry Hopkins of the National Relief Agency, writing field reports on New Deal programs. Eleanor was desperately lonely for her, and her letters take on the ache of her old correspondence with her father. She kissed Hick's picture as she took up her pen.[20] Alone in the White House, she wrote: "I wish I could lie down beside you tonight & take you in my arms."[21] And Hickok, traveling in a dreary stretch of Minnesota, wrote: "Funny how even the dearest face will fade away in time. Most clearly I remember your eyes, with a kind of teasing smile in them, and the feeling of that soft spot just northeast of the corner of your mouth against my lips."[22]

The desperate need for Hick's support faded well before Eleanor's first year in the White House had ended. By Christmas of 1933, she was writing Hick that she treasured her friendship because it was staid and middle-aged—it had "a quality of companionship not possible to youth."[23] Eleanor had discovered that she could do *more* because of her White House position—not (as she had feared) less. The discipline and opportunities of writing her daily column gave shape to her life, as did the satisfaction of earning her own money (though she gave most of it to charity). She not only broadcast her own shows, but—as the president's wife—did so for commercial sponsors. Not even the "liberated" Hillary Clinton could get away with that in later times. Cole Porter's hit show of 1934, *Anything Goes*, referred to her mattress-company sponsors:

So Missus R., with all her trimmin's,
Can broadcast a bed from Simmons
'Cause Franklin knows
Anything goes.

But the great new field for her activity was as an advocate of civil rights and the impoverished. Before, she had been able to open a small furniture factory to employ local labor around Hyde Park. Now, through New Deal agencies, she became the driving force behind the Arthurdale Resettlement Project in West Virginia, helping the unemployed reclaim land and train for jobs in new communities. She filled one great lack in the New Deal's programs—a concern for black civil rights. Her husband, who had to work with southern congressional chairmen of his own party, settled for equal pay to blacks in the federal job and relief programs. Other grave injustices to African-Americans—lynchings, segregation, denial of voting rights—were put on the back burner. But Eleanor found ways to dramatize these injustices, despite the disapproval of many in the White House. (Steve Early, for instance, Franklin's press secretary, was a traditional southerner who did not like to see blacks encouraged to depart from their imposed subservience.) Eleanor badgered Franklin to receive representatives of the National Association for the Advancement of Colored People in the White House. When the Daughters of the American Revolution refused to let the African-American contralto Marian Anderson sing in their hall, Mrs. Roosevelt gave up her DAR membership. When a policeman told her she could not, by state law, sit on the black side of an audience in Alabama, she took a chair and placed it firmly in the middle of the aisle. She spoke out on the savage lynchings that were still taking place in the South.

After her husband's death in 1945, Eleanor again feared that her life would contract, that she had lost a position from which she could affect the causes to which she was devoted. But an early concern of hers, world peace, returned to occupy her. She had disapproved of the way her husband abandoned support for the League of Nations in order to run for the vice presidency. She became one of the most eloquent advocates of the United Nations Organization, to which President Truman appointed her a delegate. There she had some famous run-ins with Andrei Vishinsky over the repatriation of refugees to the Soviet bloc. After one successful vote on the issue, Secretary of State John Foster Dulles said she had assuaged his misgivings that she would not be tough enough. Reporting this comment to Joseph Lash, she wrote: "So—against odds, the work inches forward, but I'm rather old to be carrying on the fight."[24] Yet she became the guiding force behind passage of the Universal Declaration of Human Rights in 1948. She topped the Gallup poll that year as the most admired person in the world, ahead of President Truman.

She was willing to risk her popularity against Senator Joseph McCarthy when many politicians were afraid to criticize the red-baiter. She also violated a New York political rule, that Democrats could not win by taking on the powerful Catholic cardinal of the city, Francis Spellman. When the cardinal made city schools remove *The Nation* from their libraries, because the magazine printed Paul Blanshard's criticisms of the church, Mrs. Roosevelt suggested that the cardinal become acquainted with the United States Constitution. The cardinal sent her a public letter, after which (he said) he would have no more dealings with her: "Your record of anti-Catholicism stands for all to see—a record which you yourself wrote in the pages of history which cannot be recalled—documents of discrimination unworthy of an American mother."[25] But it was the cardinal who had to back down and ask, through intermediaries, for permission to call on her in order to smooth over the controversy. Though she supported her friend Adlai Stevenson against John Kennedy at the 1960 Democratic convention, Kennedy appointed her to the chair of the President's Commission on the Status of Women in 1961.

She was never ashamed of using her connections, and her husband's, to help others. She did not think of this as privilege. In her genuine humility, she thought of it as compensating in part for her own deficiencies—her lack of higher education, her narrow upbringing, her natural shyness, the late help she had offered her own children. She was not resented by the recipients of her efforts.

It helped that she thought of herself as a worker. She wrote and taught and spoke in a professional way, keeping a schedule that any productive author could be proud of. She insisted on being paid for these activities. It was another way of breaking the dependence of her youth and early marriage. Though she and Franklin brought money to that marriage, it was not enough to support their large family in the expensive style Franklin insisted on (despite her misgivings). They depended on Sara Roosevelt to supplement their income, and Sara made that dependency as galling as possible.

She disliked having any of the young members of the family financially independent of their elders; keeping them financially dependent, she thought, was one way of keeping them at home and controlling them. . . . She did not like any of us to have regular incomes of our own . . . when I began to earn money it was a real grief to her.[26]

At a time when politicians (including her husband) used ghost writers, and politicians' wives submitted to the issuing of statements dictated by the male politician's staff, Eleanor insisted on writing all her own books, columns, and speeches. She never missed a deadline. Once, when she was sick, the president himself offered to write her column for her. She refused, and did it herself. During World War II, when she traveled without a secretary, she learned how to type her own copy. Good pay for working women was one of her highest public priorities.

Yet Eleanor did not pretend to her worker friends that she was "just one of them." The marks of her class would have made that absurd. She offered them what help she could give, which meant the power of her position. And she was careful not to undercut that position, not only because that would have hurt her husband, but because it would have limited her ability to help others.

This meant that she was always a moderate reformer. Though she was not afraid of radicals, and mixed with them constantly in order to temper their views, she was never one herself—a fact that irritated more impatient denouncers of "the system." Mother Jones would not have hesitated to break an unjust law if told she could not sit with her friend on the black side of a segregated auditorium. Eleanor would not break the law (though she could effectively mock it).

Though she was unflagging in her concern for African-Americans, she muted that concern at crucial points of her husband's legislative effort. She even asked black leaders to police their own expressions for the good of the war effort of the 1940s—and for the Cold War effort of the 1950s.[27] When she was told that Paul Robeson's appearance on her TV talk show would give Cold War "hawks" ammunition, because of the singer's pro-Soviet record, she let her producers cancel the appearance.[28] Though everyone knows that she relayed the concerns of the poor to the president, she could also serve as the conduit through which the British economist Lord Keynes warned Roosevelt against being too hostile toward big business.[29] She did not mean to overthrow the economic structure, but to make it more responsive to human need.

The moderate leader must walk a delicate line, addressing opposite camps. If Eleanor had been considered an enemy of the political system, she could not have used it as she did to help the disadvantaged. If, on the other hand, people thought she was just being kind in order to buy off criticism of her husband's administration, she would have lost the trust and cooperation she needed in order to function.

No one walked that tightrope more nimbly than the Eleanor of the 1930s, 1940s, and 1950s. A sense of the way she operated can be seen in one example of many, more fully reported than most because Joseph Lash, in his youth, was involved in its every aspect and based one of his books on it. Eleanor had a conspicuous role in setting up and administrating the National Youth Administration in 1935.[30]

The jobs and education subsidies of the NYA were denounced as an insufficient "sop" by officials of the American Youth Congress, an umbrella organization that claimed to represent every young people's group from the YMCA to the Young Communist League, but whose most influential board members were leftists. It proposed a far more sweeping (and expensive) National Youth Act, which Eleanor basically supported, though she called its financial demands unrealistic. From 1933 to 1939, she regularly addressed various youth gatherings, at a time when their strident New Deal tone was softened—less by her interventions, perhaps, than by the Popular Front mood of the time. But she had, in any case, become "the patron saint of the youth movement."[31]

Then the Soviet pact with Hitler led to a new assault on the Youth Congress. Congressman Martin Dies summoned its leaders to testify before his red-hunting House Committee on Un-American Activities. Some wanted to defy the committee, but Mrs. Roosevelt advised them it was shrewder to let the discourtesy be on the other side. She made her views known when she attended the hearings and sat with the youth leaders. When questioning became sharp, she moved to the press table and started taking notes for her column. Her presence made both sides behave better than they might have. She was not only a moderate herself but a cause of moderation in others.

At the lunch break, she took six youth leaders, including Lash, to eat with her in the White House, and returned with them, following the afternoon session, for dinner with the president. The next day Joseph Lash testified. He was the executive secretary of a Youth Congress affiliate which had followed the Popular Front line, but he was in the process of dissociating himself because of the Soviet-German pact. Nonetheless, he

"For gosh sakes, here comes Mrs. Roosevelt!"
Drawing by Robt. Day, © 1933, 1961, *The New Yorker* magazine

did not want to become an informer before the Dies Committee; so "his testimony was evasive, confused, and at times, flippant."[32] Mrs. Roosevelt, sensing his anguish, offered him the presidential lodge at Shangrila to rest and think in. Later she lent him her cottage at Hyde Park for trysts with his future wife, Trude Pratt, who was not yet divorced from a prior husband. Her attitude was motherly, but devoted, toward the man twelve years her junior—so J. Edgar Hoover added Lash to his growing list of Eleanor's lovers, male and female, black and white.[33]

Even after Franklin gave a public rebuke to four thousand youth delegates who had come to the White House at Eleanor's invitation, she kept the avenues open between the president and any students who wanted to consult with him. Her experience with the most obstructive Communists in the youth movement toughened Eleanor in her later stand against Vishinsky at the U.N. She had been criticized for even hoping to work with Communists in the 1930s. But her attitude was that the students' problems were real, and if Communists saw the problems and tried to address them, this should spur others to action. For some, this was "buying off" radicals. For others, it was giving in to them. But Eleanor dealt with *individuals*, like Lash, like others she befriended. If the New Deal worked, despite inadequate measures, in reuniting the country, it was partly because of the real concern shown by Eleanor and by other compassionate people in the federal government (many of them her friends, protégés, or mentors, like Louis Howe and Harry Hopkins). Her followers were people in and outside of government, of her own social status and from all other classes. Many succumbed to the spell of her earnestness and joined her in the work that always seemed to multiply around her.

Those who reject the moderate leader because only a radical protest is "authentic" will never understand the need more ordinary people have for help to meet life's daily problems. Nor do they see how moderates alter power by making it more responsible, less autocratic. Eleanor Roosevelt was "naive" in the eyes of ideologues, both of the right and the left, who did not understand her extraordinary appeal. But most Americans felt like the miners in Robert Day's famous *New Yorker* cartoon, men who expected that if they had any troubles, Eleanor was bound to show up.

ANTITYPE
Nancy Reagan

T he tough and effective leadership of philanthropists like Florence Nightingale and Eleanor Roosevelt should not blind us to another fact: some "ladies bountiful" dabble in charity work that is dubious in motive and effect. The economist Thorstein Veblen, in his classic work *The Theory of the Leisure Class*, called such work an example of conspicuous leisure, an aspect of conspicuous consumption. It advertises that the lady has free afternoons to spend on projects with "some specious object of amelioration."[1] The aim is less to effect real social change than to demonstrate a lady's personal accomplishments (along with her stylish wardrobe). Museum benefits attract sponsors who are themselves the most highly wrought artifacts on exhibit.

The "projects" that presidents' wives undertake are perfect examples of this form of philanthropy. Jacqueline Kennedy started it with her White House beautification project, and Lady Bird Johnson followed up with highway beautification. Pat Nixon had a kind of stealth project, which was said to exist but left no marks: it was called "volunteerism." Betty Ford concentrated on handicapped children, and Barbara Bush on illiterate children. Rosalynn Carter was supposed to have a project devoted to mental health, but she did little on it after her helper in the area, Peter Bourne, became a political embarrassment to her husband.

The idea of a project has become so important to the political wife that even vice presidents' spouses now act on it. Joan Mondale was officially concerned with the arts, Marilyn Quayle with disaster relief, and Tipper Gore with mental health (taking up Rosalynn Carter's fallen standard). Barbara Bush launched her illiteracy project in the vice president's mansion before she took it to the White House.

Most of these activities are harmless enough. It keeps the wives on the streets—it gives them somewhere to go. There is a useful element of entertainment in it all, an air of "Let's pretend." Marilyn Quayle was able to appear in some fetching work garb near disaster sites (though cleanups after the San Francisco earthquake and Florida hurricane showed no signs of her effect). Barbara Bush was able to make grandmotherly appearances with children learning to read the books she "ghostwrote" for her dog Millie.

But Nancy Reagan's "project" was not entirely benign. She was slow to come to it; Michael Deaver tailored it for her after a shaky start in the White House, when her main concern seemed to be upgrading the china used at banquets. The project finally settled on was a "Just Say No" campaign to dissuade young people from using drugs. As a former actress who played maternal parts even in her twenties, Mrs. Reagan was good at the publicity appearances this project entailed. Some money was raised and put, presumably, to some purpose—perhaps to more publicity appearances. But the program did little good and some indirect harm.

The harm came from the assumptions wrapped up in that slogan "Just Say No." It was all a matter of individual choice. Nothing systemic was causing the drug problem, just weak will in each user. The campaign resembled attempts to curb the illegitimate birth rate by telling young girls just to say no to sex. Or AIDS by just saying no to homosexuality. It was the perfect right-wing campaign. It identified an evil and blamed the victim in ways that assume perfect rationality of choice in slum-affected young people. Since it was the person's own fault if he or she just said yes to drugs, treatment of those afflicted was not a government priority. Drug *dealers* were a different matter—Ed Meese's justice department had to put them in jail. But drug users were put in spiritual Coventry by Mrs. Reagan, chided because they had failed "just" to say no. The slogan subtly announced a program of inaction, or a release for righteousness, a way of saying, "Children, *behave.*"

The Nancy Reagan program shows the danger shared by all these projects. They were given to women as something separable from the serious business of government, which engrosses their husbands. The "project" is something a lady can do in her off-hours. It is not connected with social forces to be addressed across a range of community needs. That was acceptable when Mrs. Kennedy found old furniture for the White House, or Mrs. Mondale invited in some artists for dinner at the Naval Observatory mansion. But the problems of mental health or drug addiction are matters of legislative concern, not problems to be solved by volunteerism.

Although Mrs. Roosevelt was mocked by the irascible columnist, Westbrook Pegler as a "social worker to the world," nothing could have been farther from the modern "project" than her work. She understood the structural relation of poverty to racism, the need for government action at many levels to address deep malfunctions in her society. Besides, she was a worker who actually taught in the Todhunter School, managed a furniture business at Val-Kill, wrote as a professional to support her efforts for others. She went where the need was greatest and did what she could, with no paid publicists or slogan singers. It is no wonder the Republicans who railed at her were charmed by Nancy Reagan's campaign. They were both philanthropic; but "reform" for Mrs. Reagan was a politer form of scolding. Each had her followers and was a leader to that extent. But in terms of effectiveness, inclusiveness, and lasting influence, Mrs. Roosevelt exemplifies the true reformer and Mrs. Reagan the antitype, almost the cartoon reversal. People are still inspired to follow Mrs. Roosevelt's lead in civil rights, feminist, and welfare causes. Who marches, now, to Mrs. Reagan's slogan?

4.

DIPLOMATIC LEADER

Andrew Young

The conditions of a diplomat's life seem inimical to leadership. If he serves only the government that sends him out, he exemplifies Sir Henry Wotton's famous definition of an ambassador as "an honest man sent to lie abroad for the good of his country."[1] His messages home are confidential; his communications abroad are duplicitous. If, on the other hand, he tries to serve as an honest broker between the host country and his home government, he is serving two masters—and how can they be united in a common goal? An important recommendation for any diplomat is trustworthiness. Yet his very job seems to undermine trust in him. If he is only the tool of his principal, he seems little better than a spy. If he "goes native" in the place he is sent to, the home office will consider him a liability.[2]

Duplicity is contained in the very name of the diplomat, whose credentials are "twofold" (di-ploma), sealed back on themselves. The diplomat's role grew out of the Renaissance courtier's, and the best-known study of the courtier lays a stress on ingratiation that looks to modern eyes like fawning.[3] In Baldassare Castiglione's dialogue, *The Book of the Courtier*, the conversationalists discuss the way a courtier can please his master, by falsehood if that serves better than truth.[4] The diplomat doubles the courtier's labor of complaisance. He must stay in favor at home while winning favor abroad; must represent his own government to another, yet report back on that government (which is a labor of representation, too). If, to win some goal of his own—e.g., to preserve peace between the nations—he deliberately misrepresents conditions at the foreign court (by, say, screening out its harsher conduct), he may betray both masters at once.

Yet some diplomats have been leaders, with followings in several countries. When President Jimmy Carter forged the Camp David agreements whereby Israel returned the Sinai territory to Egypt, he used a confidential diplomat of great experience, Philip Habib, in the early stages of the semisecret process. But in the high-profile final negotiations, Carter stepped forth himself, drawing on his personal credit with both Egyptian and Israeli leaders, a credit earned by Carter's innovating sensitivity toward third-world conflicts and his respect for the religious traditions of both countries. His successful effort had less to do with any constitutional or traditional tasks of the president than with diplomacy plain and simple. Some presidents have acted as their own secretaries of state. Carter was, in effect, his own special ambassador to the Middle East.

This was not the first time a president has served as first diplomat. Woodrow Wilson did that at the Versailles Peace Conference (with mixed results). Franklin Roosevelt was an ambassador of goodwill holding together the allied leaders—Stalin, Churchill, Chiang Kai-shek—at international conferences during World War II.

More conventional ambassadors have also been public leaders. When a prominent member of the American establishment is sent abroad— Averell Harriman, for instance, or David Bruce, or John McCloy—the appointment itself says that the mission is highly important and must succeed. That kind of ambassador is able to forge close ties with the foreign leader he is addressing; he recruits a clientele for joint relations even in the host country. David Bruce, as the ambassador to Germany, helped President Eisenhower and Chancellor Adenauer marshal the two countries toward their joint anticommunist crusade. This made Bruce a leader in the Cold War.

Even people who are not formally in diplomatic positions often perform essentially diplomatic tasks. When General Eisenhower was the head of the joint military forces of the Allies in World War II, he often found himself engaged less in war planning as such than in diplomatic efforts to keep military leaders from other countries placated and cooperative. He repeated this performance after the war, when he became military director of the NATO Alliance. The physicist J. Robert Oppenheimer, who was a scientific leader before World War II and a moral-political leader after, served a largely diplomatic role at Los Alamos during the development of the atom bomb. He kept the military directors of the project and the scientific workers cooperating with each other, despite stresses and dissension.

Certain jobs are almost entirely diplomatic in nature. University presidents, for instance, do little if any scholarly work. They must keep potentially antagonistic groups in some kind of harmony—boards of directors, alumni, administrative staff, faculty, students, maintenance services. Academic planning is dependent on the cooperation that can be achieved by these forces. And the president's fund-raising returns him or her to that aboriginal diplomatic role, the courtier's.

The informal kinds of diplomacy tend to be more complex than outright ambassadorships. John McCloy, as president of the World Bank after World War II, had to orchestrate the activities of forty-six nations' economic establishments, an even more delicate effort than David Bruce's hand-holding operation with Chancellor Adenauer. Peacekeepers at various levels are important factors in our social life. The director of a major opera company must bring about the cooperation of individual donors, grant-giving agencies, the board of directors, singers and their agents, conductors, the musicians, the designers and makers of stage scenery and costumes, adult choir and children's choir, ballet performers, and maintenance crews. It is a never-ending exercise in diplomatic skills of the highest order.

One of the great recent exercises in diplomacy took place where one might least have expected it, in the civil rights movement of the 1960s. That was a movement devoted to "direct action"—to provocation, confrontation, and purposeful breaking of the law. It was socially disruptive. Yet, as St. Augustine claimed, even a band of robbers must be equitable in its internal conduct. A disruptive group must not be itself disrupted. In an atmosphere of continual crisis, like that surrounding the civil rights movement, disagreements tend to be sharp and bitter. Keeping the peace is harder because of the very righteousness and moral absolutism needed to take heroic action. That is why Andrew Young, the keeper of social concord, was so necessary to a movement that lived in a situation of continuing social discord.

There were many kinds of heroism and leadership in the civil rights movement. Young's was not the most dramatic or spectacular. He was not killed like Dr. King and others. He did not go to jail as often as Ralph Abernathy, or get beaten as often as John Lewis. He was not a great orator like James Bevel. But his quiet work kept the others together and made conditions more favorable for the promulgation of their message.

Young was born between worlds, not really part of any one situation. His father was a prosperous dentist in New Orleans, the birthplace of jazz and the blues—yet Andrew was forbidden to listen to them as he grew up. His light-skinned parents had different cultural aspirations. He was taken to hear classical musicians like the singers Roland Hayes and Marian Anderson. The Youngs were prouder of their Native American ancestors than of their black ones.

The family was not even Baptist. It belonged to one of those Congregationalist parishes founded in the nineteenth century by New England missionaries to the South. Since Young's parents could afford to send him to a good nursery school, he skipped the first three grades of public school—once again putting him out of sync with his own surroundings. He was younger than his classmates, as well as lighter-skinned and richer. This age differential was even more marked at Howard University, since the campus was full of returned World War II veterans when Young arrived there in the late 1940s.

His religious vocation took Young back to the roots of his New England Congregationalism. He had been impressed by a minister from Yale who stayed with his parents while preparing to go to Africa as a missionary. When Young left for the Hartford Seminary Foundation in Connecticut, an early-fifties interest in African nations, newly represented in the U.N., attracted his attention. A professor who had served in Angola encouraged him to set his sights on that country. The woman he intended to marry on graduation, Jean Childs, shared his ambition to serve in Angola—she was studying Gandhi at her college. It was exciting to find Jean already familiar with those ideas, Young told me in a 1990 interview.

This meeting with the intellectual woman from Lincoln Normal School was in strange contrast to Young's first encounter with Martin King, in 1957. Young drove King from a college lecture he had given:

We drove from Talladega back to Montgomery and had dinner. . . . We sat around talking, and I knew he had written his . . . dissertation on Paul Tillich. I had read a lot of Paul Tillich and I had been fortunate enough to meet Dr. Tillich. . . . I wanted to talk theology, and he wasn't interested. . . . We ended up having a nice little chat about family and children; we made no comments about the social situation, nothing profound.[5]

When Young later decided to join the civil rights struggle, it was with some idea of educating the poor black preachers he had met:

> The Southern Christian Leadership Conference is made up largely of Baptist Churches and lower class Negroes. These clergy do not have the respect of the educated Negro, and there is almost no way for them to get together. They need each other desperately, though. This would be one of my objectives.[6]

Even then he was thinking in diplomatic terms, of getting people together, but with little realization of the situation he was entering. He was more condescending going back to his own South than he would have been in going to Angola. He still had not got the message of America's black culture, of jazz and the blues.

When Young graduated from the seminary in 1955, Portugal was no longer letting black missionaries from America enter its Angolan colony, so he accepted a Congregationalist parish in Thomasville, Georgia; but his talents and charm had caught the attention of church leaders, who brought him back north to serve the National Council of Churches in its youth program. He also became the administrator of the Christian Education Program for the United Church of Christ. These were important (and cushy) jobs for one so young—he was only twenty-five when he was hired by the NCC. He traveled, met influential people, continued his intellectual interests. He was a budding ecclesiastical bureaucrat. He knew the world of corporate boards, foundations, and influential charity organizations. In fact, when he decided to go south it was with a grant from the Field Foundation for a Voter Education Project (VEP). As an indication of the style he had become accustomed to, Young arrived at the VEP center in Dorchester, Georgia, on a chartered plane.[7]

The man who had come to teach had a great deal to learn. Luckily for him, he had a tough instructor on hand, Septima Clark, a woman in her sixties who had been educating people in her literacy program for decades, mainly at the venerable Highlander Folk School in Tennessee. Clark had brusque ways of bringing Young off his high horse. She began the process that would put Young in the jeans or coveralls that became the SCLC uniform for going to demonstrations and to jail.

Young was plunged into jurisdictional disputes from the outset. The VEP money and SCLC money came from different sources, though his and others' activities overlapped. Young was good at explaining such problems to donors. He was glib but courteous, sophisticated but idealistic—qualities that impressed Dr. King, who knew they could be very useful. Young was not only softer-spoken but better-spoken than most of the white officials he dealt with as King's personal representative. As a negotiator, Young represented the carrot side of the movement. People like Hosea Williams, always ready for confrontation, were the stick side. King decided which to use, and when, in every situation.

One of King's tactics was to go around the police and politicians to ask businessmen if they did not want peace for their community. Young was especially helpful here. He played a key role in forming an accord with Birmingham businessmen.[8] "As the night dragged on, both sides tended to credit the mild, unflappable Andrew Young with ideas that achieved overall balance by proceeding in mixed stages."[9]

Young believed all channels should be kept open. Some in the movement had suffered so much from white persecutors in the Deep South that they despaired of reaching anyone on the other side. Young, who had studied and worked with whites, gave them the benefit of the doubt, out of principle, but also as a tactic. The protesters would look more reasonable if they had tried to negotiate before marching. Young also believed in keeping mayors and sheriffs informed about the SCLC's intentions. Some on King's staff regretted the loss of surprise—city officials could form their own counterstrategy. But Young claimed that people get more violent if they are faced with unexpected crises. The most daring of Young's approaches involved the FBI. With good reason the SCLC distrusted J. Edgar Hoover, who hated King and meant to destroy him. But Young kept up continual exchanges with agents, trying to convince them that their own honor demanded that they avoid complicity with the oppressive local law officers. He also arranged a meeting between King and Hoover, where the two men tried to feign cordial relations.

Young's effort to defuse hostilities raised the suspicions of some of his rivals for King's favor. Hosea Williams was especially critical of Young, teasing him, mocking his willingness to see the other's side, calling him an Uncle Tom. The irony of this is that Williams was friendly with James Harrison, who actually was a paid informer working for the FBI inside the SCLC. When the movement went to Chicago in 1966, another informant, briefing the FBI agents in that city, reported to them the accusations against Young: "It is a common belief among civil rights workers that

Andrew Young is furnishing information concerning SCLC to the FBI."[10] Here was a real spy telling his fellows that they had someone else branded as a spy in SCLC.

The suspicion that a man trying to mediate is playing a double game is a perpetual threat to conscientious diplomats. Trying to make one side see how the other side views things, the diplomat can look like an advocate for the other side. But the true usefulness of a diplomat is precisely this presentation of many attitudes at work in any situation. Castiglione, in the later parts of his dialogue, says that the courtier's major task, under his omnidirectional ingratiation, is to tell the ruler truths he can hear from no one else.

> Falsehood is deservedly odious to God and to men, and more harmful to princes than [to] any other; because they have the greatest lack of what they would most need to have in abundance—I mean, someone to tell them the truth and make them mindful of what is right: because their enemies are not moved by love to perform these offices . . . [and] among their friends there are few who have free access to them, and those few are wary of reprimanding them for their faults as freely as they would private persons.[11]

King came to value Young's advice above that of anyone in his immediate entourage—a fact that caused resentment among those who had been with King longer and suffered more of the early persecutions. Young was given delicate tasks. For instance, when James Meredith (who had integrated "Ole Miss") was making a protest march and grew angry at the squabbling of black factions trying to join or manipulate him, King sent Young to patch things up with Meredith.[12]

When King went to jail, he used Young as his emissary to those outside, giving him a running series of instructions on what was to be done in his place.[13] King knew that Young could often accomplish things in his absence that King himself might not accomplish on the outside: "These fellows respond better when I am in jail or [there is] a crisis."[14] So King created a crisis, by going inside, in the hope that Young, on the outside, could resolve the crisis and settle other problems, too. This "Mr. Inside and Mr. Outside" act was an efficient division of labor.[15] David Garrow quotes with approval a SCLC staff member: "Andrew Young was Dr. King's true alter ego. Without Andrew Young, SCLC would have failed and action would have faltered."[16]

After King's death in 1968 and the partial disintegration of SCLC during a floundering Poor People's Campaign in Washington, Young won a race for a congressional seat from Georgia. While holding office, he campaigned for Jimmy Carter and was rewarded, after Carter's election to the presidency, with an appointment as ambassador to the United Nations. Back in New York, the site of his early bureaucratic endeavors for the National Council of Churches, Young was able to develop his early interest in Africa and other third-world regions. Carter told him he was appointing him because of Dr. King's standing with people of color throughout the world. The president was criticized in the South for Young's efforts to bring America out of its own colonial past—especially by means of the treaties that surrendered permanent right to the Panama Canal.

But what led to Young's forced resignation from the U.N. job was passion over Middle East diplomacy. Young felt, as usual, that channels should be kept open at all times. [17] This ran up against the Israeli-imposed taboo on talking with any representatives of the Palestine Liberation Organization. Yet the PLO had a nonvoting delegation recognized by the U.N.; so when Young was the acting president of the Security Council, he agreed to talk with PLO representatives informally at a social gathering. This provoked an angry response from Israelis. Young told me later that the Israelis were right to be apprehensive because they knew—and Young did not—of other State Department initiatives being carried on in secret. What was offensive, if anything, was those other meetings, not Young's; and to protect them, the department issued an evasive statement about Young's meeting—which Young refused to go along with. As Wolf Blitzer, then on the staff of the *Jerusalem Post*, put the story together:

> Young told Assistant Secretary of State for International Organizations, William Maynes, the truth about the exact nature of the meeting when first questioned about it on August 11. But the State Department decided to cover up . . . the entire matter probably would have blown over if Young—who told his bosses the truth—had gone along with the State Department's lie. Instead, for whatever reason, Young confided to the Israeli ambassador at the UN, Yehuda Blum, that the "official" version was not true. [18]

President Carter, already catching heat for Young's third-world contacts and anxious to keep his Camp David diplomacy successful, had to sacrifice Young to the State Department's secrecy. But the following Young had built up in Africa and other countries helped him when he was elected mayor of Atlanta in 1982. He said: "I came into office when Reagan was cutting off funds from Washington. But there is always loose capital in the world money market, and I know where it is, because of my experience as an ambassador and as a congressman on the banking committee."[19] Young was accused by his critics of "globetrotting" during his time as mayor; but he brought international business to the city, and his intense cultivation of the Olympic Committee led to the designation of Atlanta as the site of the 1996 summer Olympics.[20]

As someone who has always lived between worlds, Young has been accused by blacks of being too white, by whites of being too black.[21] He is not, in some critics' eyes, a true southerner. Some advocates of the poor called him too friendly to capitalists. He was too Africa-oriented to be really American, but too American to favor world revolutions. He has used his intermediate status to bring different peoples together, losing some people's allegiance by this very openness, but forging enough of a following in enough places, inside and outside America, to be a kind of permanent emissary for peace. He typifies the exposed position of all those who go between different factions, who must carry on with equanimity even under criticism. He still preaches on Sunday in various pulpits and considers himself basically a pastor, doing the work for which he was ordained.

Andrew Young
Ann States/SABA

ANTITYPE

Clark Kerr

When the California Board of Regents made Clark Kerr the president of the University of California in 1958, it could not foresee the student turmoil he would encounter in the 1960s. But if it had been given any prevision of those troubles, that would only have confirmed it in the choice. After all, Kerr had been not only a successful president of the faculty senate on the Berkeley campus, but (later) the chancellor of that branch of the university. Before that, he had become famous as an arbitrator of labor disputes, settling hundreds of conflicts, heading off numerous strikes. Who better to deal with a "student strike" on his own turf, where the faculty knew and respected him?

Kerr had defined the problem facing the modern university, in terms that other college presidents studied as a guide. In the spring of 1963, he codified his scattered writings in the prestigious Godkin Lectures delivered at Harvard. He said that the "multiversity" had replaced the university. The multiversity is a service center with many different roles, to be played out before many different constituencies:

> The university is being called upon to educate previously unimagined numbers of students; to respond to the expanding claims of national service; to merge its activities with industry as never before; to adapt to and re-channel new intellectual currents.[1]

The university was strategically placed at the center of what Kerr hailed as the knowledge industry.

> The production, distribution, and consumption of knowledge in all its forms is [sic] said to account for 29 percent of the gross national product, according to Fritz Machlup's calculations; and "knowledge production" is growing at about twice the rate of the rest of the economy. What the

railroads did for the second half of the last century and the automobile for the first half of this century may be done for the second half of this century by the knowledge industry: that is, to serve as the focal point for national growth.[2]

If the university was no longer a cloister of scholars separated from the busy national life, but was actually at the center of that life, then closing down a university would be a way of paralyzing the nation—and students *would* close down Kerr's university in the days ahead. For all his prescience on other matters, Kerr did not take the measure of that threat. In a passage that was omitted from the published version of his lecture, but in which Kerr can be seen on videotape delivering with great emphasis, he said:

> One of the most distressing tasks of a university president is to pretend that the protest and outrage of each new generation of undergraduates is [sic] really fresh and meaningful. In fact, it is one of the most predictable controversies that we know. The participants go through a ritual of hackneyed complaints almost as ancient as academe, while believing that what is said is really radical and new.[3]

Just a year after those comments, Kerr had to deal with student demands that were, in fact, new; that were part of a wrenching national confrontation with segregation that would alter American laws and customs. In March of 1964, Berkeley students joined a sit-in at the Sheraton Palace Hotel in San Francisco. They were arrested and tried, but they succeeded in changing the hiring practices of the hotel, ending discrimination against blacks. Emboldened by this victory, students went back to Berkeley in the fall to find their organizing center denied them. The tables with political pamphlets and calls for joint action had been removed from their traditional place at Bancroft and Telegraph streets. This muzzling of free speech on the campus gave the students an unbeatable issue. The faculty almost had to support them on this.

Upping the stakes, the activists moved their tables to the heart of the campus, Sproul Plaza. When police tried to arrest those at the tables, students flooded around a police car that held one arrested student, and kept it for thirty hours in a sea of chanting and orating young people. At last Kerr acted, negotiating a release of the police car in return for setting up a committee to consider the students' grievances. This should have been Kerr's natural arena, a negotiating session; but he let the negotiations drag on for six months, hoping the protest would die down (wasn't it just the old ritual of hackneyed complaints, like a more pretentious panty raid?). When, under pressure, the university allowed the tables back onto the campus, it was with this proviso—that no illegal actions could be advocated. That proviso hit at the heart of the civil rights movement—civil disobedience of Dr. King's sort—and violated the constitution. Free speech means freedom to say things in favor of illegal action. Once again, Kerr was undercutting his own hold on the faculty, which could hardly oppose free speech on a campus formally committed to open inquiry.

When the results of the bargaining process were announced, the students, who had taken over Sproul Plaza in the autumn, took over Sproul Hall (the administration center) in the spring, setting a pattern that would be used on other campuses to suspend university activity. The mass arrest of all the students packed inside the building caused more demonstrations, which Kerr hoped to end with a statement of university policy, given by the school's highest officials, to students assembled in the Greek Theater. Kerr's tone was one of rebuke, not conciliation: "The university supports the power of persuasion against the use of force."[4] Yet the tables had originally been removed by police force, with no administration attempt to discuss the issue of free speech. Student leader Mario Savio had asked to address the meeting in the Greek Theater, and he was refused permission. When he went to the lectern anyway, guards threw him down and dragged him off the stage. The reaction was electric. The Academic Senate of faculty members condemned the administration by an overwhelming vote. Kerr had lost both the students and the faculty. He would soon lose the support of the Board of Regents, the California legislature, and the incoming governor, Ronald Reagan. The great negotiator could not bring a single player to the table.

The year after the free speech turmoil, protest against the Vietnam War became even more bitter, as casualties went up in Indochina. Kerr had rejoiced in the close connection between the university and the federal government. This connection had been the greatest force for change on the campuses of the great universities. As he said in the Godkin Lectures, federal grants "accounted for 75 percent of all university expenditures on research." Furthermore, "six universities [California's among them] received 57 percent of the funds in a recent fiscal year," and 40 percent of that was defense-connected (even more if one included defense-related areas like space exploration).[5] In other words, by Kerr's own account of things, the university and the government were interlocked entities, and when the government went to war, so did the university. So students did not have to go to Washington to protest the war; they could confront it on the campus.

How did Kerr lose all his arbitrator's skills, exercised on the waterfront, or in corporate board rooms and union halls, when acting within his own academic domain? Apparently, he thought of the academy on an industrial model. He liked to speak of the knowledge *industry*, its *product*, and to boast that he used economic analysis to describe it. Industrial negotiation as he knew it was simply structured. It had two principal parties, the employees and the employers, and a limited set of issues to be discussed (wages, working conditions, health and pension benefits). Applying this schema to academe, Kerr acted as if the employees were the state legislature and its appointed Board of Regents, while the workers were the academic staff and faculty.

Even this simplified model was more complex than it looked. For one thing, the administrative staff (including the president, chancellor, and deans) was often at odds with the faculty. For another, the president was included in one party to the negotiations (the staff). He did not stand above the process, but was in it. Most disastrously, however, Kerr's model left no room for the students.[6] They were not the workers—faculty members were. As Mario Savio remarked at the time, the students were the raw material to be processed by a "knowledge industry" creating its "product." Blinded by this model, Kerr let the students seize the high ground of free speech. They were the ones who warned against the university's dependence on a government that pays its bills.[7] Whatever their later excesses (and there were many, as passions over the war increased and disaffected students created their own drug culture), the protesters' first actions engaged student and faculty sympathy in a way that Kerr never did. He had no empathy with the students; he discussed changes in the student body primarily in terms of the number of them "knocking at the door" to get an education.

The only extremism Kerr anticipated was that of "a few of the nonconformists" who might bring alien examples to American campuses:

They seek, instead, to turn the university, on the Latin American or Japanese models, into a fortress from which they can sally forth with impunity to make their own attacks on society.[8]

Kerr did not see that his own description of the university was not of something separate from society, but central to it, directing it. The students were not sallying out of a fortress but laying siege to it, challenging the schools' quasi-governmental responsibility for society's actions.

As a diplomat, Kerr was unable or unwilling to get inside the minds of those who should have been his followers. He hardened himself against the advice of his own faculty. And because he had lost these followers, he was unable to put the unrest down—which made him lose the regents and the legislature. Seen by some as the puppet of the regents, he was treated by the regents as a scapegoat. Under Ronald Reagan's pressure, they dismissed him early in 1967—though even toward the end, he was unaware of their hostility. Unlike Andrew Young, he was not flexible in new situations, disarming in his attitude even toward those most hostile. He sealed himself off from the students—the last thing a good diplomat wants to happen to him. Keeping as many channels open as possible is the diplomatic imperative. Kerr was not the Andrew Young of the Berkeley confrontations, but the Bull Connor, one who made his adversaries look good. Connor was spiteful, but bungling. Kerr was well-meaning— and bungling. Sophisticatedly bungling, to be sure—that is the most interesting (if disheartening) kind of maladroitness. Kerr thought he was locking a few fringe students out of the university. But when at last he got the great door turned on its hinge and slammed firmly shut, he found that he had locked himself out.

5.
MILITARY LEADER

N a p o l e o n

L eadership in the military might seem, at first glance, a simple thing. Soldiers *must* obey their officers. If a follower stops following, he or she can be shot. Desertion is against the law. Then why do we admire battle commanders? The greatest number of large statues in Washington, D.C., is of military men on horses, not of politicians on platforms.

The main challenge to a military leader is not to *attract* followers—the modern state does that for him. He must, by respected decisions, confirm his hold upon immediate followers in arms and on remote supporters of the military effort (in the government and in the citizenry). It is difficult—even if you have perfectly docile followers, ready to obey every command—to *give* meaningful commands in the blur of war's action, to keep calm enough to *see* what is needed and to *say* what should be done in ways that will be understood. The leader must keep followers, in the first place, by keeping his own wits about him—and it is hard to exaggerate the difficulty of that task.

Carl von Clausewitz, the greatest writer on the nature of war, said that war is *essentially* irrational—not accidentally, not on the edges, not by mistake or exception, but always and everywhere. It is, at the very heart of it, forever impelling itself beyond itself. To overcome combatants' inhibitions against facing death, against inflicting death, against massive violence, leaders must create a kind of psychic explosion in each soldier, but a *controlled* explosion. All the discipline of drill, uniforms, codes of conduct are meant to ignite and yet contain the forces that can keep up this unnatural psychic game of risk and wrath.

The effort at containment can never end because of what Clausewitz calls the mutual transformation (*Wechselwirkung*) of forces in conflict.[1] Each side is increasingly enraged by the other's efforts to meet violence with greater violence. Soldiers who do not break or run become explosive in new ways. The war aims themselves are ratcheted up by each blow suffered or given. Few wars conclude with the limited goals originally sought. War leaps out of control like a conflagration. Yet the commander must rein back the rage and fear in others, often wresting them into submission in his own heart and head.

A second way that war slips out of control is through what Clausewitz calls friction (*Friktion*)—the perpetual failure of all the parts of a military action to mesh because each rubs up against different obstacles, external and internal.[2] A unit supposed to advance in a straight line finds that its own elements have different fatigue points, hesitations, or degrees of self-control (sufficient to see where the line is coming apart). Each person is facing his own private demons, too distracted to perform with the poise he could summon on the parade ground. Clausewitz said the difference between moving in drill practice and moving in war is that between walking on the ground and walking under water.[3] If the chorus line of Rockettes were to do its synchronous high kicks under water, the line of limbs would be irregular, as individuals' legs, differently muscled and contoured, met different water resistance. Effortful kicks to overcome that resistance would throw off the rhythm, push legs off to this or that side, creating more eddies in the water to disturb the performance.

If this friction frays out each move in a single rank, the results are multiplied exponentially in the overall effort. Friction itself creates more friction—two irregularities higher up in the direction of maneuver cause six or seven errors down the chain of transmission. In war, something is always going wrong, and once that happens (as it is bound to), it is easy for everything to go wrong.

And so far we have considered only the friction internal to the unit's action. There is also the friction of external resistance. That varies according to the *other* side's uneven temperaments, conditioning, and grasp of the mission. An advancing line meets different levels of opposition. Ironically, even an enemy's *weakness* can hurt the attacker's efficiency—if one part of the resistance yields suddenly, it can pull the attacking line out of order, disturbing the concerted movement of the whole. Those overrunning the weak point can lose touch entirely with their own forces (less in the instance of a single rank than in the mobilization of several units to preplanned convergences).

If the effect of internal friction is like making the Rockettes kick under water, the effect of *external* friction is like having the Rockettes try to kick on the stage while people run out of the wings to trip them, pull at them, push them over.[4]

Clausewitz said that the military leader who can best control *Wechselwirkung* and *Friktion* is the one who will direct his soldiers most usefully, understandably, and firmly, making followers conceive their task and do it more confidently because the leader so clearly knows what must be done, what must be abandoned or altered, as things go perpetually awry. For Clausewitz, the man who best exemplified this kind of control was Napoleon, against whom Clausewitz had fought as an officer in the Prussian (and later in the Russian) army.

In his earlier campaigns, at least, Napoleon saw the limits of what could be done—by his enemies, by himself, by his troops—and *used* those limits to baffle his foes. Few have understood as well as Clausewitz that Napoleon did not transcend the limits of war, but beat others precisely because of his recognition that *Friktion* and *Wechselwirkung* were always at work in and around him. This is a truth that cannot be grasped by those who think of Napoleon as a kind of military genius able to impress his own will on all parts of war.

The romantic myth of Napoleon is understandable; indeed, almost irresistible. He seemed to come from nowhere and soar instantly. He became the romantic period's favorite example of towering genius. Even his oddities were part of his charm. To some he was the very embodiment—the face, the voice—of France; yet that voice always spoke a slightly accented French, with traces of his first language. The face, incandescent in elated moments, a gloomy mask in his long silences, was olive-skinned. He was small, lithe in his youth, unmistakably Italian. Enemies would brand him an outsider by persisting in the use of his name's original form: Napoleone Buonaparte.[5]

Born in Corsica, at a time when that island was outracing even France on the winds of revolutionary change, Napoleon wanted to follow the local patriot, Paoli. But his family (minor island nobles) was exiled from Corsica, despite his own radical inclinations—which were thereby tempered. He could not muster, later, any enthusiasm for the killing of aristocrats, whose doom resembled too closely what had threatened his own relatives. Only a thirst for fame exceeded, in him, a loyalty to his impoverished *famiglia*. He would take his relatives, these minor luminaries of a backward island, and put them on the thrones of Europe.

His training was French and orthodox. Like many poorer sons of privilege, he was destined for military office. He served his apprenticeship at the Brienne military academy, where a talent for mathematics, and for the engineering skills of new weaponry, advanced him in the rapidly developing field of artillery deployment. Made an officer at age sixteen, he was only mildly engaged by the Revolution until, at age twenty-four, he caught the eye of the Robespierre brothers by recapturing the port of Toulon from the British. At age twenty-six, he put down a rightest rebellion in Paris (13 Vendémiaire), and at twenty-seven he closed the leftist Pantheon Club. No one knew, yet, what he would be—though Lazare Carnot was beginning to guess.

Carnot, a geometrician who specialized in fortifications, had reshaped the newly conscripted armies of the Revolution, earning the nickname of Victory's Organizer.[6] As a member of the Directory during Vendémiaire, he made Napoleon part of his planning staff for a threefold campaign against Austria—to be carried out, mainly, by two armies on the Rhine, with a third army to press the Austrian kingdom in Italy (centered on Milan).[7] Napoleon was sent to take over this last and least body, its 40,000 ill-clothed men pinned down on the Italian Riviera. The Ligurian Hills hemmed them in by land, and the guns on British ships threatened them from the sea. If the French advanced up the shore to Genoa, they would meet the Austrians, who expected this move. If they backed off toward Marseilles, the Austrian allies under Victor Amadeus III, the king of Sardinia based in the Piedmont, would serve as a buffer keeping Napoleon from his assigned foes in Milan.

Napoleon decided to fight his way over the Ligurian Hills, at a point where he could drive a wedge between Victor Amadeus and the Austrian armies.[8] The Ligurian Hills drop off steeply toward the sea, and the French had occupied heights along this southern ridge. But to the north the hills descend, in a long anfractuous series of spurs and declivities, toward the Lombard Plain. The Sardinian and Austrian forces had advanced into the hilly lower reaches of this chain, breaking up the numerical superiority they would have if their forces were combined. They meant to block Napoleon's descent when his army was thinned by the funneling spurs and ridges. Yet these spurs also kept his enemies separated in isolated declivities, prevented by the long mountain spines from lateral movement to reinforce each other.

Napoleon decided to strike down different routes, in combinations of force, to deal out quick, numbing blows on separated units, making them withdraw toward their respective capitals—the Sardinian forces west toward Turin, the Austrians east toward Milan—opening up a gap between their troops. In a week that dazzled Europe, Napoleon seemed to win a victory every other day by these lightning raids into the foothills—right against the Austrians at Montenotte (April 12); left against the Sardinians at Millesimo (April 13); left again against the fortress at Casseria (April 14); then right against Dego. The Austrians retook Dego on April 15, but Napoleon, showing the speed of movement that would always be his hallmark, shuttled key forces from the western front (Ceva), retook Dego, then sent part of his troops back to complete the taking of Ceva. This series of discrete battles, fought with detached elements of the foe, prevented the Austrians and Sardinians from joining their preponderant numbers against him. Rocked back, the Austrians and Sardinians recoiled from each other in their movement toward separate home bases. The allies had thought they could bottle up Napoleon by holding the passes in the mountain chain; but Napoleon turned the terrain against the troops that held it, making the land itself fight for him. As Clausewitz later wrote of Montenotte, "the colossal weight of the whole French people, unhinged by political fanaticism, came crashing down."[9] At age twenty-seven, Napoleon had sent the senior generals of two nations scurrying to either side of his advance; now he could defeat them, one at a time.

The Sardinian force first. It was a detachable adjunct to Austria, not (like Milan) a part of the transalpine Austrian empire centered in Vienna. By turning his whole army against Turin, beating the withdrawing troops at Mondovì, Napoleon wrested a truce from King Amadeus on April 27, and could turn his forces eastward toward Milan. The thing had happened almost as rapidly as it could be reported.

The characteristics of Napoleonic war were present, already, in this brilliant opening to his career of conquest. They can be summarized as six in number.

1. *Victory for its own sake.* Victory in the old system of war was often of dubious (if any) benefit. Defeating an enemy did not, necessarily, win a town or port. If the defeat of others cost part of one's own army, it was

not a real gain. Armies of the *ancien régime* were precious items in themselves. An able officer corps of nobles was literally irreplaceable; it could not be expended recklessly. The officers were professionals with expensive training, and they led expensive mercenaries. The aim of such an army was not only to protect valuable territory but to protect its valuable self. As Macaulay said of Frederick the Great's father:

> His feeling about his troops seems to have resembled a miser's feeling about his money. He loved to collect them, to count them, to see them increase; but he could not find it in his heart to break in upon the precious hoard.[10]

All this was changed by the Revolution. The new force was the People in Arms, raised by conscription for mass resistance to encirclement by the combined regents of Europe. The aim was no longer to maneuver for position but to destroy attacking armies, at whatever cost to one's own troops. This is the "political fanaticism" Clausewitz attributes to the French of the period. Their officers were not the scions of noble houses, but talented men from the bourgeoisie or intelligentsia; Carnot himself was a poet-engineer, born of a notary. Armies were thrown into war with a new recklessness, once it was clear that the officers' positions could be rapidly filled again.

Wars fought between the old powers of Europe were contained spasms within a structure of stability. Neither opponent wanted to upset that structure. King fought king for this or that objective, but not to overthrow kingship itself (in which each side had a heavy investment). Not so the Revolution. It wanted to destroy not only the army it faced but the whole political system that had sent it out. It meant to remove as many players as possible from the other side, as soon as possible—a form of war that had existed so rarely in the past (e.g., in Rome's genocidal conquest of Carthage) as to be remembered ever after as something monstrous. The revolutionary armies would make that aberration the norm.[11]

2. *Attack in headlong lunges.* By the eighteenth century the art of war had become an elaborate ballet of formations, positions, and deployment. An army in the field had to be disposed for the simultaneous achievement of contending goals—to create and protect logistical support, to maintain internal lines of communication, to cover essential possessions of its own regime, and to threaten selected targets on the other side (only those worth the risk of actual clash between the precious resources of men and equipment). Napoleon shattered all this with his

almost indiscriminate charges at targets of opportunity. He sought the early engagement most generals had been taught to put off. "Come to grips, then look around" (*On s'engage, puis on voit*).[12]

This was less foolhardy than it looked. Napoleon knew that if one begins with a quick victory against one part of an army—*any* part, regardless of its strategic importance—one multiplies all the problems of battle in every part of that army. "Friction" is exacerbated on the other side, so that war itself is made to fight on Napoleon's side, as the terrain was made to fight for him in the Ligurian Hills. There, the defeats inflicted rapidly on separate units of the armies made it harder for Sardinians and Austrians to coordinate future actions. The safest course for them, almost the only course, seemed to be withdrawal from each other. Anticipating that "safe" option, Napoleon made it the most dangerous one—they were separated, now, for piecemeal destruction.

3. *Fight toward supplies*. Napoleon told his shivering and hungry troops, pinned along the Ligurian coast, that food, shoes, and clothing lay before them in the Lombard Plain. The faster they descended to that level basin, the sooner they could relieve their long stretch of destitution. One must fight *through* the enemy *to* one's reward. Much of Napoleon's mobility lay in his willingness to race beyond supply wagons, regardless of logistical routes. This entailed a new ruthlessness in "requisitioning" and scavenging—which, again, had its roots in the politics of the Revolution. The forces of legitimacy that fought each other in the *ancien régime* were afraid of turning mercenary plunderers free from aristocratic control. Keeping the troops dependent on their masters for the agreed-on rewards of predictable service was a necessary discipline. But the Revolution fought in the name of the people, and was unabashed in its willingness to live on the people's goods. Sons who had themselves been requisitioned into service by the *grande levée* were not hesitant to requisition chickens from coops, grain from barns, and ammunition from supply depots.[13]

4. *Fight only with preponderant force on one's own side*. The combined troops of Austria and Sardinia outnumbered Napoleon's Army of Italy. But by choosing his points of attack, he guaranteed that he brought a larger force to each encounter, achieving a series of ad hoc majorities until the armies were separated. After that, his was the largest of the three commands. Once Sardinia was neutralized, his troops outnumbered the Austrians two to one. Napoleon, despite his mobility, did not rely on clever ploys as a substitute for dominant numbers.[14]

5. *Simplify.* Since maintaining preponderant force was the Napoleonic priority, he did not like to disperse his forces in feints, ambushes, pincer moves, and complicated evolutions.[15] For the same reason, he did not make long-term plans with any rigid claims on him.[16] Such planning inhibits improvisation, which takes advantage of new situations unfolding in the course of a battle. Napoleon kept himself ready to strike at targets of opportunity, to turn away from unexpected concentrations of the enemy, to pick and choose his next points of conflict as they were revealed to that "sweeping eye" (*coup d'oeil*) that Clausewitz says each commander should have.[17] The accidents of war become opportunities to the one who cooperates with them, instead of simply resisting the way they disrupt prior plans. Friction itself fights for such a commander.

6. *Keep moving.* The older warfare supported static regimes, and the military system reflected this preference for stasis. It held to fortifications whenever possible, with their prepared water supply, strategic positioning, assured billeting, and other factors that must be created anew on the march. For the same reasons, armies in the field, when they found strong positions, clung to them as long as possible.

Napoleon surprised his early opponents by reversing all such preferences. He needed movement as the shark does; it was his way of breathing. His army was always seeking a foe, and new supplies, and a way *around* fixed points. He was less vulnerable because no one could be sure where he would be (even, sometimes, himself). Morale was sustained by new opportunities. He avoided the boredom of long billeting and sieges.

Other leaders were drawn to the classical siege. A professional army must be posted and fed somewhere—why not in front of a town, where its mere presence can seal off and starve out a foe? Napoleon undertook only two sieges in his whole career—Mantua (1796) and Danzig (1807)—and the first one he broke off, even spiking his siege guns, to resume his mobile war on the Austrians crossing the Alps to relieve the siege.

Breaking off the siege at Mantua is one of the few acts in Napoleon's early career that made Clausewitz doubt that he had "thought the matter through."[18] By sacrificing the siege train in order to move out, Napoleon prolonged the fall of Mantua for almost six months. Clausewitz thought Napoleon was just yielding to his preference for boldness. But other scholars have pointed out that Napoleon's need to live off foraging would have made it necessary to send detached units away from the siege party, where they could be picked off. His greater priority was to keep the mass of his troops united. That is why he would not divide them into siege section and mobile section. By doing one thing at a time—attack the relief armies first, *then* resume the siege—he kept the army united. One sees here how simplicity entailed all the rest of his program—move fast, but together; do not disperse troops; maintain morale by cohesiveness. [19]

The man who had entered the Lombard Plain from the southwest in April of 1796 was knocking on its northeast Alpine passes by October. He had taken all of Austria's Italian kingdom, defeated four campaigns sent through the Alps against him, and was in a position to reach Vienna before the two French armies on the Rhine could attain that objective. His very success frightened the reeling French Directory, which tried to divert him to a smaller command in central Italy. He threatened to resign unless he retained his forces in the North, and he was too valuable to be dismissed. This left him in charge, not only of the military resolution of the war with Austria, but of the diplomatic terms for concluding hostilities. Napoleon returned Venice to Austria in exchange for all the rest of his Italian conquests.

Napoleon has been criticized for not pushing through to complete the assault on Vienna. [20] But here Clausewitz gives him the very highest marks. In a demonstration of the way analysis (*Kritik*) should determine strategy, Clausewitz says that at the first and most obvious level Napoleon *should* have crossed the Alps, since his army—added to the two on the Rhine—could have crushed the entire Austrian military establishment. "But the critic may take a wider view," as Clausewitz says repeatedly in this analytic exercise. Napoleon heard from the Directory that the two French armies to the north could not be sure of joining him for another six weeks. The Austrians could detach enough troops to meet Napoleon in the Norican Alps and defeat him.

But "if the critic takes a still wider view," he will notice the exposed state of Vienna, to the east of both the French and the Austrians who were contesting the Rhine. A run by Napoleon's army for the Austrian capital could have made it fall to his single assault. The pendulum seems to have swung back, in favor of action. But Napoleon himself was a doubter of the essential nature of fixed points, even capitals. "What would have happened if the Austrians had abandoned Vienna and withdrawn into the vast expanse of territory they still controlled?" [21] Napoleon, Clausewitz feels, already realized the genius of the new warfare he had fashioned—that one fights not for position or terrain but to destroy the opposing troops. When that was not foreseeable, Napoleon consolidated his gains by the Treaty of Campo Formio.

The possibility that Clausewitz discusses here—of Austria fighting on after the loss of Vienna—offers a prevision of the campaign that broke Napoleon, when Russia fought on after the loss of Moscow, fifteen years after the Treaty of Campo Formio. Clausewitz himself had foreseen that Napoleon might be tempted toward the impossible by invading Russia. He wrote in 1804:

> If Bonaparte should someday reach Poland, he would be easier to defeat than in Italy, and in Russia I would consider his destruction as certain.[22]

The Russian campaign of 1812 will always compel the mind by its fatality. Here are all the marks of the Napoleonic genius for war, now turned against him. He seeks battle for its own sake, advances in mass, neglects his supply train, minimizes planning, and waits for opportunity. Yet all these things, which had been instruments of victory in the past, became the manacles of destiny now. By 1812, Napoleon was no longer the master of a single army, one in which he lived his entire life, but of many forces deployed throughout Europe. He had been emperor since 1804, a civil legislator and administrator, as well as the military chief of armies in Italy, Spain, and his mainland empire, and of the navy in the Caribbean. He could not improvise on the spot, maintaining his own cohesive fighting force.

When Napoleon invaded Russia, the czar's army practiced what Muhammad Ali called "rope-a-dope" boxing tactics. Ali, relying on his stamina for receiving punishment, would let a contender burn himself out throwing unopposed blows—then, when the opponent was exhausted, Ali would come back to life. Tolstoy argued that the Russian general, Kutuzov, drew Napoleon into a trap out of some mystical sense of the deep reserves of redemptive suffering the Russian people were capable of.[23] Clausewitz, more skeptical, says the Russians were forced to give way for want of any better alternative.[24] Actually, the Russians were extending a strategy that France's enemies had naturally arrived at by 1812—they tended to yield to armies under Napoleon's direct command while fighting the ones he had to place under subordinates.[25]

At the outset of his career, no one understood better than Napoleon the intrinsic limits of war—the friction that grinds up an army by its very movement, by its very successes. Much of his daring came, paradoxically, from that knowledge. He would not risk dispersal, difficult maneuvers, tricky communications; so he attacked whenever he had the numbers to do so. He foraged because he knew the encumbrance of logistical trains. He shied off from engagement with larger forces.

But Napoleon failed to see the longer-term reality of friction. Since war is paroxysmal, it is hard to maintain it as a *normal* condition. He could bring his troops up to the challenge of the revolutionary wars of the 1790s, with hope of gain and zeal for *liberté*. But as he became the emperor, betraying the Revolution, fighting for aggrandizement of his empire, the endless wars ground back toward the routine of fighting under the *ancien régime*. And, through it all, Napoleon himself had changed. War was no longer an exhilarating challenge but a kind of addiction—something he needed more as his energies declined. His was the plight of the great fighter who fights himself out. When Hannibal invaded ancient Italy, and lived off the land by constant fighting, Fabius the Delayer (Cunctator) gave the Romans the first "rope-a-dope" advice, telling them to let Hannibal "grind himself down in war, since an athletic body kept at the stretch and overworked, quickly loses its edge."[26] After the Romans had kept Hannibal in frustrating movement for many years, Fabius could at last engage him, "easily frustrating the wrestler's moves, since his grabs and holds had lost their tension."[27]

War, over time, takes a tremendous toll even on a victor's energy, concentration, nerves—that is why we send such youngsters up in jet fighters, men with the reflexes of earliest manhood. Napoleon had prodigious reserves of stamina and concentration—which Clausewitz considered a necessary precondition for all other skills in a commander.[28] But even his powers had to decline during fifteen years of battle on a scale and of an intensity never known before. That would have been true of him even if all his energies had been focused only on military matters. But he had the distractions of his civil and political life added to the fighting burdens.

The political tasks of Napoleon show how he lost his grasp on that other limit of war, the external one, the relation to policy. Internally, remember, friction chews at an army even in success. Externally, the *military* transformations (*Wechselwirkung*) cause a disconnect from the *political* uses of war. Clausewitz's most famous dictum is that "war is merely the continuation of policy by other means."[29] By its internal dynamics, war runs on hate and a desire to destroy; but that should be checked by the external needs of the society that supports the army. In his early days, Napoleon seized the authority, as general, to make political settlements with the Sardinian and Austrian forces in Italy—but he did so with a clear grasp of the political benefits to be gained by his actions. He did not pursue his victories toward the Austrian capital. He consolidated his gains in Italy by ceding some conquests to achieve stability. He was acting "out of line," but wisely.

After Napoleon became first consul for life—and then emperor—he merged the highest military and political authority in himself, and his military talent and appetites outran their real usefulness to the French nation. He found, like the autocrats of the later Soviet Union, that he could best maintain his authority by a constant premonition of war, an endless preparation for it, even when not actively waging it. (This is the logic of war-created authority that is carried to its ultimate absurdity in Orwell's *1984.*)

After Napoleon's overextension in the Russian campaign, the combined kings of Europe were able to defeat him at the battle of Leipzig (1813), forcing his abdication. All the conquered territories were stripped from France. His prior victories had undone themselves. Peter Paret asks what would have happened to the Revolution without Napoleon:

> Without his insistence on the immense exertion, demanded by European wars, the government would probably have been content with conserving France's "natural" frontiers—in itself a very considerable expansion of French territory . . . the Revolution and the transformation of war would still have left France the most powerful country in Europe, but a country integrated in the political community, rather than dominating and, indeed, almost abolishing it.[30]

Napoleon could not, in his civil capacity, control war because war controlled him. He was imprisoned in his own skills, a slave to them:

> He had studied war, he had experienced it, he was born of it, and it never ceased to shape his life. Condemned [for long] never to be compelled to make peace or even to lose an important battle, he continued to up the ante with each new round.[31]

He won enough to make winning a treadmill he could not escape until it wore him out.

I have talked here of Napoleon's *military* leadership, because it was the basis of his civil leadership. Only as the man in arms could he become the man crowned. Jacques-Louis David, in his portrait (now in Washington's National Gallery), shows him completing the Code of Civil Law, with his sword doffed for the late-night labor—but he is about to resume the sword now that he has risen from his chair.

As a military leader, Napoleon appealed to a wide range of his soldiers' motives. His foraging policy offered immediate gain to those who took more territory. But he appealed to the ideal of glory as well as gain. He told his men that, as agents of the Revolution, they were vindicating the Rights of Man. He ennobled patriotism with imagery taken from Roman antiquity, rallying men to eagle standards. His grasp of the essence of war made him a master at creating morale. Since he relied on preponderant numbers, he gave his soldiers a sense that they were not called upon to do the impossible. His insistence on massing troops and avoiding tricky maneuvers meant that few men were left in small detachments, where fear and panic breed. A tight formation keeps spirits up. Napoleon's need for personal control kept him close to his men at the outset, as did his professions of *fraternité*. It was the French nation that fought as a whole, and everyone was part of that. Napoleon had a sense of theater, of the magnanimous gesture, that made his marshals sharers in his glory.

These gifts had less room for display in his imperial role—which explains his need to reconsolidate his position by a constant recurrence to military leadership. But solidarity with his troops was harder and harder to maintain as he drifted upward above them into regal grandeur and began to think himself invincible. He lost the sense of war's uncertainty. That is why he fulfills Clausewitz's maxims in his fall as well as his rise.

Napoleon's sense of theater turned later to imperial display, to the grand portraits where he heaps every symbol of rule upon himself— eagles, fasces, Charlemagne bees, scepters, orbs, and the crown. The Ingres portrait in the Invalides is a virtual catalogue of devices for eliciting submission. This gross appeal to followers' awed allegiance lacked the force of his earlier appeals to the Revolution. He was no longer calling them to a shared goal, but to direct reverence for his person.

Napoleon's career confirms Clausewitz's dictum that there are no rules for war. The six characteristics of Napoleonic fighting that I listed earlier were effective for *that* leader, dealing with *those* followers, in *that* kind of war and at *that* stage of the war. When the situation had changed, not even Napoleon could prevail by using those characteristics of battle. They worked then because Napoleon saw, in the concrete details of his position, how to cope with *Friktion* and *Wechselwirkung*. To cope with those in a new situation he would have had to make a new analysis (*Kritik*) and act on it. Clausewitz said, "What genius does is the best rule"—and Napoleon had ceased to be a military genius by 1812.

The failed general loses his followers literally—they die because of his mistakes. Or else the threat of that happening makes his civil superiors remove him, his fellow officers isolate and neutralize him, his subordinates desert or ignore him. Napoleon lost his followers and his throne. Yet his legend perdures because of the brilliance he brought to battle in the early days. He will always be studied as a great leader in that light, even though his procedures cannot be applied routinely to other situations. His goals were, at the outset, revolutionary; that tempered everything about his actions. A stabilizing authority is at odds with the style of revolution—a thing he learned too late as emperor.

The best images of Napoleon's military leadership do not come from the many paintings he commissioned, all of them completed after he had become consul (and then emperor). The young Napoleon is better caught in an early sketch by Jacques-Louis David, done in 1797. The filmmaker Abel Gance picked Albert Dieudonné to play Napoleon in his 1920s film because of the actor's resemblance to this sketch. There is more of the spirit of Napoleon in that movie than in the ponderous celebrations of Napoleon by Ingres and David. Napoleon comes alive in the motions of Dieudonné's head, turning with quick eagle glances, or pressing its sharp profile through the montage of horses' hoofs and stormy waves during the Corsican scenes. Gance continually films Napoleon's face canted at an odd angle, cutting athwart a scene, looking on from a new perspective, *in* the picture but including it within the sweep or sudden fixing of his gaze. He is all eye, all steady gaze. I am reminded of the way Muhammad Ali carried his head high, swerving from punches, not ducking, unblinking. Most fighters fight blind a good deal of the time, in the ring or in the field. Ali, like Napoleon, had Clausewitz's *coup d'oeil.*

Poster from Abel Gance's *Napoleon*
The Kobal Collection

ANTITYPE
George McClellan

T he dashing George McClellan seemed destined for glory. Everyone was certain of that, none more than McClellan himself. At the beginning of the Civil War he was only thirty-four years old, and he looked younger—something he liked to emphasize.[1] He had already been a success in two fields, military and business. As a graduate of West Point, he served honorably in the Mexican War and was sent by his country to observe the conduct of the Crimean War. As a businessman, he had shot to the top of the "growth industry" of his day, becoming president of the Ohio and Mississippi Railroad. Back in the army, he anticipated a call to replace President Lincoln—he would do so, he admitted, but only as dictator: "I will never accept this Presidency—I will cheerfully take the Dictatorship," he confided to his wife.[2]

Given credit for a battle he watched rather than waged at Rich Mountain in West Virginia, he was hailed as "the Young Napoleon of the West," and there were apparent grounds for such a comparison. Called by Lincoln to take command of the Army of the Potomac, he trained and developed raw recruits with panache and efficiency. He insisted on the massing of troops, and feared the worst of any encounter. On the surface, this looks like a vivid apprehension of Clausewitzian "friction." But Clausewitz equips generals to expect and cope with the uncertainties of war. It makes them realize they will fight always in a fog, or as if moving under water. This freed Napoleon to act swiftly, putting the heavier burden of the unexpected on his foe.

For McClellan, the doctrine of predominant numbers was a principle of paralysis. He felt he *never* had enough troops, well enough trained or equipped. Clausewitz says that enemy numbers are always exaggerated, out of fear.[3] But McClellan took this tendency to new heights. He doubled or quadrupled the probable numbers of Confederate troops.[4] Where nothing is certain, he worked from a "worst case" scenario—which prevents a general from acting at all. So great is the magnifying force of rumor in war, Clausewitz said, that the general must, as a matter of self-discipline, force himself to "give his hopes and not his fears the benefit of the doubt."[5]

If McClellan had to act, he preferred the slow and stationary operation of a siege—the very form of war Napoleon renounced.[6] In the open field, McClellan longed for some ruse or supreme tactic that would obviate the need for pitched battle. Trapped, almost, into a victory at Antietam, he pressed no farther than he had to, not following up the advantage he was given. Earlier, he had pushed deep into southern territory by way of a massive troop movement down the Chesapeake Bay. This seemed to menace Richmond, but it also gave him a clear route of escape up the bay and a daily convoy of food and supplies. He made less contact with the enemy that far south than would have been possible, at many points, more to the north.

If he failed to grasp the internal friction of parts in the operation of war, he was just as obtuse on the external relation of war to policy. While not forcing his own military operations to a conclusion, he gave constant political advice to the president and tried to undercut or control generals outside his line of command. He let his own antiabolitionist sympathies show before his men, undermining their confidence in the Union's civil commanders.[7] When the Emancipation Proclamation was issued, he told his men to protest it politically under cover of ordering them to obey it militarily.[8] He considered Lincoln a "despot" for issuing it, and radiated contempt for the man he called "a baboon," a "gorilla," an "idiot," and a "coward."[9]

Thus McClellan, despite the loyalty he inspired in his pampered troops, never led them to the *goal* of military leadership, victory. He misunderstood himself, the nature of war, his relations with the president (who treated him with lenience, fooled for a long time by the warlike rhetoric that covered inaction). McClellan, professing concern for his troops, followed his own followers, in a circle of self-referential compliments, isolating himself from contact with his own fellow generals and the enemy's inferior forces. McClellan, in effect, spent his whole war dressing up for a battle he never attended. Those who look mainly to such "qualities of leadership" as dashing appearance, noble rhetoric, thorough preparation, and a sense of destiny, would have to give McClellan high marks. But those qualities are useless if they do not mobilize people toward some goal. McClellan *immobilized* his followers.

6.

CHARISMATIC LEADER

King David

General George McClellan, dashing in appearance, loved by his subordinates, groomed for a great political future, was what people now call "charismatic." Heads turned when he entered a room. He showed flair; he had his own unmistakable style. What else do we want from "charisma"?

The popular use of this term grew up around John Kennedy's presidency, to describe the glamour that succeeded Dwight Eisenhower's frumpy reign. Now the word is used of any celebrity, attractive businessman, or headstrong athlete. It means something like "attention-compelling."

But the scholarly world had been using "charisma" for some time in a harder, more specific sense, one introduced by the sociologist Max Weber. He used it as one of his three main categories for the structure of social authority. The charismatic order was to be distinguished from the traditional order and the legalistic order. In the first, authority derives entirely from one person, because of his privileged position with God.[1] The "grace" (*charisma*) of this divine authority is enough to serve as the ordinating principle of a whole society. In Weber's terms, McClellan was a flashy guy, but not a charismatic leader.

Weber's meaning for charisma is useful because it makes us look not just at a leader's charm (or other qualities) but to the whole social context—one in which followers recognize a *personal* authority as the principle of organization for their entire society. The charismatic ruler is not merely a king but a founding king. The successors in the king's line, if any, will be recognized because they are derived from him. Their authority is no longer peculiar to their own person, but is *traditional*. It has been "handed down." The first Dalai Lama was a charismatic ruler. The subsequent ones have been traditional rulers.

When tradition comes into question, when it ceases to bind, then authority is established by *agreement* and becomes legalistic, Weber's third social category. The three orders not only call for different kinds of leaders but for different kinds of followers. Awe is the proper response to charismatic authority. Dutiful deference is given traditional rule. Challenge and arbitration are the acts of a responsible citizenry in legalistic regimes.

The style of the leaders varies according to the structure of authority. The charismatic ruler is original in the most basic sense, originating an entire social order. The style of the traditional ruler is ceremonial, evoking memories of past obligations incurred. The style of the legalistic ruler is forensic, proceeding by dialogue with all the agents who work out the social contract.

Which of these three orders is the controlling one in American politics? Clearly, the legalistic—which is called the *constitutional* order here. The forensic style of such an order is reflected in the importance of presidential press conferences, congressional hearings, committee reports, party conventions, citizens' forums. Thus no American president, no matter how personally charming, can be a charismatic leader in Weber's sense.

Lincoln, for instance, had a great moral authority derived from his own genius. But his legal hold on followers was circumscribed by the terms of the contract ruling American society. He had to be elected, to hold office for a stated term, and to deal with other bodies whose authority was also derived from the contract (Congress and the courts). A lawyer himself (like so many leaders in our system), he was a deft compromiser and coalition builder. He helped put together the Republican Party by trimming and hedging, often sacrificing his personal convictions in a way that a charismatic leader would disdain. As president, he placed great emphasis on preservation of the Union, the framework of the old order under the single Constitution.

In another kind of society, his skills would have been blunted or turned to detriments. To those wanting to be awed by the divine authority of a Simeon Stylites, Lincoln would have seemed too tentative to be speaking for the One Truth.

The cult of personal qualities in leaders has led many to speak of the charismatic as the only "real" leadership. It is *complete* mastery, outside the trammels of oppressive tradition or compromising legalism. Such talk reflects the small regard given to followers, who are most docile in charismatic regimes and most participating in legal ones.

For all the participation of the followers in a legalistic order, there can be great electoral leaders—as Lincoln and Roosevelt demonstrate. Conversely, a person who tries to be a charismatic leader in a noncharismatic social structure will botch things, as always happens when a leader neglects the social goals of his time and the followers capable of seeking those goals. In fact, each of the orders described by Weber has its own strengths and weaknesses. Charismatic rule easily turns weird, traditional rule stodgy, legal rule dithery. Drama, decorum, procedure mark the three regimes, respectively. These different emphases can be shown in a simple table:

	Charismatic Authority	Traditional Authority	Legalistic Authority
Basis:	Preternatural	Natural (Sacred)	Natural (Secular)
Evokes:	Awe	Dutifulness	Criticism
Strengths:	Originality	Continuity	Adaptability
Style:	Personal	Ceremonial	Negotiatory
Prized:	Performance	Deference	Compromise
Dangers:	Idiosyncrasy	Stagnation	Gridlock

Weber suggested a chronological progression in the ordering of the three societies. The sacred figure occurs often at the establishment of a social order—for instance, the divine lawgivers of antiquity, lined up in the opening pages of Plutarch's *Parallel Lives*. When a Solon or Lycurgus has given laws to Athens or Sparta, by virtue of his own conversings with the gods, he goes off to let traditional successors uphold what has been fixed. When these fixed traditions come under heavy questioning, the questioning process itself is made the basis of a new, a *legal*, order.

But Weber knew there was no internal necessity for this succession. Charismatic figures can occur at any point in national history—a Cromwell in the seventeenth century, a Napoleon in the nineteenth. What is normally true, however, is that the breakdown of other forms of authority opens a space for charismatic leadership. In Cromwell's case, England was caught between the fading of a traditional monarchy and the faltering rise of a legal (parliamentary) order. Cromwell's rule of "the saints" filled this gap. Napoleon entered, in the same way, through the crevice opened by a fallen king and a faltering revolution. Modern charismatic figures are, in fact, regularly the products of failed revolutions. The proclaimed dictatorship of the proletariat leads to the one-man rule of a Joseph Stalin, Mao Zedong, or Fidel Castro.

This latter point answers one objection to Weber's concept. Since it was derived, originally, from religious regimes, based on literal "divine grace," Carl Friedrich argued that it only makes sense when confined to that kind of role.[2] Cromwell, with his soldierly "saints," would thus be charismatic; Napoleon with his marshals would not. But students of charisma in the postcolonial "third world" of our time have shown that leaders do not have to be expressly theological in their "grace" to found new orders on their personality.[3]

Some feel that the cult of figures like Mao became, in effect, a pseudoreligion. The Mao posters were icons. His Red Book was a bible. His word was thought to be infallible. But we should not quibble on theological matters like "true religion" and "pseudoreligion." The charismatic ruler is one whose *person* is the source of power, outside the restraints of tradition or legal agreements. He or she will be seen as in *some* way superhuman. The test is structural. Churchill was a great war leader, like Stalin; but Churchill served king and Parliament, and was turned out of office, without appeal, after the war. He existed within a firm constitutional order, as did Roosevelt. But there was no turning Stalin out of office. *He* was the authority he served.[4]

Of course, Stalin claimed, like Mao, to be serving the Communist Party; but he had become its sole voice. The saintly charismatic claims to be serving God, but as his oracle. Adepts of Marxism as a school of thought can say that Stalin distorted the meaning of his own dogma. A theologian can, with equal force, say that Simeon Stylites was misinterpreting the Bible. But Stalin and Stylites, in the eyes of their followers, embodied the only authority that could be appealed to. God spoke through Simeon, as History spoke through Stalin.

These reflections lead to an interesting paradox. Though "charismatic" has become a term of praise, in our looser forms of political discourse, leaders who meet Weber's tests for real charismatic authority have not been the sort liberal democrats admire.[5] Charismatic leaders—from Stalin to Sihanouk, from Mao to Fidel—make up a kind of rogues' gallery of recent history. Hitler himself, though he began as a legal ruler elected by the people, later broke out of that restraint and qualified, progressively, as a charismatic leader: no other element of the German state could prevail against his personal authority.[6]

If one is not to prejudice the analysis of charismatic leadership, it will help to find a more sympathetic model than the clearest recent instances offered us. To do that, I have chosen one of the charismatic rulers Weber named—King David of Israel.[7] Weber did not develop his thoughts on David's charisma.[8] But David is as good an exemplar of Weber's concept as any I am familiar with. Admittedly, the David of the Bible is part legend and myth; but all charismatic leaders exist in a glow that fuzzes their image to awed followers—and the followers' reaction is the test of the leader's authority.[9] Besides, David's court historian has a good claim to be the founding father of western history.

> The work's detail, tone and focus point to a text which was written much earlier [than the final redaction of the books of Samuel]: how else did the author know so much court detail and geography, tell it relatively straight? I share the general view that behind these chapters [on David and Solomon] lies an early history which was composed from court sources . . . a court narrative which was based somehow on primary knowledge of its personalities. It was written either in Solomon's kingship, or later on the strength of a detailed earlier memoir. Long before Herodotus, therefore, we must reckon with the world's first historian. . . .[10]

David began his rise to kingship as a biblical Robin Hood:

> David made his escape and went from there to the cave of Adullam. When his brother and all his family heard that he was there, they joined him. Men in any kind of distress or in debt or with a grievance gathered round him, about four hundred in number, and he became their chief.[11]

Charismatic figures subvert or stand outside the regular forms of authority. David had to go into hiding when King Saul discovered that he was a center of dissent within his court—even winning over Saul's own son (Jonathan). When David had fought for Saul's armies, it had been as an independent guerrilla leader with almost magic invulnerability. As Weber says, unarmed peasant resistance to the heavily armored Philistines is the point of the Goliath story.[12] The mobile, light-armed David can skip in and find the gap in Goliath's armor, where the eyes need to remain uncovered.

The king was bound to see such a free spirit as a threat. Saul tried to murder him, under cover of the javelin exercise going on in his military camp. David escaped, with Jonathan's help, and set up his rebel band in the hills. Saul hunted him persistently, instructing his spies and pursuivants:

> Find out exactly where he is and who saw him there. They tell me that he by himself is crafty enough to outwit me. Find out which of his hiding places he is using; then come back to me at such and such a place, and I will go along with you. So long as he stays in this country, I will hunt him down, if I have to go through all the clans of Judah one by one.[13]

This David in the hills resembles Fidel Castro assembling his rebels in the Sierra Maestra. Harried out of one place, he moved to another—like Mao Zedong seizing control of the men forced out of Kiangsi to make their Long March of 1934.

The emasculating of Saul's power by David's hijinks is symbolically enacted several times:

> When Saul returned to the pursuit of the Philistines, he learnt that David was in the wilderness of En-gedi. So he took three thousand men to the east of the Rocks of the Wild Goats. There beside the road were some sheepfolds, and near by was a cave, at the far end of which David and his men were sitting concealed. Saul came to the cave, and went in to relieve himself. He himself [David] got up stealthily and cut off a piece of Saul's cloak.[14]

Mutilating clothes was a sign of violation or humiliation.[15] An even clearer symbolic castration occurs at I Samuel 26.5–12, where David sneaks into Saul's camp and takes the spear stuck into the ground by the sleeping king.

The picture of David as a Robin Hood extends to the seizing of royal property for redistribution. Saul fears that his own men, like his son Jonathan, are ready to join David:

He said to them: "Listen to me, you Benjamites: do you expect the son of Jesse to give you all the fields and vineyards, or make you all officers over units of a thousand and a hundred? Is that why you have all conspired against me? Not one of you told me when my son made a compact with the son of Jesse."[16]

The popular leader of a robber band, David shared booty equitably with his men. He said, after one attack: "Those who stayed with the stores shall have the same share as those who went into battle. They shall share and share alike."[17] David was at one with the countryside, blending into it like a guerrilla. He would fight or hide in forests like Hareth or Ephraim (I Samuel 22.5, II Samuel 18.6). In hills like Hachilah (I Samuel 23.19, 26.1). In "wildernesses" like Maon or En-gedi (ibid., 23.24, 24.2). In riverside promontories like Adullam (ibid., 22.2, 24.23).[18] In caves like that of the Wild Goats (ibid, 24.3). Places were named for his escapades on the site (ibid., 23.19).[19]

David even played Saul off against his enemies the Philistines. At first the Philistines did not trust David—he had to escape their camp by playing the madman (I Samuel 21.11–15). But later they took him on as a mercenary. David was engaged in a double game with these new masters, pretending to conduct raids on the Israelites but actually preying on the Israelites' non-Philistine enemies. To keep the Philistines from discovering his duplicity, he took no prisoners on his raids, killing all possible witnesses (ibid., 17.9–12).

David lived a "charmed life," as people loosely say. But the Bible gives to that notion a theological density that does not apply to Robin Hood. David is literally the favored of God. When the people chose Saul as their king, the prophet Samuel knew that a better king was in store: "The Lord will seek a man after his own heart" (ibid., 13.14). When Samuel anointed the boy David, "the spirit of the Lord came upon David and was with him from that day onward" (ibid., 16.13). When others began to notice David's versatility as poet-warrior, they considered this a sign of God's favor: "I have seen a son of Jesse of Bethlehem who can play [the lyre]; he is a brave man and a good fighter, wise in speech and handsome, and the Lord is with him" (ibid., 16.18). That sentence is a virtual definition of charisma. The divine favor marked David off from all other men—he is the one after God's heart. His future exploits are further pledges that "God is with him" (ibid., 18.14).

To emphasize that David's power is entirely charismatic, he is pointedly deprived of all other forms of authentication. He is a ruler so little traditional that his father's line is obscure, and even in this family David is the despised younger son—the prophet Saul must brush aside his likelier brothers to find David in the Cinderella role (ibid., 16.8–13). To contrast his authority with legal rule, David's kingship is made to come from God while Saul's comes only from men. Wanting protection from the Philistines, the people had clamored for a king, and they chose Saul. Samuel calls this a contractual (legal) relationship, to be canceled if its terms are broken:

> Samuel then explained to the people the nature of a king, and made a written record of it on a scroll which he deposited before the Lord. . . . If you *and the king* who reigns over you are faithful to the Lord, well and good.[20]

Unlike Saul's election, done by the people in defiance of sacred tradition, David's election by God was sealed in secret. It would become effective only as David's special powers were manifested in action. David first won attention as a warrior; but after Saul's death, he emerged as a statesman, winning over the dead king's army. As a sacred leader, he had already rescued a priest (Abiathar) from the purge Saul conducted, and escorted him to safety. In his own kingdom, he restored Abiathar's priesthood, so he could conduct the divine service in its new site: Jerusalem.[21]

Jerusalem is the perfectly charismatic place for David. No prior Israelite worship had occurred there, since it had been immemorially in the hands of the Jebusites. After capturing the city (typically by a ruse—infiltrating the city through its water conduit), David takes this centrally located town as the place around which to unite the divided tribes of Israel. Jealousy over separate places of worship is solved by appeal away from them all to the radically new religious establishment, a temple, in Jerusalem.

David also helped unite the tribes by marrying well and often; but his harem created troubles for him. This often happens in the crackle of sexual electricity that attends charismatic leaders (even Gandhi).[22] The affair with Bathsheba is David's most famous erotic exploit, but the rivalry of sons sired by different mothers in the harem created the regular problem of charismatic power—difficulty in achieving orderly succession.[23]

The revolt of David's first son, Absalom—who capitalized on unrest among the tribes as David's reign became more centralized and demanding—reveals another danger of charismatic rule. So long as the charismatic leader is performing wonders, few doubt his semidivine powers. But when conquest yields to stabilization, youth to age, fabulous exploits to everyday reality, how can charisma be "routinized"? English translators have normally used "routinization" for Weber's more vivid "everydaying" of authority (*Veralltäglichung*). Since this kind of ruler did not rise by traditional or legal agreement, but by the wonders he performed, there can be a swift draining of power from him if he stops performing wonders. Then the aging leader, deprived of traditional and legal tools for revalidating his authority, resorts to extraordinary measures that are *not* charismatic—using spies, secret police, secret trials and executions. This is the story of aging charismatic leaders like Stalin and Mao. And it is partly the story of David. When he tried to impose administrative accountability through a census, the people considered this a departure from his charismatic trust in God. He was becoming a bureaucrat, and an oppressive one.

The gunfighter who has not killed anyone recently is rumored to have lost his speed or nerve or hunger, and challengers begin to move in on him. Absalom brought an army against David's proudest possession, Jerusalem, and David had to abandon the city. On the run again, hiding as in his outlaw days, he returned to his old skills of deception, guerrilla assault, and "doing the impossible." He left a friend behind him to mislead Absalom's troops. Hushai gave them false intelligence about the king's forces:

> Your father and the men with him are hardened warriors and savage as a bear in the wild robbed of her cubs. Your father is an old campaigner and will not spend the night with the main body; even now he will be lying in a pit or in some such place. Then if any of your men are killed at the outset, anyone who bears the news will say, "Disaster has overtaken the followers of Absalom." The courage of the most resolute and lion-hearted will melt away.[24]

Hushai advises Absalom to wait until he can gather a greater army before he assails the king's picked troops. Actually, time is on David's side—he has nothing like the forces Hushai attributes to him. The fact that Hushai's advice is taken, not the wiser counsel of Achitophel, shows that David's charisma has again descended on him: "It was the Lord's purpose to frustrate Achitophel's good advice and so bring disaster on Absalom."[25] David, given time to dispose his forces in the forest of Ephraim, again makes the terrain fight for him: "The forest took toll of more people that day than the sword."[26]

If the glow fades from the charismatic leader himself, once he ceases to perform miracles, the bestowal of his entirely personal magic on a *successor* is still more difficult. Weber lists four expedients, all more or less feckless, that have been tried for transferring the original magic to another vessel—anointing, oracular induction, sortition, ceremonial trial.[27]

In David's case, a conspiracy to defeat other heirs had to be combined with the prophetic pronouncements of Nathan to bring Bathsheba's child—Solomon—to the throne. Solomon was no warrior who could manifest David's charisma. He tried to institute a traditional succession in Jesse's line—and failed. Despite his own long and prosperous reign, he could not hand on a united kingdom to his heir. The kingship fell apart, and has not been restored. The charismatic power of David had departed long before, replaced by Solomon's bureaucratic skills—those at the farthest distance from charisma.

That is the grimmest lesson of charismatic rule. It is always unstable, often short-lived, and at odds with its own foundation. The divinely graced person is supposed to be above failure—so each failure undermines the very *raison d'être* of charismatic rule. No one expects a traditional or legal ruler to be successful in everything. But why should *divinity* fail? There is an implicit pledge of infallibility in charisma. The gunfighter has to win *every time*. God cannot be only occasionally successful. If his favored one is bested, then God himself loses, and chaos is come again.

The conflict between the demand for continuous order and spontaneous exploit was worked out in all the later imagery of David. Christian theology seized on him as the supposed progenitor of Christ and put him in "the tree of Jesse" as a hander-on of patriarchal tradition. In the Middle Ages, he is most often the white-haired king seen as a progenitor.[28] But the Renaissance returned to the ideal of his charismatic individuality. In a brilliant series of Florentine statues, he became the naked slayer of Goliath, young, beautiful, needing no armor but God's protection.[29] The culminating image in this series is Michelangelo's "miracle," by which he turned a "ruined" piece of stone into the poised strength and calculation of the guerrilla fighter choosing his enemy's vulnerable spot.[30] The torque of his body within its confines (the statue was originally meant to stand in a narrow niche) prefigures the drawing of his sling. David will explode with action when his plan, forming behind the fiercely concentrating brow, is perfected. This is the charismatic man par excellence, relying on nothing but his own supremely graced right arm.

David—*Michelangelo*
Alinari/Art Resource

ANTITYPE
Solomon

T he opposite of charisma is bureaucracy—a topic much studied these days. Max Weber is *the* theoretician of bureaucracy, just as he is of charisma. Analysts still draw on him, but most of them connect bureaucracy with the intensified rationalization of modern legal systems. One might almost think, from these studies, that bureaucracy is a peculiarly modern phenomenon. Weber, however, knew that bureaucratized agrarian, hydraulic, or military systems go back to the origins of all complex societies. He treated bureaucracy, for instance, as the essence of feudalism. One of the earliest examples he gives is Solomon's reign:

> Already under David the Hebrew monarchy had begun to resemble a Near Eastern government based on labor services, and under Solomon the basic features of that system clearly emerged: a fortified capital, accumulation of a royal hoard, a foreign bodyguard in addition to the national levy, and public works for which the supervisors were important and the material was collected from labor services.[1]

All these activities required standardization of services and fees, professionalization of overseers, and extensive record keeping.[2] Solomon acquired stores of chariots and horses—something made useful by his creation of roads connecting fixed urban centers.[3] He standardized cult practices around the temple, and moved toward a royal monopoly on the lore that had been decentralized before. Now wisdom was officially the king's domain:

> The glory of God is to keep things hidden, but the glory of kings is to fathom them.[4]

As all lyrics (the Psalms) were attributed to David, all wisdom sayings tended to be associated with Solomon. And the burden of that wisdom was conservative, pessimistic, retentive:

> The words of the Speaker, the son of David, king in Jerusalem: Emptiness, emptiness, says the Speaker, emptiness, all is empty. . . . All things are wearisome . . . and there is nothing new under the sun.[5]

Where charisma is free to improvise and expect the new, bureaucracy reduces everything to system and recurrence. Even Solomon's harem —more ambitious than David's, reflecting alliances with Egypt and other peoples—was more orderly in its administration.

There is a general revulsion from bureaucracy in the scholarly as well as the popular press. But a Solomon, growing up in the turbulence of David's court, knew the uses of routine. Bureaucracy is an attempt to make administration automatic, not dependent on the comings and goings of personalities.[6] It can protect as well as burden the subject. Most of us would prefer, as defendants, the cumbersome procedures of jury trials to the "creative" law enforcement of lynching, police impulse, or ruler's whim. The tax mechanism is resented; but arbitrary requisitioning, confiscation, and grants of exemption would be resented more. Punching a time clock validates one's claim on wages. The employer of the parable at Matthew 20.1–16 pays on his own private scheme of value—no union would accept those conditions. Charisma inspires people, but also exhausts them, with the unexpected. Bureaucracy holds people together on a predictable schedule. One would not want the sun to rise (or not) on a whim, to set (or not) at unforeseeable times. Bureaucracy is as much underrated, as an ordinating principle of life, as charisma is overrated as the source of *real* leadership.

Can there be bureaucratic leadership, or is that conjunction absurd? One would think so from the pejorative use of the adjective in other contexts. But what is a good army lieutenant if not a bureaucratic leader? The military is the most bureaucratic imaginable existence short of a prison. People are standardized—the name "uniform" is significant, as are all "general issue" items. Workers must report on time; soldiers not only rise on time, but are overseen doing it. They not only obey superiors, but advertise their duty to obey each time they encounter an officer and salute him or her. And one salutes the uniform, not the person (an anticharismatic norm if ever there was one). The aim is to make people go on, automatically, if one officer falls in battle and another steps in.

The Napoleon, at the top, can be creative and charismatic; but his plans are worthless if subordinates do not predictably carry them out. All the way down the line, the subordinate is not expected to challenge orders, improve them, decide on which are worthy of fulfillment. People are numbered ("dog tagged"), treated as units, tested by set forms, promoted or reduced against career deadlines that make civil service rules in government look very lax indeed. No wonder Tennyson spoke of the "*armies* of unalterable law." If there is a romance to the military, that just shows there can be a romantic side to bureaucracy. Solomon's conservation of the kingdom was less dramatic than David's creation of it. But rabbinical tradition would find an administrative magic in Solomon's judicial sweep and authority.

7.

BUSINESS LEADER

— · —

Ross Perot

Go into a major bookstore—I just checked the shelves at Kroch's & Brentano's in Chicago's Loop—and look at the business section, books on management, marketing, sales. They tend to be inspirational, with a great emphasis on leadership. Most purchasers of books about becoming a leader come from the business community. There are thousands of titles in print, and hundreds of them are on the shelves of any fairly large bookstore. One could get the impression that leaders exist mainly in corporations—or that leadership problems exist only there. If that is where the leaders are, why are so many books needed to tell them how to lead?

This cheerleading literature treats the business world as the last arena of frontier initiative in America. It contrasts private enterprise with governmental inertia. The leader can still accomplish things in the private sphere because bureaucracy has not taken over there. Yet a very different body of literature is devoted to "corporate man" as a cog in a giant entity. Which is it to be?

The corporation is itself a bureaucracy—which makes some people claim that only "small business" can foster independence and creativity. Yet the successful small business *becomes* the larger business. Is success here really failure, canceling the conditions of its first existence?

We should begin by questioning the romanticism that finds no good in bureaucracy. The principles of bureaucratic organization—standardization, regulation, review—are more beneficial than harmful in their first application (though all procedures tend to grow perfunctory). Eddie Rickenbacker, the great car racer and pioneer aviator, used to rebuild, service, and perpetually refashion the engine in his own car or airplane. His pockets were full of parts he rubbed and rejiggered, in his spare moments, to ensure perfect fit when parts were not being uniformly machined. But when he became the president of Eastern Airlines, we did not want his corporation's mechanics to be making up their own parts as they went along, rubbing individual ball bearings to make them rounder. We want uniform parts, and uniform operators of those parts. We do not want a "creative" mechanic reinventing the plane we are about to fly.

Thorstein Veblen said that modern manufacture is at odds with the instinct of workmanship.[1] The individual worker does not stamp his or her own personality on the product—in fact, he often does not touch more than one part of the machine process that assembles the product. The foreman is not there to encourage "self-expression" in the thing produced—as Ruskin claimed that Gothic chiselers could create their own ornaments while working on a cathedral's fretwork. The foreman exists to enforce regular procedure, to make sure each person does that part of the process assigned to him or her, in the proper way and at the proper time, so that a quota of measurably standardized product is turned out. And automation multiplies these pressures.

The foreman, or floor manager, or plant supervisor thus oversees an impersonal process, even though a worker's difficulties and morale have to be taken into account. The laborer's immediate leader is much like an army sergeant or second lieutenant, as Peter Drucker long ago pointed out.[2] There are real leadership challenges to being a good sergeant or a good foreman; but these are posts of *bureaucratic* leadership—not at all what most books about business leaders want to praise.

The books tend to focus on higher executives, and especially on the chief executive officer, who seems to be the leader par excellence in the business hierarchy. He or she has technical superiors—the board of directors that hired and can fire him or her. But the CEO is hired precisely to make the day-by-day decisions on which the health of the corporation depends, and the CEO is fired for not making the right decisions. Getting hired as CEO may involve "selling oneself" to the board—in that broad use of the term "selling" that business people love. (Many executives echo, by quotation or unconscious imitation, IBM's Thomas Watson, who liked to claim that "the best sale I ever made was of myself to my wife.")

If the CEO is not quite the leader of his own board, whom *does* he lead (to adapt the generic "he" for a while)? The workers? Charles Wilson, President Eisenhower's secretary of defense, famously said, "What is good for General Motors is good for America." Whether that was true or not, executives of that corporation like to believe that what is good for General Motors is good for General Motors workers. But that is not necessarily true. It depends on how the employers use their profits. Employers *should* treat their workers well, if only out of self-interest: well-treated workers are more cooperative. But the same argument was made by defenders of slavery: it is in the interest of the master to treat slaves well, so they will be healthy, willing to work, less restive or resistant or rebellious. That notion gave small comfort to slaves. Though it might have been to his own ultimate advantage for a slave owner to be a "good master," not all of them were. And though Peter Drucker can make a good case for corporate executives to treat workers well, he found executives who rejected his arguments.[3]

It is true that a CEO sets the policies for research, design, production, and marketing. He chooses the proximate goals (under the ultimate goals of winning a profit and putting out a decent product). In the same way, Charles Wilson as secretary of defense set the policies of military appropriation, mobilization, training, and so on—but few privates in the army really thought of him as their personal leader.

Nor does the CEO have the same commonality of interest with his workers that Wilson had with army recruits. Wilson and the military inductee did share a common goal—to provide the nation with defense. The private also wants pay and fair treatment, and has personal goals; but the goal to which the leader mobilizes response in the military is one shared in some measure by most citizens, and certainly by most patriots.

The same cannot be said about workers and their employers. The boss may say, "We all want to make GM's cars the best on earth." But if workers get better pay and working conditions, better health and retirement benefits, from Ford, they will change jobs unless some accidental barrier stops them. After all, Lee Iacocca changed from being a Ford executive to being a Chrysler executive when his own pay and work conditions were improved; why should others fail to do the same thing? The contrast with the military is clear. American sergeants cannot normally join other nations' armies if the pay is better. In that sense, corporate workers are less like military bureaucrats and more like mercenaries in the days when professional soldiers' services could be purchased in an international marketplace.

The relationship between boss and worker is not that of collaboration toward a common goal but of barter—and barterers have a common transaction but different goals within that single transaction. The worker trades time and skill for compensations of various sorts. It is to the advantage of the employer that the workers have continuing satisfaction from the terms of any agreement, but that does not mean they are working toward a common goal. The worker wants dignity, reward, good relations with his fellows and his work. The employers want the most work to be had, under such restrictions, for making and selling products and services that reward owners or shareholders of the business.

By our definition of leadership—mobilization toward a common goal—the CEO is not directly a leader of workers. A leader's skills may be deployable in the bartering of benefits to elicit labor from employees—as a leader's skills are useful to actors, celebrities, or artists, without making them leaders in the strict sense. In fact, many of the employers' claims of leadership are insulting to workers—the claims that "we are all one family" at IBM (or wherever) is patriarchal; it assumes that executives are fathers who know what's best for their immature charges. Union leaders, in turn, offend employers by challenging that stereotype.

If employees are not the same thing as followers, then who *does* follow the CEO? Is it the customers, those who buy the company's product or services? Some locutions might suggest that. "Hertz is the leader in the field"—meaning more people rent its cars. But are the renters actually following their leader, the Hertz CEO? This is even more clearly a case of barter—one transaction with differing aims: the person doing the renting wants a safe, dependable, affordable car's use, with ease of servicing; the company wants the best price it can get for furnishing these. It is true that good service will make return business more likely (the old "good master" argument); but the barter relationship will lapse whenever the purchaser no longer likes the terms.

Who else makes up the potential followers for a CEO? Department heads? Here we are getting closer. The CEO must not only make policy but work with those responsible for implementing decisions. At primitive stages of any business, this relationship is close and a leader's skills are exercised directly—Ford actually making cars with his first shop assis-

tants, Edison inventing alongside his original team, Disney (briefly) drawing cartoons beside his animators. But as the concern grows more
complex, the executive has to withdraw from its actual operation to the
setting of policy and hiring of personnel—the personnel coming, increasingly, from objectively credentialed backgrounds, at first from the company's own training schools, and then from independent credentialers
(especially the universities). IBM boasts of the number of Ph.D.'s working for the firm. Talented people with such credentials become scientific
mercenaries able to sell their skills to the highest bidder. Barter rather
than leadership has sneaked in again.

Are we running out of people for the CEO to lead? There is, of course,
the immediate executive team of the CEO—his highest assistants, the
most important department heads, especially those who are responsible
for *marketing* the company's product or services. This is what keeps the
company customer-oriented, that ultimate test of success. Thorstein Veblen said it best:

> Salesmanship is, in a way, the whole end and substance of business en-
> terprise; and except so far as it is managed with a constant view to profitable
> bargains, the production of goods is not a business proposition.[4]

You can make the world's most perfect product, yet be a failure if you
cannot (or do not) sell it. The CEO's mobilizing ability is best demonstrated in the sales division, where it reaches past the department heads to
affect ordinary workers, the actual salesmen and -women. Here there is
a common goal—to sell more products, individually and in the aggre-
gate—and a team spirit exists in those who succeed. Even when leadership is exercised in other departments, it is usually (when it goes beyond
mere management decisions) based on some analogy with the sales division's slogans, values, and practices.

The heroes of the corporate world are usually revered for their capacity
to inspire sales. Wizards in accounting may be crucial to the firm's
success, as may researchers in their labs, or foremen on the line; but the
stamp of corporate personality is usually placed there by the sales division.

This explains the legendary status of John Henry Patterson in the
modern corporate world. Patterson, born in 1844, graduated from Dart-
mouth in 1867 and kicked around in odd jobs for two decades. He was a
storekeeper in Dayton when he saw the instrument for his rise in a

primitive cash register. This machine, invented by James Retty, kept track of each transaction when the store's cash drawer was opened. It was meant to prevent pilfering by clerks. Patterson saw a grand future for this lowly tool, and took over the shop manufacturing it in 1866. Patterson's brother was put in charge of producing the machines, while Patterson trained the sales force of what he called the National Cash Register Company.[5]

The nineteenth-century "drummer" was not a respected figure. He peddled goods that had no warranties, little brand recognition, no independent endorsement. He depended often on a fanciful "line," on gimmicks, on "giveaways." Rootless and undependable men were drawn to this odd living, which gave rise to legends like that of the traveling salesman forever seducing farmers' daughters. The traveling salesman was a notch below traveling actors in social regard. Patterson meant to change all that. He dressed his salespersons in the expensive luxury (in the ill-laundered nineteenth century) of detachable white collars. He gave them scientific arguments for his machines. He enforced a puritanical code against drinking or sexual transgressions. He made his salesmen exercise and keep fit. He wanted them to seem moral paragons. He was, after all, sending them out to convince store owners that they needed cash registers to protect them against dishonest clerks. A man traveling by had to seem more trustworthy than the workers who stayed behind when he was gone.

Thomas Watson, Jr., who inherited his father's office as the CEO of IBM, called John Patterson his "spiritual grandfather," since Watson senior was a graduate of Patterson's sales school:

> Patterson's genius was to figure out how to take crude, partly educated, ambitious commercial travelers like Dad and mold them into America's first national sales force. . . . Being a salesman at the turn of the century was an ignoble job, but under Patterson it became almost a profession.[6]

Patterson aspired even higher—he said he was making sales a science. He is generally credited with either inventing or institutionalizing all the basic practices of modern sales forces—the sales manual, the standardized sales speech, the quota, the exclusive region, the training school, the simulated sales situation (he even built mock-ups of different kinds of stores in which to demonstrate cash registers), the sales convention with annual awards. His protégés went on to spectacular careers in or outside his own company.[7]

Despite all his claims for salesmanship as a science, Patterson's genius was to understand the psychological needs of the seller. The salesman does not make a product or plant a crop. His stock in trade is personal persuasiveness—his charm (if any), his persistence despite refusals to buy (always far greater than sales "closed"). The salesman (again the generic he) must identify with his product—a situation that can be embittering even if he succeeds (am I just this refrigerator) and crushing if he fails (the product refused is the man rejected). Arthur Miller rang some changes on these themes in his 1949 play *Death of a Salesman*. The salesman is constantly being "graded" in terms of the commissions he earns. That is why so many of the books on selling are devoted to building and sustaining self-confidence. An example at hand is typical when it devotes a section to "The Champions' Five Attitudes Toward Rejection."[8] So important is the development of ego in salesmen that the fear of becoming obnoxious reasonably haunts them. (Miller's Willy Loman fears that he talks too much, is not liked, cannot let well enough alone.)

Patterson's sales school encouraged team morale by having salesmen share their experiences of rejection, plan responses to them, encourage each other. Patterson had a "buddy system"—experienced salespeople helped beginners or those having trouble. He developed a paramilitary attitude toward defeating rivals—one that got him and his prize pupil Watson in serious trouble with the law. Under Patterson's direction Watson built flawed typewriters (called by their makers "knockout machines") and peddled them under the brand names of NCR rivals. This was part of a general pattern of sabotage and "disinformation" directed at holders of competing patents. When disaffected NCR employees revealed the practices in 1912, Patterson, Watson, and three others were convicted in federal court of conspiracy to violate the antitrust laws and sentenced to a year in jail.[9] The company won an appeal for a second trial, but by that time Patterson had fired Watson (one reason so many of his disciples had to succeed in other companies was Patterson's fear they might replace him). Watson, severed from the other defendants, was asked to sign a consent decree renouncing the illegal activities, but he avoided this by arguing he could not engage in illegal activities for a company that had fired him.

Despite the blow to Watson, who had done Patterson's dirty work for him and been fired as a reward, Watson remained a true believer in Patterson's methods. Almost all the identifying marks of Watson's own success at IBM were based on Patterson's practices. The famous THINK sign that became Watson's trademark was developed at NCR (along with many other inspirational slogans). The white collar, the disparaging of alcohol, the pep-meeting annual events, the emphasis on sales (and especially on sales morale)—all these were Patterson's devices. Watson copied even accidental aspects of Patterson's regime. When Patterson sought a more pleasant locale for his sales school, he put the first class there into tents rather than keep it at the gloomy earlier site. Watson held annual sales meetings in tents (lavishly furnished) in imitation of the master.

Though Watson had to seek work under the disadvantage of his anti-trust conviction (still unresolved at the time), he had the good fortune to meet another flamboyant mentor, Charles Flint, who had his own way of skirting laws. A munitions trader, much involved in developing the United States Rubber Company, Flint was an imaginative entrepreneur intrigued by technological developments—in weapons, aviation, communications. On a hunch, he had bought up thirteen companies that worked on various kinds of tabulation. As president of the joint venture, which he called the Computer-Tabulating-Recording Company (C-T-R), he could force on a resisting board the convicted felon Watson (whose legal troubles did not disappear till he had been on the job for a year).[10]

The most valuable component of C-T-R turned out to be the Tabulating Machine Company, which owned the patent to a device Herman Hollerith had developed to speed the taking of the 1890 Census. The machine quickly sorted file cards by a pattern of holes punched in them. Hollerith combined the coding of sequences for player-piano rolls with a device for sorting by way of holes (based on the Jacquard automatic loom). For its first fifty years, the basic tool of IBM would be the punch card, first sorted by pins, then by electrical impulses. Speed-sorting of the cards (20,000 an hour) allowed mathematical processes to be done in a flash. Watson sought new areas in which to prove the usefulness of such an investment, and found them in the academy or the military. Faculty members at Columbia University used the card sorters to work out long equations in astronomy.[11]

The tie-in with the government, and especially with the military, was even more crucial to IBM's growth. That the bureaucracy was a natural client had been clear from the use of Hollerith's machine for the 1890 Census. The New Deal, denounced by some businessmen, was a boon to IBM (and Watson became a great fan of President Roosevelt). IBM machines were used to record Social Security information, National

Recovery Administration codes, and the resources for works projects.[12] War brought new uses. IBM machines worked equations for the Manhattan Project and helped break enemy codes.[13]

When vacuum-tube computers came along—bulky, expensive, prone to overheat—the needs of the Korean War led the government to supply the capital for such instruments.[14] It is not surprising, then, that a young naval lieutenant who graduated from Annapolis in the last days of that war should meet an IBM salesman on the ship he was assigned to. The IBM gospel of servicing equipment sent its representatives out to learn and to teach wherever they sold computers. (These follow-ups, along with the noncompatibility of IBM parts and the exclusive use of their cards and other software, helped IBM control the market, which made the Securities and Exchange Commission keep a perpetually wary eye on its monopolistic tendencies—an echo of Watson's trouble at NCR.)

The naval lieutenant was named Ross Perot, and he liked what he saw in the modern IBM man. If Patterson had turned rubes into professional experts on cash registers, Watson had made his sales team into diplomats of the new technology. But the puritanical personal standards were still straight out of Patterson—dark suits, white ties, no beards or long hair. That cookie-cutter image was offensive or amusing to some, but not to Perot, a man who admires discipline, order, and routine. Even the navy was too sloppy and unbuckled for him. He tried to get an early release from his postacademy service, partly on the grounds that shipboard profanity and shore-leave laxity offended his moral sensibilities.[15]

Perot was drawn to IBM by elective affinity. As soon as he took off one uniform, he put on another. It was a good time to join up (1957). The company could not keep up with postwar demand for computers. Perot likes to boast that he sold his yearly quota in the first month of 1962, but that was not unusual in those heady times. By 1962, Perot had exhausted the possibilities for rapid advance at IBM. Just as he gave several versions of his reason for seeking early discharge from the navy, he has given a largely self-serving account of his departure from IBM. In his version, he saw IBM failing to help buyers of computers to program software. IBM had fallen down on its own "gospel of service," just as the navy had fallen down in its discipline. Perot would go out and help the little guy puzzled by the new technology. He set up, in 1962, a firm to tailor software to particular firms' uses, and then to maintain the program at a monthly fee. Perot had to use his wife's savings to meet the thousand-dollar incorporation fee in Texas.

It was not quite like that. Perot left IBM in 1962, but he went to work for Dallas Blue Cross and stayed there until forced to resign in 1967. This was a typically "big guy" operation, the kind computers were sold to from the outset:

> It was public utilities, insurance companies, and railroads that became the earliest users of punch card machines, for they dealt with vast quantities of records that required periodic updating and tedious sorting.[16]

Perot worked part-time at Blue Cross for five years, drawing a salary of $20,000. He was telling the company how to exploit the new computers. He was simultaneously developing a computer-service company that would meet just the qualifications he was establishing as an in-house advisor. When a Blue Cross employee revealed the conflict of interest, Perot had to resign from Blue Cross; but by then he had used his employment there to launch EDS (Electronic Data Systems), whose first corporate residence had been his office in the Blue Cross building.[17] By then, too, he had sold his services to his employer, without competing bids.[18] Since Blue Cross was drawing federal money for the Medicare program, Perot had in effect been paid by the government to develop a private service he would then sell back to the government.[19]

As he piggybacked off IBM (getting the skills he sold to Blue Cross) and off Blue Cross (getting the inside knowledge of services he would supply from outside), so he piggybacked off other people's computers. Since he had no "hardware" of his own, he developed software programs on computers not being used. His teams would enter buildings at night—a famous incident led to the first woman employee's having to scale a high fence to get into the locked building where a computer was idle.[20]

To perform these tasks, Perot recruited a "lean, mean team" of (primarily) men with military experience. Perot had an even better right than Thomas Watson, Jr., to call John Henry Patterson his "spiritual grandfather," since Perot revived the paramilitary spirit that had made the senior Watson create "knockout machines" to do in the competition. Perot derived from IBM the inspirational and slogan-centered style of leadership that made his sales-service team willing to work weekends, travel at the drop of a hat, observe a dress and sexual-behavior code. Perot was lavish with personally granted gifts and rewards to his employees, but blocked attempts to set up guaranteed benefits. He kept and increased the IBM emphasis on secrecy—employees were not even supposed to divulge to one another the amounts of their salary.[21] Perot rewarded early employees with stock in the company—which made them rich when the stock went public, artfully managed to sell "at more than a hundred times earnings, the highest price yet" (in 1968).[22]

Like most good leaders of sales teams, Perot is a homilist, a thinker in punchy slogans, a dramatist, especially a self-dramatist.[23] John Henry Patterson, famous for his chalk talks to salesmen (he used red chalk), would do anything to get his men's wandering attention—at times he crumbled the chalk and rubbed it onto his face like war paint.[24] Patterson, who had volunteered as a teenager for Civil War service, also loved military discipline and procedure. He had his own "cavalry" of early morning NCR riders and he called the executive dining room the Officers' Club.[25]

Perot's leadership was proved when volunteers from his own firm undertook a dangerous rescue mission to Iran, where some of their fellow employees were being held hostage in 1979. The shrewdness and daring Perot had used in launching his company were given a larger sphere. Perot also tried to duplicate Thomas Watson, Jr.'s diplomatic feats. Watson became the United States ambassador to Moscow after retiring from IBM. Perot tried to negotiate the release of prisoners from Vietnam and to rally support for President Nixon's Vietnam War policies in a gala television broadcast. (Perot's later political career is outside the purview of this chapter, which deals with business leadership.)

Perot proves that in a corporate world—where IBM's computer card message, "Do Not Fold, Bend, or Mutilate," seemed to overwhelm individual initiative—a man can maneuver in the interstices of the giant operations and become tremendously successful. The irony is that in doing so he serviced the giants and made them more gigantic. The lineage of NCR-IBM-EDS—of John Patterson, both Thomas Watsons, and Ross Perot—is one of the epic tales of modern sales leadership. Business writers like to tell this story in terms of personal imagination and creativity. But look what the men were accomplishing. NCR was meant to replace the personal transactions of fallible and peculating clerks with an "incorruptible cashier."[26] The cash register is considered the beginning of automation in the merchandising field. IBM, under the Watsons, served the New Deal and the government's bureaucracy. Perot's great contracts were with the successors to Social Security, government health programs (Medicaid and Medicare). The fruit of all this business leadership was to set up automatic processes that do not depend on personal leadership.

Taken from control of his handpicked team, Perot's management skills were not successful at General Motors, to which he sold EDS in 1984, nor on Wall Street, where he tried and failed to reorganize the brokerage firms of duPont Glore Forgan and Walston & Company in 1971–1974.[27] Perot blames these failures on others, but it is hard to imagine his idiosyncratic brand of leadership working in large, less autocratic, less secretive, less "inspirational" contexts. (After selling EDS to GM, Perot tried to prevent the parent firm from auditing its own subsidiary.)

Perot's mastery of EDS was a triumph of leadership. Even his tall tales about himself were part of the inevitable mythmaking that goes into sales. As Veblen noted, it is not enough simply to produce a product; one must create a saleable *image* of the product as well.[28] That is even more true of a man selling a *service*—trust in the servicer is part of the total package being purchased. This makes salesmanship a traffic in what C. Wright Mills called "the personality market," which is just as important as the product market.[29]

Yet skill as a salesman was not enough to make Perot a leader. The salesman impresses buyers. The leader must field a whole team of followers who are inspired by him or her to make sales on their own. Despite his autocratic ways, Perot was very good at instilling pride in the people he called his "eagles." When I interviewed him in 1988, he told me, "I never had any ideas I used." He is quick to give credit to others—a knack he applies to politics, where he calls himself the servant of the voters. Perot perfectly blended his own preferred image of himself with that of his followers when he adopted as his company's motto: "Eagles Don't Flock, You Have to Find Them One at a Time."

Ross Perot
Shel Hershorn, print courtesy of TIME INC. PICTURE COLLECTION

ANTITYPE
Roger Smith

R oger Smith was a brilliant financial planner who had risen through the ranks of General Motors to become its CEO in 1980. Put in a position where he had to lead instead of manage, he floundered. No man can lead a sales force who commits what most sales people consider a primal sin—Smith did not look his interlocutors in the eye.[1] When Smith closed GM plants, he could not go before the public and explain his act—a fact that was memorialized in a satirical documentary film, *Roger and Me*. One can imagine how a Ross Perot or Lee Iacocca would take to the airwaves, choosing his own forum, making preemptive publicity strikes. Smith thought he was doing his job if he just made good production and design decisions.

Even those decisions were flawed by Smith's lack of a sales orientation. Smith wanted to automate GM car making. He moved toward a basic car design that could be recomputered to produce the variants represented by GM's several name brands. The result was a line of barely distinguishable cars. Yet GM had built its sales strategy on the class differences in its cars.

> Over a lifetime, a family would start out with a little Chevrolet, then move up to a Pontiac, then Buick, then Oldsmobile, and ultimately, if things went well, to Cadillac luxury. And there were many who developed life-long loyalty to a single division—"Dad's always driven a Buick."[2]

By 1985, the Young & Rubicam ad agency could make a Ford ad for TV dramatizing an attendant's problem retrieving a Cadillac from a parking lot—first he brings a Buick, then an Oldsmobile. Efficient design and production are useless if you cannot sell the efficiently designed product.

Smith knew what he was lacking. Apparently unable to develop sales-manship in himself or his staff, he tried to acquire some flair from outside. At first he turned to a jet-set entrepreneur in Germany, Horst-

Dieter Esch, the director at IBH, a holding company on the rise. Smith originally tried to get Esch to buy a GM subsidiary, Terex, which made earthmovers. Since Esch had no ready cash, he bought Terex with IBH shares and, once GM was involved with his company, he coaxed Smith into promising further investment—a promise Esch used, in turn, to get loans from a Saudi millionaire. When IBH folded and Esch went to jail for fraud, GM lost $40 million, and Smith was in danger of prosecution under German law for his involvement in Esch's affairs.[3] Smith had continued his association with Esch, despite the misgivings of associates, because he was fascinated by the man's style. It was like a nerd's idolatry of the star footballer.

Smith did not learn his lesson from Esch. He succumbed, even more disastrously, to Ross Perot's dynamism. With Esch, Smith was trying to sell Terex. With Perot, Smith was trying to buy a new company. EDS was just one firm on a list of prospects drawn up for GM by Salomon Brothers, the investment bankers. Perot was not interested in selling, but he prolonged negotiations as a way of scouting out the computer needs of GM. The more Perot said no, the more Smith was impressed by his firmness—this was just the kind of commanding personality Smith wished he had, and just the kind GM needed. Smith kept escalating the offers, promising Perot the sky—he could come in as a board member of GM and use the absorbed EDS as an intelligence center to reform GM's whole operation. Perot sold EDS on those terms.

When Perot took Smith at his word, chiding GM in public, prodding the huge company he called an elephant, praising his own EDS team and belittling the computer operators in place, the situation became untenable. The GM board backed an effort to buy Perot out. Perot once again escalated his demands, making them so exorbitant that they *could* not be accepted—the shareholders would rebel at the extravagant payoff.[4] Perot was mounting a coup—Smith would have to go, not Perot. But to Perot's amazement, the board stuck with Smith. He was not a glamorous leader. But neither was he a loose cannon.

It was unrealistic but understandable that some at GM had hoped to combine Perot's salesmanship with Smith's knowledge of production. But the two men were not oil and water. They were gunpowder and fire. Their breakup shook the huge corporation to its foundation and convinced Perot that his talents would have to find a new outlet. Commando raids are not the style of corporate executives. It had been Perot's bad luck to attract, in Smith, his perfect antitype.

8.

TRADITIONAL LEADER

John XXIII

Of the three social structures described by Max Weber, the *traditional* is the least studied or regarded now. *Charismatic* leadership, though treated as primitive, is yet prized for its "transformative" effect. *Legal* leadership seems the highest form of social ordering, since it is based on reason and voluntary consent. But tradition is stuck between these two. It seems to have no inner principle of action, only the force of inertia, like a cannonball still moving though the explosion that launched it is over.

Yet tradition is a necessary element, even in the other two forms of society. David was a charismatic leader, but he needed the prior respect for Jewish cult to explain his charisma in theological terms. Even a contractual system like the United States Constitution has its tradition-preserving aspect. One of the three departments of the government, the judiciary, is devoted to preservation of the laws. All the trappings of a traditional order are used to emphasize this function. People entering a court of law are made to observe a decorum that amounts to liturgical choreography. Judges are seated on high. They wear ceremonial garb. Silence is enforced on all who do not have the court's permission to speak. Lawyers approach the bench only if permitted by the liturgical forms or the judge's command. Ritual cries open and close the proceedings. Ancient oaths are administered.

This traditional way of applying old laws to new situations is cumbersome. The procedures make for what Shakespeare called "the law's delay." Little room is left for improvisation, or the inspiration of the moment. "Charismatic" law enforcement is done by fiat—the king's mercy or swift punishment, the crowd's rescue of a prisoner (or its lynching of him) based on authentic feelings of the moment. Most of us prefer the procedurally more clumsy workings of a trial.

But the courts are preserving a set of laws reached by contractual process. Tradition is subservient to a legal-rational society. When tradition is the *main* source of authority, the society looks (in our eyes) retrograde or irrational. We think that John Locke refuted Robert Filmer's case for the patriarchal traditionalism of kings in the seventeenth century. Only romantics yearn back toward the day when people pledged themselves blindly to a liege lord, knights in absolute service to their king. There was something generous about that, no doubt; but something foolish as well.

In only one area is traditional leadership still honored (and not always there). *Religion* has a traditional structure, for several reasons. Since God in most theologies is absolute in his claims on man, there can be no bargaining with Him. Though He forms contracts with humans in many religious structures, these covenants are *granted* on His side, not wrested from Him (as concessions were wrung from King John in Magna Carta). The idea of protection from a ruler's injustice does not apply (in believers' eyes) to God, who is Justice personified. Priests may misinterpret what God demands—but that is a different problem. Usually, religious forms preserve the memory of some revelation—Torah, New Testament, Koran, Book of Mormon, *Science and Health.* That is the "handed-on" thing (*tradition*).

It is not surprising, then, that even in the twentieth century, traditional leaders could still be found in religious communities—the Dalai Lama, the Ayatollah Khomeini, Billy Graham. But the official who extends the longest tradition of religious office into our time is the pope in Rome. He claims to have the authority of Peter, Jesus' first disciple, handed on through a direct chain of representatives. The dynamic of traditional leadership can be studied in a pope who renewed the tradition with some success, Pope John XXIII, who ruled his church from 1958 to 1963.

Angelo Roncalli was born (1881) on a farm outside Bergamo, the birthplace of the opera composer Donizetti. Because of his peasant origins, and because his sunny personality could not have been more different from the chilly poise of his predecessor, Pius XII, too much can be made of Roncalli's earthy "commonness." He did have a regional loyalty for Lombardy, the countryside of his birth, but he thought of that countryside in terms of his favorite novel, Alessandro Manzoni's *The Plighted Couple* (*I Promessi Sposi*). The peasant lovers of that tale are rescued from their trouble by two aristocratic clergymen. Roncalli wanted to resemble those clerical paragons.

After attending the local seminary, and finishing his studies in Rome, Roncalli came back to Bergamo to serve as his bishop's secretary. His career was launched, not as a parish priest, but as an ecclesiastical bureaucrat—and that is what he remained, despite some intervals of teaching canon law. His role model, taken from the local history of his area, was Charles Borromeo (1538–84), the canonized bishop of Milan whom Lord Acton could never forgive for his use of execution as a penalty for heresy.[1]

Borromeo was the nephew of Pope Pius IV, whom he had served as secretary of state, helping to direct the third session of the reforming Council of Trent. Installed in the diocese of Milan, he made his realm a model of the disciplinary reforms called for by the council, consulting his clergy in meetings (synods) and making inspection tours of all one thousand parishes in his custody—including Bergamo, where he established the seminary Roncalli would attend. Angelo conceived, early on, the idea of editing the records of these "visitations," a scholarly work he labored at for three decades, snatching time from his other duties, proudly producing the fifth and final volume in 1957, the year before he was elected pope.

After the Bible itself, no other guides were more important to Roncalli than Borromeo and Manzoni's novel. At each of the ecclesiastical domains he took over, Roncalli imitated Borromeo by using little councils (synods) and visitations to reform the religious life entrusted to his care. The idea of a *general* council as the vehicle of church reformation was inspired by Roncalli's admiration for Borromeo's work at the Council of Trent. The ability to use historical models in modern revivals was part of Roncalli's training for the papacy—to which he came, in his seventies, better equipped than most of his critics (or, for that matter, his friends) realized. The historic seat of Milan, whose archives he had haunted, was central to his life, and he would find in its resident cardinal of the 1960s—Giovanni Battista Montini—an important ally during his own council's sessions.

The Manzoni novel enters into this Milanese connection. Though the novelist went to Florence to polish the Tuscan diction of his story's third and final version, its most exciting events take place in and around Milan. In the seventeenth-century fictional setting, riots and plague threaten every form of social stability, and heroic churchmen are the principal props of the community. A relative of Charles Borromeo, Federigo Borromeo, had become the cardinal of Milan in the time covered by the novel, and Manzoni makes a Capuchin friar repeat Charles Borromeo's brave service to the plague-stricken. All these aspects of the story gave it special force for Roncalli.

The Plighted Couple is a national epic that means as much to Italians as *Don Quixote* does to Spaniards. The book is dearer to them than *Madame Bovary* is to the French or *Huckleberry Finn* to Americans. Verdi's devotion to Manzoni is famous—the composer began his career by setting Manzoni's religious verses to music, and his life work was crowned by composition of the *Requiem Mass* in Manzoni's honor. When the musician from Busseto finally met "the Saint," he was awed as by no other encounter of his life.[2] Manzoni achieved some magical blend of modernity and tradition. His novel codified an Italian identity just as it was taking shape in a national unification (Risorgimento). By rewriting the book in purest Tuscan, Manzoni helped give the new realm a common language. He won the allegiance of secular patriots and pious seminarians alike. Manzoni's mother, the daughter of the great Enlightenment thinker Cesare Beccaria, had run off with a Frenchman to Paris, where she moved in the circle of "Idéalogues" that met at Mme. de Staël's salon. Taken with her into this atmosphere, the young Allesandro lost his early faith in God; but he married, in Paris, an evangelical Protestant from Geneva, Henriette Blondel, whose piety helped provoke his conversion back to Catholicism.

Despite his piety, Manzoni remained a shrewd satirist of the church's venal or self-deluding members. He despised Jesuits—omitting them from his novel's seventeenth-century milieu is one of his more deliberate historical distortions.[3] The novel's cowardly curate, the sadistic mother superior of a convent, are searing portraits.[4] He never mistook piety for mere churchly conformism. The psychological sophistication of Angelo Roncalli was formed out of a lifelong contemplation of the human comedy contained in *The Plighted Couple*. The book served, too, as a school of manners for the man from rustic Bergamo. The influence of Henriette Blondel made Manzoni conceive a "gospel Christianity" not confined within sectarian structures. His Federigo Borromeo is a subtler version of Victor Hugo's good bishop in *Les Miserables*. Roncalli's ecumenical attitudes of the midcentury were prepared for by the latitudinarian spiritual ideal of Manzoni.

Another influence on Roncalli was the bishop he served as a secretary in Bergamo—Giacomo Radini-Tedeschi—whose social liberalism Roncalli praised, after his death, in a monograph (*My Bishop*). This publication set off alarm bells in the conservative chambers of the Vatican bureaucracy, the Curia, and may have helped shunt the rising church diplomat into "backwater" assignments in Bulgaria and Turkey. He spent a decade in each place, his prime years, from his mid-forties to his mid-sixties, and he chafed at the assignments though they served him in the long run. By being in Bulgaria during the 1930s, he escaped the Fascist involvements of those left in Italy. By serving in Turkey during the war, he had the opportunity to give Vatican visas to thousands of Jews whose lives were saved by this timely passport. The aristocratic German ambassador to Turkey, Franz von Papen, collaborated with the Vatican legate in these acts of mercy, as each could later testify of the other— Roncalli in a deposition for the Nuremberg trials and von Papen at Roncalli's beatification process. Roncalli was sufficiently cooperative with Pius XII's policy, however, to advise the Curia against Jewish transportation to Palestine, which might challenge Christian possession of the Holy Places.[5]

After the war, Pope Pius finally brought Roncalli into the center of European diplomacy. As the papal delegate to France, he helped moderate Charles de Gaulle's efforts to purge the French hierarchy of bishops who collaborated with the wartime Vichy government.[6] Even more unhappily, he was instructed from Rome to cool or discourage the intellectual revival of Catholic art and philosophy in France—resisting, for instance, de Gaulle's appointment of the liberal theologian Jacques Maritain as the French ambassador to the Vatican.

Roncalli's best biographer in English doubts that he ever really understood the subtleties of French thought in that postwar era of existentialism and phenomenology. His attitude toward the Jesuit paleontologist, Teilhard de Chardin, was probably typical of his response in other cases: "Why can't he be content with the catechism and the social doctrine of the church, instead of bringing up all these problems?"[7] Roncalli was not by temperament a repressive person, and he managed to escape the scene when some of Rome's harsher measures were being promulgated. Appointing Roncalli's successor, Pius XII said, "Don't be like your predecessor—he was never there."[8] Roncalli, put in the middle, was agile enough to maintain good relations both with Rome and with the French leaders of church and state. Despite his portly girth, he proved surprisingly elusive. As Archbishop Maurice Feltin of Paris said: "He could be subtle, perspicacious, and far-sighted; and I could give plenty of examples of the way he slipped through the grasp of those who sought to exploit him."[9]

Nonetheless, it was with great relief that he ended his decade in Paris and held his first residential see as the patriarch of Venice in 1953. He was seventy-two. After three decades in three foreign posts, he was coming home—presumably to his final position. Bergamo was on the edge of the Veneto, and had actually been ruled by the Republic of Saint Mark in the seventeenth century of *The Plighted Couple*; so Roncalli, now Cardinal Roncalli, greeted his new assignment to Venice with Renzo's cry, in the novel, "Long live St. Mark!"[10]

Though personally unpretentious, Roncalli loved the ceremonies, processions, and rites of the church. He was very happy in the theatrical atmosphere of Venice, where he blessed gondolas, married the city and the sea in the pageantry of Ascension Day, lifted the ban on Catholic participation in art and movie festivals, and got along well with socialists trying to organize the poor mainland workers of the Veneto. He also threw himself into visitations and synod preparations, like his Borromeo heroes (Charles and Federigo). Here he finished his life work, the edition of Charles Borromeo's inspection tours. There seemed nothing further to accomplish.

Though Pius XII was eighty-two and sickly, his death came as a surprise in 1958—he had been so rigidly disciplined that nothing seemed to dent his iron-spectacled control. Ill for the last four years, he was kept in hope by the injection of lamb tissue that a Swiss gerontologist called "living cell therapy."[11] When he died at his summer palace, Castel Gondolfo, the customary evisceration was delayed until the body was returned to Rome. As his cortege reached the pope's episcopal seat as bishop of Rome, the Lateran Basilica, a loud boom issued from the casket—it was the pope's body exploding. His personal physician (an ophthalmologist) had used an "experimental" embalmer, who worked to undo the damage that night. But the next day, when Pius's face was exposed, it was green, and the day after that his face developed dark blotches and a rotting odor spread from the casket.[12]

In medieval times all these signs would have proved that the devil had taken possession of the unfortunate cadaver. Even modern Rome is not entirely proof against superstition. The curial forces that wanted to celebrate Pius as a way of electing a conservative heir to his policies (perhaps Domenico Tardini) were thrown off their stride by these unsettling events. The sense of an ending, the need for a new beginning, made the conclave look for someone outside the tight Roman circle Pius had pulled around him. Some even wanted a non-Italian Pope—Gregory Peter Agagianian, of the Armenian rite. Roncalli later told some Armenians that his name and Agagianian's had gone up and down in the conclave's balloting like two *ceci* (chickpeas) in boiling water.[13] But on the eleventh ballot Roncalli was chosen, as a man of amiable mien, one who could serve as a "transitional pope" until a younger man was groomed for the real leadership of the future. Roncalli was seventy-seven years old, a hard worker at his desk, overweight (despite frequent prayerful determinations to diet)—he would not last long.

Cardinal Alfredo Ottaviani, the head of the Holy Office (formerly called the Inquisition), had supported Roncalli as a stop-gap, probably believing that he could control the genial but not "first-rate" conciliator from Bergamo.[14] For a time, it seemed that Ottaviani was right. The newly named Pope John confirmed Ottaviani in all his powers, much as American presidents used to renew J. Edgar Hoover's hold on office. Though John began his customary shake-up of the Roman diocese by undertaking visitations leading to a synod, the international actions of the Vatican continued for some time in the Pius tradition. Teilhard de Chardin was given a new "warning" (*monitum*). The worker-priest movement was finally dissolved in France—there were credible reports that Roncalli had promised this move when cultivating French cardinals before his election.[15] Vatican "wisdom" soon had the new pope pegged. A jingle went around:

> *Angelo regna,*
> *Carlo informa,*
> *Alfredo sorveglia,*
> *Domenico governa,*
> *Giovanni?—Benedice.*

> Angelo presides,
> Carlo spies,
> Alfredo oversees,
> Domenico does the governing,
> And John?—He blesses it all.[16]

Angelo Dell'Aqua was deputy secretary of state.
Carlo Confalonieri was secretary of seminaries.
Alfredo Ottaviani was head of the Holy Office.
Domenico Tardini was secretary of state.
And John? He was the man who noted this jingle in his diary.

He knew what was going on. He did not fight the Curia on its own ground; he would go around it, in two ways—through encyclicals, and through a universal (ecumenical) council, two ancient instruments.

Encyclicals (circular letters) were a device of the patristic era whereby bishops conducted a kind of rolling epistolary council discussing doctrinal matters.[17] After long medieval neglect, Benedict XIV revived the term in the eighteenth century for missives sent by the pope to bishops. These became more important, and extended often to political matters, in the nineteenth and twentieth centuries. Pope John, after issuing some routine letters, changed the encyclicals' focus drastically in his letters *Mater et Magistra* (1961) and *Pacem in Terris* (1963)—the letters are known by their opening words. These were addressed not narrowly to bishops, or even to Catholics alone, but to all "men of goodwill." They were not defensive of church rights or doctrine, but concerned with the common problems of mankind—the first with the need for economic justice, the second with world cooperation to ensure peace. The first encyclical, challenging the secular autonomy of a free market, prompted William Buckley to write *"Mater sì, Magistra, no"* (based on the Castroites' slogan of that day, "Cuba sì, Yanqui, no").[18] The other encyclical tried to call off the Cold War.

In preparing these documents, Pope John reached out beyond the curial experts he had inherited—to people like Giovanni Battista Montini in Milan, who had disturbed Pius's circle by his friendship with Aldo Moro, the Christian Democrat who sought an opening to the left (*apertura alla sinistra*). John was also consulting with Augustin Bea, the Jesuit cardinal who was a leader in ecumenical relations with non-Catholics. These were among the bishops he would support at key moments in Vatican Council II.

There was nothing necessarily liberating about calling a council of all the world's bishops. These had begun as ways of deciding and imposing orthodoxy. Early councils, like that which the Emperor Constantine summoned to Nicea (325), had given secular rulers great power to intervene in church affairs. Later, conciliarism was a movement used against some popes. But the last two councils before John's had been instruments for maximizing papal authority—Trent (1545–63), which set up the Counterreformation's discipline, and the first Vatican Council (1869–70), which rubber-stamped Pius IX's desire to be declared infallible.[19] There was no guarantee that this would not prove true of John's council, especially with the Curia preparing the "talking papers" (*schemata*) for each subject.

On the other hand, calling a church council is something like calling a constitutional convention in the United States—it risks opening up unforeseen questions and becoming a "runaway" body. The Curia worked hard and long to anticipate and prevent such breakaway developments. John, with his genuine trust in the Holy Spirit, hoped that some providential afflatus would strike "the bark of Peter" and drive it in new directions. John was not a "liberal" in any consistent or temperamental sense. He loved church ceremonies as they were, and had no desire to change them. He delighted in ecclesiastical Latin, the medium through which he had communed with his hero, Charles Borromeo, across the centuries. His idea of a good council was Borromeo's Counterreformation council, Trent, which modern liberals distrusted. He never intended change in areas of sexual asceticism—he took contraception out of the hands of the council and he showed hostility to the idea of married priests (even worker priests were not true to their celestial status in his eyes).[20] Personally, he got along with traditionalists in the Curia. (It helped that Cardinal Tardini could quote whole pages of Manzoni from memory.)[21] He differed from them only because he believed more deeply than they in traditional doctrines like the divine inspiration of the church. The hereditary ruler must accept the validating myth of his own office if he is to use it effectively. John gambled with history because he was so sure that God was on his side. Next to this man's divine recklessness, the calculating Pius XII looks like an unbeliever. Those who want hereditary rule to express only the virtues of stability undermine that very rule.

Vatican II did "run away." The assembled bishops rebelled against the straitjacket the Curia had woven for them. The same thing had happened at Pius IX's council, where the pope broke the rebellion. This time, the pope intervened to relax curial restraints. When a significant (but not a legally binding) majority objected to the rigid formulation of the first doctrinal matter, the relative authority of Scripture and tradition, John sent the *schema* back for reconsideration. Then liturgical reform was brought forward, ahead of time, to fill the gap created in the schedule. The proposal to substitute vernacular languages for Latin in church ceremony unleashed strange passions. Though this seemed a mere matter of church practice, it had great symbolic significance. Latin had been an instrument of domination at Vatican I, where noncurial bishops, unfamiliar with church Latin (or its Italian pronunciation) had been bemused onlookers while the pope's team chattered its doctrines into place.[22] John, who had called in a classicist to brush up his Latin before the council, accepted the move toward vernacular Masses; yet he would not have proposed it himself.

Though no outsiders were aware of it, John knew he was dying of cancer during the first session of Vatican II. He would not live to see its later meetings. He had not called the bishops together to "ride herd" on them. The image of Peter that he clung to was not the seated ruler in majesty but the trusting man who left the boat to walk toward his Master when summoned (Matthew 13.28–33). He did not have his own program, even at the slogan level others invented for him. It was said he meant to "open the windows" of the church, to air it out—but his secretary denied that he would use such language. He hated drafts, and closed himself up tight, even in Roman summers.[23] He did use the word *aggiornamento*, "updating," but that had been the announced aim of his visitations in Venice, patterned on the spiritual renewal Borromeo recommended.[24] He never deserted his first masters.

In fact, the council would go farther in its next sessions than he ever foresaw. It changed the official position on freedom of conscience, on the people's right of self-government, and on Catholic relations with other believers (and unbelievers). But there was something in each of these developments that reflected John's spirit and attitudes. His churchly critics said he trusted too much to natural goodness; he did not give enough weight to original sin. The truth is that he trusted God's power to reach and touch anyone. During the Cuban missile crisis, he sent his peaceful urgings as hopefully to Nikita Khrushchev as to John Kennedy—and it was Khrushchev who responded. Seeking a way to back off, the Soviet leader had a pope's message—of all things—printed on the front page of *Pravda*. Later, in "openings to the left" that might stagger an Aldo Moro, the pope received a visit from Khrushchev's daughter and son-in-law. The community he could find with them depended on natural goodness and the shared human things that God has created for everyone. He told Stalin's son-in-law, Alexis Adzhubei:

You are a journalist, and as such you know the Bible and the story of creation. The Bible says that God created the world and on the first day he created light. Then creation went on for six days. But the days of the Bible, as you know, are whole epochs, and these epochs last a very long time. We are looking into each others' eyes and we see the light there. Today is the first day of creation, the day of light, the day of *fiat lux*. It all takes time. Let me say again: the light is in my eyes and in your eyes.[25]

In the Communist's eyes. In the disbeliever's. When the Nameless One (*Innominato*), the great sinner, comes to see Federigo Borromeo in Manzoni's novel, he expects some kind of reproach or preaching; but instead the cardinal, embracing him, apologizes for not having gone first to visit *him*. A hapless curate, standing by, reacts exactly as the Curia did to the pope's cordial relations with the Kremlin:

I'm telling you, saints and thugs! They have so much quicksilver running in them that, not able to keep still themselves, they have to make everybody else dance around as well.[26]

When John turned to Khrushchev's daughter, he said:

Madame, I know you have three children, and I know their names. But I would like *you* to tell me their names, because when a mother speaks the names of her children, something very special happens.

She pronounced the names: Nikita, Alexei, Ivan. He said something nice about each name, saving Ivan for the last, since Ivan is the Russian form of John.

That is the name of my grandfather, my father, the name I chose for my pontificate, the name of the hill above my birthplace, the name of the basilica of which I am bishop. When you get home, madame, give all your children a hug, but give Ivan a very special one—the others won't mind.

To connect a distant Russian boy with a hill *he* had looked at as a boy—that was said like a diplomat, of course. But some forms of diplomacy are indistinguishable from basic humanity. There have been powerful popes—shrewd ones, brooding ones, maligned, misunderstood, or malevolent ones. But everyone, far off or near him, grasped the fact that this man, whatever one thought of his office, was the good pope. It became so inevitable a usage as to form a new title: Good Pope John.

A shallow reading of Pope John's impact would say that he succeeded by deserting tradition—so how can he be called a traditional leader? Certainly the conservatives of the Roma Curia thought he had betrayed tradition instead of upholding it. They and their successors are still bitterly opposing the effort to canonize the Roncalli pope. But John embodies the paradox of all traditional leadership. If it relies *only* on tradition, the thing handed down becomes something different, at the end of the process, from what it started as. G. K. Chesterton put it this way:

> Conservatism is based upon the idea that if you leave things alone you leave them as they are. But you do not. If you leave a thing alone you leave it to a torrent of changes. If you leave a white post alone it will soon be a black post. If you particularly want it to be white you must be always painting it again. . . . Briefly, if you want the old white post you must have a new white post.[27]

What people celebrate as "tradition" is usually a thing that has been blackened by time. The church the Curia celebrated as "changeless" embodied all the changes that had crept into the church in its long history. The Christian church *began* with a vernacular liturgy, an experimental ministry, a gospel expectation of apocalypse. The Latin liturgy, the celibate priesthood, and other things to which the conservatives clung, were late encrustations. Pope John knew that the church must always be in a process of renewal (*ecclesia semper reformanda*) to get back to its original inspiration.

It is a commonplace that religious orders decline from the zeal of their founders with routine and rigid formulae. That is why "reform Benedictines" have kept one of the oldest orders alive by making it the newest order in different centuries. Protestants face the need of reforming the Reformation. Those who rely on inertia have to face the fact that inertial movement decreases of itself. "A frequent recurrence to first principles" is recommended to politicians. Corporations have to recover their early energies. All things that resist change *are* changed by that resistance in ways undesired and undesirable. The tradition must be repristinated if it is to be *worth* following.

The temptation of the papacy, as of all traditional leadership, is to think of its strength as derived from immobility, from sitting still. The pope's office is defined as his see (seat), the *sedes apostolica*—and St. Peter as pope is shown seated. But only a dead thing is immobile. Pope John often meditated on the risen Jesus' words to Peter in the gospel of St. John (21.18):

> I tell you this in very truth: when you were young you fastened your belt about you and walked where you chose; but when you are old you will stretch out your arms, and a stranger will bind you fast, and carry you where you have no wish to go.[28]

St. Peter was a married man ignorant of Latin—someone Pius XII would have had a hard time recognizing. But John, whirled through the changes of modern times, went back to the *origins* of the Christian tradition. His only steadiness—like that of the man scrambling out of the boat in Tintoretto's picture of St. Peter in Washington's National Gallery—comes from the gyroscopically upright figure of Jesus in a scene where everything else tilts and pitches out of true.

Christ at the Sea of Galilee—*Tintoretto*
National Gallery of Art Washington, D.C.
Samuel H. Kress Collection

ANTITYPE

Celestine V

One obvious antitype to Pope John is Pius XII, a tradition-alist who clung to the tradition as it came to him, black-ened over time. But a subtler antitype is the lover of tradition who fails to be a leader out of *entire* trust in the original inspiration. This degree of trust in others leads to the renunciation of power. The best example of this is Pope Celestine V (1215–96), the only pope who resigned his office. In 1294, in the seaside fortress-castle of Naples, he stripped himself of the honor he never desired—an act so out of the ordinary that it speeded his canonization as a saint.

Jesus told Peter, in the gospel of Matthew (10.16), to combine the dove's simpleness with a serpent's wiliness. Pius is a figure of contrast with Pope John, coming at him from the side of wiliness. But Celestine offers as stark a contrast from the side of dovelike simplicity, proving that holiness is not, of itself, a quality of *leadership*. For that, one must effect the difficult combination John achieved.

While others were calling Celestine a saint, Dante called him a coward. Traveling through hell with Vergil as his guide, Dante encounters those too fainthearted to live while they were alive, including the man who

> renounced from littleness of soul large powers.
>
> *Che fece per viltade il gran rifiuto.*[1]

Another Italian poet, Celestine's contemporary and fellow cleric, Jaco-pone da Todi, thought his mistake was not so much in giving up the papal office as in accepting it:

> I was crushed by shared distress
> When I heard your fatal "Yes."
>
> *Grande ho auto en te cordoglio*
> *Co te uscio de bocca: "Voglio."*[2]

Jacopone was part of the Spiritual Franciscan movement that treated as a prophet Pietro del Morrone, the hermit raised to the papacy as Celestine V. In the apocalyptic atmosphere of the late thirteenth century, Pietro was a famous ascetic who rebuilt churches and founded an order, like St. Francis. He starved and scourged himself, and issued urgent moral exhortations taken as prophecies. It was one such "prophecy" that brought on him the calamity of great power. The papal throne had stood empty for two years while the Colonna and Orsini families, who controlled it, refused to let the other's man take a turn in office. Pietro issued a denunciation of this unedifying situation, and the little camp of a dozen cardinals, moving about Italy to avoid the plague, decided to intermit skulduggery with salvation by hauling the saint down from his mountain cell and clothing him in grandeur as the pope. (It was not a terrible risk, since he was eighty-five and sickly.)[3]

Pietro resisted, but the populace loved this fairy-tale rewarding of the good by the hopelessly stymied bad. As soon as Pietro accepted the papacy, a competition arose to flatter and manipulate the bewildered holy man—a game made not too difficult by his ignorance of Latin. The cardinals tried to spirit him off to Rome, but Charles II, the Angevin king of Sicily, intervened and got him ensconced in Naples, where he induced the pope to appoint a batch of cardinals subservient to the king. Celestine was wise enough to know he was being used, but not wise enough to know what to do about it. Even the good he did led to greater disaster. He recognized the Spiritual Franciscans as the legitimate branch of their order—which led to a ferocity of repression after Celestine left the scene. (Jacopone da Todi was thrown into jail, and elaborated his lament over Celestine's folly.) He installed his own order (the Celestines) at the historic monastery of Monte Cassino—which angered the Benedictines, driven out of their founder's site.

Cardinal Benedetto Caetani worked with King Charles to bring about the puppet pope's resignation after Celestine had been used to thwart the Colonna and Orsini. Caetani was elected Boniface VIII as soon as Celestine stepped down. Dante felt that Celestine's yielding to Caetani was a submission to the devil, and many saw in Boniface the AntiChrist, another harbinger of the world's end the Spirituals were preaching. After all the harm done by corruption, Celestine stands as proof that even holiness can be an earthly bane.

9.

CONSTITUTIONAL LEADER

––––

George Washington

Max Weber's third social order, the legal-rational type, is not as spectacular as the charismatic order, not as ceremonial as the traditional order. It can seem as dry as the shuffling of a lawyer's briefs. People *contract* with their rulers to set the terms of their submission. This is not an easy accomplishment, as history shows. Revolutions meant to overthrow charismatic or traditional monarchies, meant to reach the ideal of limited rule under law, veer off into dictatorships that are eerily similar to the first evil. The Russian czar is overthrown, only to bring in a tyrannical Stalin. The French king, Louis, gives way to the French emperor, Napoleon. Charles I is beheaded, and Cromwell takes up powers even greater than his.

The most successful transition from monarchy to republicanism took place in America. A cluster of brilliant men, favored by historical circumstance, accomplished that change. But it could have gone awry if the central figure in that transition had been a man of different ambition or less tempered shrewdness. It is one of the most mysterious imaginable cases of successful leadership. Though George Washington rose from dim origins, nothing was more wildly improbable than his return to a quiet private station at the end of his dizzying career.

In 1754, the well-armored powers of Europe crunched around in each other's proximity like wary crustaceans, ready for outright assault. None of them suspected that two slim antennae would touch, half a world away, and jolt the main bodies at home. A young colonel blundering through the back forests of America mistook a diplomatic delegation for an advance French war party, leaped upon it in a sneak attack at dawn, and let his Indian allies scalp the dead French officers—one of whom carried diplomatic credentials.[1]

Outnumbered, later, by the French he had been stalking, this twenty-one-year-old Virginia colonel retreated into a badly situated fortress, suffered casualties, and surrendered on terms that admitted his crime against the dead diplomat. His defense was that he had not understood the French text he was signing.[2] When British regulars were censorious to the young man, he resigned his commission in the colonial militia—Washington's first (and the only nonproductive) withdrawal in a long career of resignings. Without knowing it, he had touched off a world war that would remake the imperial maps of France, England, and Prussia. The young colonel's captured diary was published and execrated in France, and censured in England by King George II. He was a world-famous bungler. Learned men debated whether he was vicious or merely ignorant. His wounded pride took years of salving, and the preservation of his dignity became an overriding concern. He was in Cassio's mood:

> Reputation, reputation, I ha' lost my reputation! I ha' lost the immortal part, sir, of myself, and what remains is bestial. . . .[3]

His fellow Virginians did not judge Washington harshly. He was too useful to his land-developing patrons of the Fairfax family faction. That is why he had been pushed prematurely into such a responsible position. He was a strong and resourceful surveyor of the unknown regions where English land companies competed with French *coureurs de bois* for control of the river system between the Great Lakes and the Gulf of Mexico. Washington was trustworthy, forceful though somewhat tongue-tied, gigantic even by Virginia's standards, a Natty Bumppo, a John Wayne, a natural leader of men. He, in turn, was dazzled by the educated leaders of Virginia. He was smitten with Sally Fairfax, the married mistress of Belvoir plantation. Young colonials, lacking other entertainment centers, fell in love easily with their hostesses, the versatile managers of huge households—Thomas Jefferson made advances to the married Betsey Walker, and Philip Fithian, a tutor of Nomini Hall, adored his employer's wife from a distance.

Washington had little prospect of advancement but the military. His father, Augustine, had sent two sons by his first marriage to be educated in England; but the five children of his second marriage—including George—were stranded when Augustine Washington died during George's eleventh year. There would be no education in England for them; and the modest family estate (twenty slaves, only seven of them good workers) was entailed to sons of the earlier marriage.[4]

George was not resentful. In fact, he had a hero worshiper's regard for Lawrence Washington, the half-brother who was fourteen years his elder. Lawrence had served in the Caribbean "War of Jenkin's Ear" under the illustrious Admiral Edward Vernon (Lawrence renamed the family plantation after Vernon). Tobias Smollett sailed with the same 1740 expedition, and described its reverses in the novel *Roderick Random*. Lawrence had already been part of the imperial world his half-brother stumbled into so ingloriously in the next decade.

On his return to Virginia, the charming Lawrence moved as an equal in Fairfax circles and paved the way there for his admiring young relative. But Lawrence was already dying of tuberculosis. The teen-aged George accompanied him on a trip to Barbados, where his brother sought health from the sun and the medical baths. George himself fell ill of the smallpox during this one trip off the American continent—fortunately, since the ordeal gave him immunity to the disease when it was ravaging his troops during the Revolution.

With both half-brothers dead, George fell heir to the renamed Mount Vernon, a small stake to begin with, but one he expanded by marriage and by managerial dedication. In a world of debt and gambling, Washington understood his own "credit" in the broadest sense. He would take the same view of the young republic's credit abroad—he knew it must have financial steadiness at its base. Washington ran his plantation as he would later run his armies, with an eye for detail, for morale, for future contingencies. Respect for him grew. His advice was sought when he entered the House of Burgesses. When Virginia sent its most impressive representatives to confer in Philadelphia on Parliament's aggression, Washington stood out even in that galaxy of talent.

He had, despite his own misgivings about a lack of education, a sense of his own worth and a theatrical flair for impressing others. Even as a young colonial militiaman, he had designed his special uniform.[5] As a civilian at Mount Vernon, he summoned Charles Willson Peale to paint him wearing it. When the time came to choose a colonial commander in chief of the military, Washington declared his availability by appearing uniformed in Philadelphia. After his bad beginning in the Seven Years'

War he had proved useful to General Braddock, and acquired the respect and friendship of British officers like Robert Orme. He would have the same success serving with French officers (like Chastellux) in the Revolution. In his remote colonial station, he had become important to the two opposed imperial armies of his era. His central role in the opening scene of conflict between them had been modified in a way no one expected. He had been with the British victors when they wrested Canada away from France. And he would be with the French victors when the seaboard colonies were snatched from British control.

Even in the earliest days of the Revolution Washington had a large *national* vision. Others fought for their individual states. He worked to forge, out of the state militias, a *continental* army. Despite his friendship with Lafayette, he secretly undermined that young officer's attempt to draw British Canada into the fray.[6] Washington knew that reinstating France on the North American continent would hem in the new republic's prospects. Much as he needed French naval and diplomatic help, he would not tie the new country to a second superpower in order to slip out of the first one's orbit. Like the leader of a "non-aligned" third-world country during the Cold War of this century, he played the great powers off against each other.[7]

Even while he created military unity, strengthening Congress's hand over the state legislatures, Washington was working for postwar political unity. At the war's end, he surrendered his military commission, and withdrew from all political office, to back up his final letter to the state governors asking that they create a strong union of the states. When the weak Articles of Confederation disappointed these hopes, Washington kept his pledge to remain in private life for six years. After that, he let himself be "drafted" to serve at the emergency convention in Philadelphia, but only in response to the most strenuous actions taken by Madison and others to secure his attendance.

Directing the "runaway" convention at Philadelphia was the most revolutionary act of Washington's life. He knew that it was acting illegally under the amending provisions of the Articles.[8] That is why the convention kept its proceedings secret until it was disbanded. Washington, elected president of the body, enforced its secrecy with vigor. When it became known that the plotters were repudiating the Articles (the law of the land), only Washington's and Franklin's great reputations saved delegates from the odium of treason. Opponents decried the mobilization of the two men's glory for such a cause:

The great names of Washington and Franklin have been taken in vain and
shockingly prostituted to effect the most infamous purposes.[9]

The denunciation would have been even harsher and more effective if the
critics had known everything that went on in the convention—a development the plotters were careful to prevent: they voted that Washington
take the minutes of the convention back to Mount Vernon and keep them
away from public scrutiny.

When the Constitution was, with difficulty, ratified, it was in part
because Washington had stood by it and was foreseen as the first president
under it. Had he aimed at a dictatorship—a normal development when
governing becomes difficult after a revolution—he might have worn that
title, at least for a while. He made clear, by contrast, his respect for
Congress, his determination to live by the new law's letter, and his desire
to serve only one term. A farewell address—composed by James Madison—was prepared for his resignation after the first term; but once again
Washington was drafted into further service, even critics admitting that
his country needed him. The same thing was urged after his second term;
but this time he was adamant. His published farewell address, drafted by
Alexander Hamilton this time, returned to his old message from the
war—that America should not be drawn into the imperial struggles of the
great powers. The new republic must not form its ethos in the midst of
military adventures. The Napoleonic wars tempted Anglophiles like
Hamilton and Francophiles like Jefferson to join the kings or the rebels
in ideological conflicts over European legitimacy. Washington's counsel
was so far heeded that when Jefferson took office, five years later, he did
so with a pledge against "entangling alliances" that is often misattributed
to Washington's farewell address. It conveys that document's meaning,
though not its phrasing.

Washington's refusal to bring about a strong central government by
seizing power is his greatest legacy to the nation. He who began as an
agent of the Fairfaxes kept clear in his mind that he was an agent of the
Congress when leading warriors, and an agent of the people when governing. He wielded power by yielding it. His fame spread through Europe
as the new Cincinnatus, the ancient Roman who left his army to return
to the plow. His reputation, the dearest thing to him, was bound up in
service. To seize power in any way that hurt his reputation would be felt
as the greatest defeat by Washington. His honor and the nation's were
mutually pledged, one worthless without the other.

It had been the dream of some political theorists, ever since Plutarch's time, to vindicate classical myths of the legendary founders of states—Lycurgus, Theseus, Solon, Numa—as men able to establish power they could walk away from. Guicciardini criticized the "realist" Machiavelli for retaining the vision of such an ideal ruler.[10] Yet Madison found the ideal realized in the Philadelphia convention, which intervened where ordinary procedures were of no avail, produced a new law, and then disbanded itself. In a crisis unprovided for by previous law (the Articles of Confederation),

> since it is impossible for the people spontaneously and universally to move in concert towards their object, it is therefore essential that such changes be instituted by some *informal and unauthorized propositions* made by some patriotic and respectable citizens or numbers of citizens. (*The Federalist*, No. 40)

The convention performed the role of the Lawgiver as described in Rousseau's *Social Contract* (2.7): "He holds no office, and does not partake of the sovereign. His task, which is to institute the republic, has no place within that republic's constitution."

Washington, the president, protector, and guarantor of the Philadelphia convention, was the lawgiver supreme—holding no office at the time, bringing a plan from nowhere for the people to accept, then stepping away from the ratification process. Even as the first executive, he stayed only to make sure the plan was firmly in place. Then, like Romulus, he disappeared—not amid rumors that he was spirited off to make sure that the law (rather than a man) should be obeyed.[11] Washington left of his own free will, living up to the legends only approximated by mythical figures. The man whose life began in an obscure scuffle of the major European powers fulfilled, at last, classical Europe's dream of a figure who might create a state without ensnaring himself in its very structure.

His accomplishment was so great and unusual that it is hard to estimate at its true worth. Washington has managed to become dull—though his contemporaries thought him the most exciting man in the room, even when the other men in the room were Franklin and Jefferson, Madison and Hamilton. Both scholars and most Americans tend to rate him second to Lincoln among United States presidents. But Lincoln had less than a decade of greatness (1858–1865), after an otherwise undistinguished life. Washington was "the indispensable man" (as James Flexner puts it) in crisis after crisis—the Revolution in the 1770s, the formation of the republic in the 1780s, the conduct of the nascent government in the 1790s. He was what Henry Lee called him, "first in war and first in peace." He was a shrewd judge of men and had a self-knowledge that never carried him into the excesses of ambition or despair. Others have *conducted* constitutional government well. He set up such a government, established its precedents, faced all its problems, with no guidelines based on earlier performance.

During the early struggles of the nation, Washington was himself the unifying icon, the symbol of the whole process. He had to replace his own glamour with the more impersonal symbols of power—the Constitution, the flag, the offices of government, the courts. He learned an elaborate language of tact and protocol, receiving respect because of his office, not his person. He stripped away as soon as possible all emblems of his military glory. He would not wear the medal of the Society of the Cincinnati, the elite club of revolutionary officers—and he threatened to resign if that body did not cease to be hereditary. It was typical that, at the inauguration of his successor as president (John Adams), the newly sworn-in vice president (Thomas Jefferson) stepped back to let the ex-president follow Adams out of the chamber—but Washington refused the honor, recognizing Jefferson as the current official of the people. This is the paradox of leadership in a legal system—it asserts authority by deferring to it, as Washington wielded power by giving it up. The authority is that of the contract—in America's case, the authority of the people. It was mentioned earlier that all American presidents are, under the Constitution, legal-system and not charismatic leaders, however glamorous they might seem. That is preeminently true of Washington, who did have (initially) a charismatic authority, of which he divested himself in order to establish the *republic's* claims. A look at the table on page 104 will make it clear how Washington moved from the role in the left column to the attributes in the right column.

In all of this, Washington—who was as entirely self-educated as Lincoln—showed a profound understanding of the nature of representative democracy. Though he presided over the convention that drafted the Constitution, he stepped down daily when it formed a "committee of the whole" to go off the record. While a committee chairman presided, Washington made few but telling interventions. Most of the time he was listening to the intense discussions that none of his contemporaries outside that room would ever read. (We know them from Madison's extensive notes, not published until 1840.) Washington absorbed Madison's vision of the republic's leaders as distillers of the wisdom and virtue of the whole people. It was an intense seminar Washington took with the principal theorist of the Constitution taking shape.

To speak for the nation, Washington had to transcend his own limits. Leading the revolutionary army, he ceased in some measure to be a Virginian looking to his own state's interests. He forged a corps around him that was *national* in its outlook, a prefiguring of the government he would later lead. At the head of that government, he distanced himself from the regional peculiarity of slavery, not letting his servants be seen by the public. By building up a fund for the purpose, he managed to free his own slaves at his wife's death—his estate was still paying for the freed former slaves' support well into the nineteenth century. It was his belief that a leader must *be* virtuous in order to represent a virtuous people. Yet representative leadership does not mean unquestioning subservience to those who are represented. It means the enlightened quest for what is the *best* interest of the people, a quest subject to that people's final judgment, one helping to shape that judgment in a dialogue between the elected and the electors. What Madison said of the Senate's role in our system could also be taken as a description of Washington's neutrality policy at a time when various factions in the new-born republic clamored for war:

> An attention to the judgment of other nations is important to every government for two reasons: The one is that, independently of the merits of any particular plan or measure, it is desirable on various accounts that it should appear to other nations as the offspring of a wise and honourable policy. The second is that, in doubtful cases, particularly where the national councils may be warped by some strong passion or momentary interest, the presumed or known opinion of the impartial world may be the best guide that can be followed. (*The Federalist*, No. 63)

Washington won the respect of "the impartial world" as few leaders of a new nation ever have.

What made for such leadership? His contemporaries gave it the simple but majestic name of "virtue." They meant by that *public* virtue, republican virtue, a devotion to the commonweal, as in the mythical Rome celebrated by the Enlightenment.

If we look at other revolutionary leaders, from Caesar to Cromwell to Napoleon, we have to conclude that it is even harder to give up power than to acquire it. Napoleon began as "Citizen Bonaparte" and ended as the emperor. Washington began as a client in the aristocratic circles of the Fairfaxes, went on to be the first general to win a modern revolutionary war, then the president of an entirely new nation—and he ended up as Citizen Washington. Washington's massive determination, yet principled submission, is perfectly captured in the Roman bust Houdon created on classical models.

George Washington
National Portrait Gallery, Smithsonian Institution/Art Resource, NY

ANTITYPE

Oliver Cromwell

Oliver Cromwell (1599–1658) moved from a legitimate to a charismatic role, reversing the course followed by Washington. Yet there were surface similarities in their careers. Both led military rebellions against English monarchs—Cromwell against Charles I, Washington against George III. Each took local militias—the "train bands" of Cromwell, the colonel levies of Washington—and forged professional armies on a national scale. Each infused a new ethos into his troops—a religious spirit in Cromwell's case, a postcolonial American identity in Washington's.

Cromwell's rebellion was a more rending affair altogether. Washington withdrew from the king some of the Crown's colonial possessions. Cromwell not only overthrew the king, but killed and replaced him. Though he did not intend this at the outset—or for a long time after hostilities began—events swept him into the reenactment of some of the executive arrogancies that the Civil War was launched to remedy.

Cromwell had entered his forties by the time the Civil War began. A great horseman and falconer, though he had no military experience, he showed a natural genius for cavalry movements. The royal troops were best in that arm, and had their best leader, Prince Rupert, in command of it. But successful English cavalry charges tended to dissipate themselves in pursuit of the broken enemy. This showed how desultory had been England's insular fighting of the early seventeenth century, when the dispersal of ragged mobs was the chief task for the king's guards.

Cromwell checked the headlong charges of his cavalry. His men rode so close that "every left-hand man's right knee must be locked under his right-hand man's left ham."[1] This meant that he could react in midcharge to new developments, continue to shape the troop's action after it had broken through the enemy line: "Cromwell, after a first charge, could succeed in getting his men together for a second, while Rupert could not."[2] This gave him, in effect, a reserve force *within* his attack force, something new on British battlefields.[3]

Religion was important to this military achievement. The King, who had imposed bishops on resisting Presbyterians, found himself faced with a "preaching, praying, and drilling" army.[4] The Parliament called to finance Charles was opposed to bishops, and it financed, instead, the antimonarchical force being raised at the time. When the king was in captivity, the army refused to disband itself until it had received full pay, and at Newmarket it dictated terms to Parliament in its Solemn Engagement (1647). This rebellion of the military against the civilian authority resembled the mutiny of Washington's officers at Newburgh (1783). But Cromwell, after some hesitation, promoted the Engagement at Newmarket.[5] Washington rebuked and broke the rebellion at Newburgh. From those two acts, the men's successive careers diverged. Washington retired to civilian life and supported the creation of a strong but legal government. Cromwell used the army to break, discipline, and finally dissolve Parliament. As lord protector, he summoned, packed, and dismissed Parliaments in ways more high-handed than Charles had ever dared to.

Though Cromwell toyed with the idea of the crown, the reluctance of the army made him put it aside. Yet he adopted the style of a king's court at Hampton Palace, and he appointed his son to be his successor. Carlyle said of Cromwell that he could "not get resigned" from the duties his time thrust on him, and contrasted him in this with "George Washington, no very immeasurable man."[6] It is true that few who rise by military rebellion can give back the power they assume in that process. Caesar, Napoleon, Stalin, Fidel, Mao all go the way of Cromwell. They cannot *get* resigned. This shows the tremendous originality of Washington, who brought legal rule out of the false dilemma posed in revolutionary times— either charisma or chaos. His dull legality is the brilliant exception where brilliant supermen have been routine.

10.

INTELLECTUAL LEADER

Socrates

Intellectual *leadership* is as rare as intellectual *influence* is common. Lord Keynes said that we are ruled, without knowing it, by dead economists.[1] That does not mean we are the followers of people we cannot even name. We are influenced by the impact of their theories, just as we are by Einstein's theory of relativity or Freud's theory of the unconscious. Though Freud has many disciples, they are not the few people he recruited to collaborate in his work—the later disciples are under his influence, though he did not personally mobilize them toward a goal.

Intellectual distinction, at its purest, disregards followers. It seeks the truth for its own sake, apart from its impact on others' lives. That was the charge made against some nuclear physicists, who gave no thought to the weapons their theories might bring into being. Yet disregard for the applications of theory is a point of pride for those—from Galileo to Freud—who try to reach the truth even though the truth might disturb social arrangements. The seeker after truth often secludes himself from others, to avoid being deterred by such considerations.

This tendency is not confined to experimental scientists. The young David Hume withdrew from society while he worked out his lasting contribution to philosophical method, the *Treatise of Human Nature* (1739). After he published that work, Hume did want followers, but he found none—the book's influence would be exerted only over a long time and at some distance (initially in Germany). Hume then changed his whole mode of life and did become an intellectual leader—through his enormously popular *History of England* and his moral and political essays. He exemplified in his own life the two tendencies of intellectual excellence: (a) toward a severe and lonely quest for the truth, or (b) toward a less exacting but more accessible truth, one more to be disseminated than discovered. The best intellectual work is done by the first route, but *leadership* is made possible only by the second.

Most people do not have the flexibility of a Hume, they remain crusty discoverers *or* affable disseminators. The first group is made up, often, of antisocial or "maladjusted" persons—idiosyncratically "absentminded" about things outside their field of concentration. Stories and legends grow around such people, who can be absorbed in trances or follow a line of thought for hours. They use a technical language that precludes questioning from those not up to the high demands of their discipline. They often neglect their income and their families. They do not attract a wide following, though a few disciples may be able to join their elite quest. These thinkers often have the widest later *influence* just because they do not strive for an immediate *following*. The strongest and longest claims to later attention are often lodged by "neurasthenic giants" like Kierkegaard, Nietzsche, or Wittgenstein—people who, in effect, toss their thoughts out of the caves where they are hiding.

Leaders, on the other hand, are "outer-directed." They go toward potential followers, cultivate them, satisfy their needs. They show a "healthy" openness to others' concerns; they give up their own project's schedule to accommodate others' demands. This makes them more admirable in some ways, but less focused on purely intellectual matters. It is a commonplace in universities that the faculty member who takes an administrative post is "ruined" for later scholarship. The shift in gears toward ingratiation, persuasion, and negotiation is not easily reversed. An endless response to other people's unpredictable problems interrupts "the single rush of his own mind" that creative intellectual work demands.[2]

> The brain of a great administrator is naturally occupied with the details of the day, the passing dust, the granules of that day's life; and his unforeseeing temperament turns away uninterested from reaching speculations, from vague thought, and from extensive and far-off plans.[3]

The need to be popular discourages daring concepts that could embarrass: "People dread to be thought unsafe in proportion as they get their living by being thought to be safe."[4]

A bold person who suggests a matter of principle, or a difficulty of thought, or an abstract result that seems improbable in the case "before the board," will be set down as a speculator, a theorist, a troubler of practical life.[5]

Those are not the concerns of a Nietzsche, the influencer without followers. Intellectual leaders often feel they cannot afford the luxury of intellectual concentration. William F. Buckley, Jr., unquestionably an intellectual leader of the modern conservative movement, said that he had to give up theoretical work himself and found he had "lost the capacity for reading scholarly prose."[6] The same might be said of Buckley's counterpart on the left, Arthur Schlesinger. Both men were interested in mobilizing followers to a goal—not only to vote Republican or Democratic, but to do so from a consistent intellectual position, of conservatism or liberalism as the case may be.

Scholars will condemn such people as intellectual "popularizers." But popularizing is the task of leadership. Nietzsche had no dealings with followers. He was too busy torturing himself with truth. Intellectual leadership is not the highest form of intellectual activity. It can be exercised by people capable of the highest activity, but normally at a different stage of that thinker's life. Benjamin Franklin, like David Hume, first did his original research (into electrical theory) and only later became a popularizer. Bertrand Russell, after spending nine reclusive years on his most influential work (*Principia Mathematica*), went out into the world and became a social activist. It is hard to find an intellectual leader whose own deepest and most creative work was carried on while he or she exercised leadership. St. Augustine did it, preaching views as a bishop that reforged Christian thought. Voltaire did it, refining his critique of scholastic philosophy and monastic Christianity while propagating his views in drama and history and epic. So did Martin Luther, spreading while formulating his theology—in hymns and sermons and Bible translations. But perhaps the best example of this rare ability to create an intellectual world and, simultaneously, to lead others was Socrates.

That Socrates was a leader is proved by the reaction to him. He would not have been killed for misleading the young if he had not actually *led* some of them. And though he was as eccentric as any lonely genius, he was not withdrawn into rarefied study. He wrote nothing, he is not described as reading anything. He learned where he taught, in the rough-and-tumble of daily life. He was public-spirited, though he refrained from some citizen activities. He was, in particular, a famously brave soldier, who fought for Athens at Samos (440), Potidaea (430), Delium (424), and Amphipolis (422). At Potidaea he rescued a fallen Alcibiades while his armored phalanx was in retreat—the moment when a phalanx was most vulnerable, and when self-control was hardest to maintain.[7] At Delium, his self-command when others were fleeing so impressed the general Laches that, in Plato's dialogue *Laches*, the general recommends Socrates to fathers who want their sons trained in military prowess.[8]

This soldiering over the decades tells us a good deal about Socrates' social standing. A hoplite (heavy-armed) infantryman could not be one of the poorer class of citizens (*thētes*). He had to buy his own armor, all eighty or so pounds of it, and be free enough from business cares to spend his summers on military campaign. He was attended in the field by a slave "batman" (*hypēretēs*) who handled his armor's upkeep and the buying of provisions.[9] Socrates, whose father was admired by Athenian aristocrats, obviously had an estate sufficient to support his wife and their sons, with their slaves. Because Socrates told the court trying him (in his seventies) that he did not have enough money for a large fine, some people have pictured him as a kind of inspired bum, without means of support. But his high degree of oral education was an aristocratic privilege—he even paid the sophist Prodicus for some early instruction, and he advised wealthy men on the training of their children.[10] Nicias, for instance, the successor to Pericles as the leader of the democracy, consulted Socrates on the musician he should hire for his sons' training.[11]

The long experience of war tells us, as well, that the independent Socrates could submit to a discipline of the most homogenizing sort. A hoplite warrior was folded into a unit of men, with overlapping shields in shoving density, where mutual dependence rarely allowed for individual heroics. It is hard to think of a person good at this kind of performance as "out of step" with his fellow citizens.[12]

It is true that Socrates taught in an idiosyncratic way, talking with anyone who cared to converse with him. But he haunted the normal place for such disputes—the gymnasia attended by the sons of well-born citizens, metics (foreign residents), or traveling scholars.[13] The form Socrates' teaching took—intellectual dueling before a sportive audience— looks much odder to us than it did to Athenians, whose whole culture was based on the contest (*agōn*), formal and informal, physical, intellectual, and legal.

The agonistic quality of Athenian life is impossible to exaggerate. Boys competed in athletics, music, and seductive technique from their birth.

Politics was competitive to an extent that must strike us as absurd. Even the passage of laws was staged as a contest between the proposed law and the one it would replace, with five defenders of the old law acting in an adversarial procedure as if the prior law were on trial for its life.[14] Trials themselves were legal duels, with rules framed more for equal contest than for finding valid evidence. Citizens competed with each other to subsidize the state or to avoid subsidizing it. A characteristic institution was the exchange (*antidosis*)—a man asked to pay a state levy could propose that another citizen was better able to, and accept the other's wealth in exchange for his own if the challenge failed.[15]

In every field, the Athenian was an agonist (contestant). The lead actor in the dramatic contest was the first agonist (*protagonist*), but all those participating were contestants. Aeschylus wrote a play in which his chorus of satyrs, sent by their master to the Isthmian Games, cannot resist getting into the games, despite the master's anger.[16] The Athenians were constantly ranking each other, drawing up lists, debating who is first—in oratory or drama (and their subcategories, like *trial* orations or tragic *pathos*). Who is this season's leading beauty? Who leads war best? One of their recurrent poetic devices is a list—what is the most daunting of things (man), what is the most beautiful thing (a loved one), what is the best thing (water), and so on.[17] It is not so strange, in this world, that Chaerophon, a "cheeky" (*sphodros*) follower of Socrates, should go to the Delphic oracle on one of its "clearance answer" days and submit the question "Is anyone wiser than Socrates" to answer-by-sortition. Out came the bean signifying *no*.[18] Socrates claims he was surprised at the answer, but Plato presents him as "taking on" the wisest even before the oracle's response was given. There is an air of watching a gunfighter go up against "the fastest man in Hellas" when people gather to see Socrates confront Protagoras. The fighting spirit is acknowledged by Socrates after Protagoras scores a point and is greeted by applause.

> At first, like one punched by a skilled boxer, I blacked out and went wobbly, from his words and the bystander's applause. Then—frankly I was buying time to consider the matter—I turned to Prodicus. . . .[19]

These bouts pleased Athenians. Indeed, Plato's own disdain for such popular encounters is a guarantee of their authenticity in the early dialogues devoted to Socrates.[20]

Socrates talks about the need for putting on a good show for others.

Trying to lure Gorgias back into a fray, he says that unskillful competitors do not stick to the points in dispute but "end up exchanging random insults, insulted and insulting, so that bystanders are disgusted with themselves for having listened to such poor contenders."[21] One should win by art, without departing from the matter at issue—but one should win.

Aristotle describes the atmosphere of such mental prizefighting when he says the aim was to "break one's opponent down into incoherent muttering of the same thing over and over."[22] The model for this is clearly the athletic contests in Homer, where the vanquished is rolled in dust or dung, weeping ineffectual protests.[23] The parallel between physical and mental "agonizing" was underscored by the fact that sophists put on competitive displays at the great religious games of Hellas. In Plato's *Hippias Minor,* Socrates joins one such fray, and even offers Hippias an ironic little "victory ode," the equivalent of Pindar's songs for the physical contests: "What a monument of wisdom your glory has raised to your city of Elis and your ancestors!"[24] It is not surprising, then, that Plato sets many early dialogues at scenes of physical contest—in or near a wrestling school, or at a military dueling ground, or where a horse race is about to be run.[25]

Plato clearly meant for us to see Socrates in an agonistic context. His man has a relish for the fray, and he plays rough. When Socrates stretches the rules, his modern admirers claim he is just satirizing the sophists' methods.[26] But it is *his* method to demand that others respond briefly, and say only what they truly believe, while he engages in long and hypothetical arguments.[27] He takes up role-playing, saying for instance that he wants to take lessons in defeating the person he will impersonate.[28] He accuses others of cheating, and is accused in turn.[29]

The Greeks with the most lasting reputation as intellectual cheaters were those foreign experts who flocked to Athens and bore the general title "sophists." ("Sophist" meant "expert," with a possible sneer to it, suggesting "know-it-all".) Plato presented the sophists as corrupters of Athens; but most of the time they just taught Athenians to do better what they were already doing—to compete in mental *agōnes*. Where the sophists did differ from some Athenians, Socrates was often on the sophists' side—for instance, in a fascination with technical expertise. The older Attic education stressed a wisdom (*sophia*) handed down from inspired ancestors and absorbed from inspired poets.[30] Socrates argues that such "inspiration" is just another word for fuzziness.[31] At least the carpenter or cobbler knows how to *do* something. The sophists took these plebeian experts for their models.[32] This defied the prejudice Athenians had against *banausia,* demeaning work with one's hands—a thing tainted by the fact that slaves did it.[33]

Plato, condemning both Athens and the sophists, tried to exempt Socrates from his criticism by pitting him against both the Athenian mob and the foreign wiseacres.[34] Later students of Plato naively assert that Socrates was interested in justice and the sophists were indifferent to all morality.[35] This simplistic view leads to retaliatory simplisms—to reactions like I. F. Stone's claim that Athenians were modern liberals and Socrates an enemy of free discourse.

If we try to escape anachronistic celebration or condemnation of Socrates, what are we left with? Clearly, for all his similarities to other sophists, he was a highly original man who made a deep impact on many Athenians, not only on Plato. Why? His impact on others is suggested in several key places.[36] In one, Nicias—who was, at the moment imagined in the dialogue, the most powerful politician in Athens—warns a fellow army general what he is in for if he talks to Socrates:

> Anyone who encounters Socrates and gets drawn into a verbal exchange with him, no matter how the exchange begins, will find that Socrates maneuvers him continually to a point where he can ambush him into giving a report on the life he is now living and has lived in the past. Once the ambush is sprung, Socrates will not let the man out until he has tested his every assertion through and through. I know his ways, and know what I must put up with from him. Yet I welcome his approach, Lysimachus, since I think it is useful to be put on notice if our actions now or in the past were improper. A person goes away more reflective about his actions if he has not escaped Socrates' treatment but accepted it, and resolved to keep on learning no matter how long he lives, not assuming that age of itself confers knowledge on a man. So I am not surprised or displeased to find myself put to the test by Socrates—in fact, I knew all along that these boys would not be questioned by Socrates without our being questioned too.[37]

Fierce moral inquest—that is the principal note of Socrates' words. He searched his own depths as well as others'—in fact, he prosecuted the one inquiry to keep up the other:

> You react, Critias, as if I were claiming to know what I am examining and could explain it to you if I wanted. Far from that, I am seeking along with you, on the matter proposed, since I at least lack knowledge of it. . . . How

can you think I have any other goal, when I hector you for the truth, than to hunt myself down, from fear of thinking I know what I do not, in fact, know?[38]

It is the passionate desire for personal wholeness that makes Socrates throw others back on themselves, forcing them to examine the true state of their desires and knowledge. One finds the same challenge mounted to others in the self-purifications of a Ludwig Wittgenstein. But where Wittgenstein offended with his outbursts of perfectionist demand, Socrates was ingratiating: as Laches said, he drew others into his toils, and questioned them from an earned intimacy. His followers, we can conclude from Laches' remarks, joined him in a quest for self-knowledge. This, too, was a traditional Greek goal, reflected in the Delphic admonition, "Know yourself." But Socrates took it to new and unsettling depths. He taught his followers to question everything, *especially themselves*. (Plato believed the sophists questioned everything *except* themselves). The *Apology* (23c) gives us a glimpse of Socrates' followers in action, unsettling others with their fierce pursuit of honesty about self-knowledge:

They like to see men being drilled and, in imitation of me, they try their hand at drilling others—to find, I'm afraid, a vast supply of men claiming knowledge but having little (if any). With the result that those under drill get angry at me, not at them, and say, "That damned Socrates is making delinquents of our youth!"

Apart from such "drilling" of the citizens, Socrates' doctrines—his famous paradoxes—are ways of intellectualizing an internal need for transpicuous purity of intention. He argued that all virtue is one, that knowledge is the same thing as virtue, that his lack of perfect knowledge was an almost perfect ignorance. He took an all-or-nothing approach to integrity. His break with Athenian morality was made in the name of high demands made upon his own purity—he *owed it to himself* not to retaliate evil for evil, and to prefer suffering wrong to doing it. His sense of high duty to his own worth resembles that of the heroes he invokes—Achilles, who met the terms of *his* mission, and Ajax, whom Socrates longs to meet in the next world.

There are rational arguments to be made for Socrates' paradoxes—Gregory Vlastos has made them well. And Plato, in developing his own thought, took those arguments into later intellectual formulations far in spirit from their origin. But the *psychological* unity of all those insights comes from the kind of moral absolutism seen in certain religious figures—St. Francis with his *entire* nonviolence, or Gandhi, or the Baal Shem Tov. Socrates' piety was intense, though idiosyncratic. Being true to himself was being true to gods he honored for their *morality*, not their *power*.

The intensity of his quest, not the perfection of his argument, is what gave Socrates his incandescence—the presence that made others go away from him feeling they must change their lives. It is true that he pursued his moral aims by rigorous *intellectual* exercises—turning the sophists' own tools to the task of radical self-questioning. This moral aim is often missed in modern treatments of the man. His refusal to escape from prison is, for instance, discussed in terms of a contract theory of the state. But the "tacit consent" to laws is the least important of four different arguments sketched in *Crito*—and the most important is the least attended to now. Socrates *owes it to himself* not to return evil for evil. His reverence for the city despite its mistreatment of him will not let him wrong it by his escape—any more than he would have deserted his hoplite rank when he fought for the city (in imperial wars, it should be remembered, of dubious morality).[39]

Vlastos has defended with legalistic nicety Socrates' irony—maintaining that he was sincere in his professions of (qualified) ignorance. But Kierkegaard, despite much vaporizing on the subject, touched perhaps the deepest point of the Socratic irony—that it makes *all* the worldly professions around it ring hollow. There is something deeper to holiness—or to the world for that matter—than anything we say about it.[40] The real puzzle of Socrates is that, understanding this, he still found useful things to say about the world *while* proclaiming his own statements' inadequacy. He was an *intellectual* leader—as opposed, say, to St. Francis, whose moral fervor took no philosophical form—because he used the mind and its powers as the principal instruments of moral action.

Continual questioning came, for Socrates, out of a continual *need*, a *lack* of knowledge. Only the thirsty person is desperate to drink, only the person needing love will go out to seek it. In this way, ignorance is the *genuine* motive for Socrates' quest, not a mere pose or tactical profession, a feigned puzzlement used to embarrass those he interrogates. That is the paradox of intellectual leadership. It must come from a sharp perception of the *absence* of knowledge. The great teacher is the strategically igno-

School of Athens, *detail—Raphael*
Alinari/Art Resource

rant person, one who knows the power of negative thinking. Others spread a knowledge they have and can dispense, as from a storage tank. Socrates *knows* only as he interrogates, as he keeps questioning, going deeper and deeper. His professions of gratitude, in *Crito*, for all the city has done for him are not insincere. Only Athens could have supplied him with competitive youths so ready for intellectual exercise.[41] To the extent that these youths' appetite for knowing was sharpened by the sophists, Socrates was the sophists' debtor, not their enemy (as Plato would later make him).

Socrates is the archetype of all those who learn by teaching, who keep up the energy, curiosity, and intellectual freshness to ask the basic questions all over again, not merely as a pedagogical technique, but as a genuine way of advancing their own moral understanding. There are few such teachers, for all the talk of "Socratic method" in law schools and elsewhere. Almost every serious thinker, like Plato, retires into refined and esoteric research, speaking to and for elite knowers. It would be unauthentic for such people to pretend they are still learning from beginners. In fact, it is rare that the truly great intellectual leader is found in a classroom. Voltaire in his salon, Samuel Johnson at tea, Paul traveling through Asia Minor—these are the sons of Socrates. Or St. Augustine preaching from his episcopal chair: "So great is the tie between those similarly disposed that when listeners are moved as we speak, we are reciprocally moved. We change places as it were, they speaking what they hear, we learning what we teach."[42]

Socrates spoke from a *personal* authority rather than in formed tenets. The most familiar picture of him is David's painting of his death, where he is at the center of pious disciples. But a better sense of his restless mission, his perpetual questioning, is given by Raphael in *The School of Athens*, where Plato and Aristotle preside, like a secular Peter and Paul, over the great airy temple of reason—while Socrates is seen, off to the side, engaging unidentified people in dispute, counting off arguments on his fingers.

ANTITYPE
Ludwig Wittgenstein

L udwig Wittgenstein (1889–1951) has often been compared to Socrates, and there are some striking resemblances—the trances of concentration they went into, the sharp questioning of those who professed to know, the search for purity of language and life.[1] But the contrast is sharper than any such comparisons. Wittgenstein is a powerful example of the separation of modern philosophy from ordinary life, a separation he deeply regretted but could do little to remedy. Unlike Socrates, who engaged citizens in philosophical self-examination at public meeting places, Wittgenstein could not bring himself, very often, to meet with a small circle of students. He feared that not even those select Cambridge philosophers could understand him.

The son of an artistic and wealthy family of former Jews who were thoroughly assimilated into Christian Austria, Wittgenstein was convinced that he must display genius to make his life justifiable. Short of that, he would follow his three brothers' example and commit suicide. After a false start in the study of engineering, he was drawn to the most abstract study of philosophical mathematics. In this esoteric field, he rapidly surpassed his mentor at Cambridge, Bertrand Russell, and felt the isolation of one whose new ideas could not be followed even by Russell.

Wittgenstein regularly sequestered himself—often in a remote house he had built in Norway—to ponder his theories. While serving in the Austrian army during World War I, he began the shift from mathematical to linguistic philosophy, and also cultivated a mystical bent that made him consider joining a monastery. After the war, wanting to serve mankind humbly, he became an elementary schoolteacher—though impatience with the students' mental slowness made him hit them in frustration.

Returned to Cambridge (where he had not even bothered to take his undergraduate degree), Wittgenstein became an instructor and then a professor, concentrating now on ordinary uses of language—but with no ordinary theories or methods of teaching. His attempts to form ties with common people were well intended but clumsy. His interest in popular culture was entirely escapist—Hollywood westerns and pulp detective fiction.

There was a moral urgency to Wittgenstein's quest for an entirely perspicuous language. He saw the total honesty of speech as a question of integrity. He went through Dostoyevskian efforts to achieve a purity of life—as when he returned to the village where he had been a schoolteacher and went door-to-door apologizing to the pupils he had beaten. He urged others to reform themselves and seek lives of service—diverting philosophy students into humble jobs as nurses or manual workers.

Even those who admired Wittgenstein's genius found it hard to put up with his oscillating moods of proud rebuke and abject contrition. He feared intimacy with his own disciples, renouncing some for whom he felt too powerful an attraction. Only toward the end of his life did he reach some internal accommodation with his own homosexuality. He hated teaching, since it just underscored his inability to find people who could understand his theories.

Wittgenstein has become the most influential philosopher of this century. Yet he personally *led* few even of his small group of students—as we have seen, he mobilized some of the best toward goals other than philosophy. He was not an intellectual leader who learned by teaching. His theories were largely wrested out of himself in periods of seclusion, or while serving in the army, or in menial jobs (where his mind ran on a different track from his body's mechanical functioning). He was a Socrates in intent without the theory or the methods that lent themselves to interaction with others.[2] He succeeded as a thinker almost in proportion to his failure at life—a situation he was the first to consider grotesque. To Socrates the voluble he stands in tongue-tied contrast, an observer on the margins of human society, not a man busy in the midst of life.

11.
CHURCH LEADER

Mary Baker Eddy

The person who has had the greatest influence over western culture in the last two millennia is probably Jesus. More properly, reports of him have had that influence. It may seem odd, then, to exclude him from my list of leaders. But he falls outside the definition of leadership I have been working with. Who were his followers and to what goal did he mobilize them? Even in the first Christian accounts of his life, his closest followers fail to understand what he meant by his goal, "the kingdom of God." And even those followers deserted him before his lonely death.

To Christians, "the historical Jesus" was a failure during his lifetime. Only the risen Jesus rallied the deserters and sent them out to create a following that was large and lasting. This risen Jesus, acting after his death, is not a subject for historians but for believers, mystics, and theologians. The first great Christian leaders, for the historian, were early preachers of the risen Christ, and preeminently Paul. He roughed out doctrine, organized churches, and evangelized, in a marvel of energy and creative intellection.[1] This does not mean he is the founder of Christianity. Peter and others also proselytized—they just did not write powerfully, as Paul did, so we know less of them. And all of them claimed no more than to be passing on the doctrine of the risen Christ. Jesus exists somewhere back of them as a mystery, a savior, a redeemer, something darker or higher than a mere leader. In this respect, Jesus differs from other bearers of revelation who were also leaders—Moses, for instance, or Muhammad.

Paul was a church leader, something different from a saint (like Dorothy Day—see chapter 16) or a keeper of tradition (like Pope John XXIII —see chapter 8). Paul did not proclaim himself, but Jesus; yet he was an innovator; he had to create church bodies from scratch. Later church leaders have also had to refound their churches in some measure—to form new communities of belief, in service to an old gospel. Luther and the Reformers are good examples of such church leadership. So are the founders of Catholic religious orders—SS. Benedict, Francis, Dominic, Ignatius, and others. In one sense, Christianity is constantly being refounded by leaders of their stature. They go beyond the work of John XXIII, who had no positive reforms to advance, but who held his office open to the spirit of reform. A Francis of Assisi has startling new values of his own to spread among his followers.

"New" Christian churches in America have gone farther than mere refashioning of clerical lifestyles. Shakers, Mormons, Christian Scientists, Adventists, Amish, all draw on the Christian gospels, but reinterpret them drastically in a new situation. Church leaders like Ann Lee of the Shakers, or Ellen White of the Seventh-Day Adventists, repeat the early struggles of Paul in a modern context. Of these, the most influential may have been Mary Eddy—not because of the size of her following (the Church of Christ Scientist, always less than 1 percent of America's population) but because she formed a body of belief at once more receptive of the "healthy-minded" climate of her times and reciprocally more determinative of that climate's future than was the case with more closed systems, like those of the Shakers, Mormons, or Amish.

William James, in his influential Gifford Lectures of 1899, published as *The Varieties of Religious Experience*, divided nineteenth-century religious concepts into two main schools—one working from a sense of "the sick soul," the other from a reliance on "healthy-mindedness." Those in the first school emphasize mankind's separation from God, the corruption of nature, the inheritance of guilt and "original sin." Those in the second school emphasize God's creation of the world as His own good domain, His desire that people be saved and be happy, and the access offered to Him by His benevolent nature, on which human nature is modeled.

America's intellectual heritage was at first indebted to thinkers of the "sick soul" variety—Puritan divines, Calvinist theologians, and New England preachers of "jeremiads." But in the course of history, an American emphasis on opportunity, resourcefulness, and individual initiative led to optimism about man's ability to reshape the "virgin continent," to do God's work unhindered by satanic interference. This attitude came as a liberation to those pent up in a punitive Calvinism—not least to William James himself. James's father had been an enthusiast for new spiritual-isms, especially that of the Swiss mystic Emmanuel Swedenborg, who enjoyed a great vogue in his time.[2] William, the son, felt a therapeutic power in inspirational thinking that had to do with his own psychological liberation from New England pessimism.[3] He was acutely responsive, therefore, to the "healthy-minded" movements that swept over the English-speaking world during the second half of the nineteenth century. These movements brought a sense of progress to a theological scene that was beginning to look retrograde and irrelevant.

The Victorian crisis of religion occurred on many fronts.[4] Geology and biology seemed to be destroying the historical basis of the Bible. Anthro-pology equated Christianity with other "primitive" salvation cults. Indus-trialism removed the mystery from life, rationalizing and depersonalizing civilization. Manchesterian economics destroyed the spiritual value of charity and altruism. Torn in many directions, tugged backward toward the jungle by evolutionary theory and the scramble to survive, sped headlong into the future by railroad trains and steamships and telegraph wires, some people responded with a deep if blind will to believe again—to believe something. Wordsworth spoke for them when he said that, rather than be smeared with trade and choked by manufacture,

> I'd rather be
> A Pagan suckled in a creed outworn.[5]

Many creeds, new-minted, not outworn, were brought to comfort such forlorn souls—romanticism, transcendentalism, theosophy, mesmerism. All of them rose above the gross and mechanical in nature, searching for an ethereal vitality untainted by the materialism of the times.

Women played a prominent role in this proliferation of spiritualisms. They had been assigned a cloistered position in society, one that sealed them off from the bustle of "manly" initiative. In a rationalizing age, they were not admitted to higher education—it was said that hard mental work would jangle their delicate systems.[6] Women could not be "captains of industry," scientists in the laboratory, explorers on expedition. Assured that they were subject to hysteria and "the vapors," they were given a regime that confirmed that diagnosis. They were not healthy enough to exercise—so, for lack of exercise, they became unhealthy. Cramped by stays and bindings, hobbled by long skirts, loaded under pounds of uncut hair, shut up in rooms that excluded "dangerous" fresh air, Victorian women were cared for by male doctors proud of their "no-nonsense" dismissal of female complaints. Dr. Henry Mandsley put motherhood and childbearing in perspective:

> Looking at the matter objectively in the dry light of reason, could anything be more ridiculous than all this affectionate fuss about what is essentially an excretory product?. . .There is nothing nice in the process of parturition nor in the base services which the child exacts.[7]

And Mandsley was considered an expert in the care of women!

One of the most interesting developments of the nineteenth century was the way some women took the dark room they were sealed into and made of it a powerhouse. Alex Owen has traced that story in England; but she emphasizes the transatlantic connection between the women spiritualists of England and America. If they were to be the more "sensitive" gender, they would become sensitive to sources of power men did not guess at. Women mediums and spiritualists used their gifts to recover health and competence on their own, in defiance of male medicine. They specialized in mind cures, often based on a healthier regimen as a psychic boost. Dismissed by some as gloomy and reactionary, as shrinking from the new rationalism, they were often working for "optimism, radical ideas, and democratic principles."[8] Louisa Lowe, for instance, was a leader of the Lunacy Reform Movement, which opposed the easy consignment of women to insane asylums. Lowe had been tricked that way by her husband, who profited financially from a declaration of her incompetency. She had suffered what she would later oppose. Many of those who gave health to others had been sickly themselves, and rebelled against the conditions promoting their sickness.

Mary Eddy was the greatest of these sickly leaders. Certainly she is best understood as a sister of that company. When she experienced a cure from her famous fall on the ice in 1866, the event from which she dated the birth of Christian Science, she was not only recovering from that one accident but from a lifetime of various disorders. Opponents of Eddy later produced an affidavit from her doctor saying that the fall had not caused serious physical harm. But Eddy claimed, two weeks after the fall, that misguided friends were "forming, [in] spite of me, the terrible spinal affliction from which I have suffered so long."[9] Her psychic cure was from a primarily psychic illness, one widely shared by women submitted to the debilitating culture and medicine of their time.

The woman who fell on the ice in Lynn, Massachusetts, was forty-five years old and had been married twice—her first husband died, her second deserted her. She had been physically disabled all her life, despite or because of all the pharmacological attentions of the period's medical practitioners (including regular doses of morphine). Only when she went to a nonmedical curer, Phineas Quimby, did she find relief. Quimby, a clever inventor, had become interested in the scientific claims of "electrical" cures effected by hypnotists. He acquired all the techniques of Franz Anton Mesmer, the pioneer hypnotist, but was unsatisfied with the pseudoscientific explanations of "animal magnetism." He performed rudimentary experiments of his own to show that the mind works on suggestions made to it. His use of healing suggestions made him a success at mind cure.

Though he used "manipulation" at times—soothing strokes or massage—it was only to visualize the suggestion process for his patients. Among other things, his manipulation relaxed patients. In the case of women, it also made them take off their stays and unbind their heavy ropes of hair. He used water on his fingertips to massage the temples and scalp or to stroke the diaphragm—women had to take down their thick hair to dry it after his water treatment.[10]

Many of Quimby's patients were women. Unlike some doctors, he did not condescend to them as "the weaker sex," but reinforced their own desire to take control of their lives. He believed that women were superior to men.[11] If a woman was sickly, it was usually because the culture had imposed itself on her by a use of her superior suggestibility. Quimby's sense of such *cultural* power over the mind was his shrewdest insight. He used it to explain how even children can be suggested into sickness before they have the conceptual power to frame thoughts of their own. It is their *subconscious mind* that receives signals of what the culture expects of them. Quimby came to this conclusion after seeing a five-year-old child replicate the symptoms of its mother—which showed "the effect of mind upon mind." Since people have a "mental atmosphere," in which their minds engage the circumambient sociocultural attitudes, "persons affect each other when neither are conscious of it."[12]

Though Quimby was not a believer in the churches of his day, he believed that Jesus had a Truth (which Truth was "the real Christ") that others can share—that is how Jesus cured people.[13] The gospel tales of demons "cast out" were cases of evil suggestions countered by good ones, and were therfore no miracles. They were what Quimby himself did. That is why he called his cures experimental and nonmiraculous—operations of what he called "Christian Science."[14]

Eddy was first cured by Quimby in 1862. In 1864 she had a relapse, and, after being cured again, became his propagandist and disciple, returning to visit him in 1866, shortly before his death. That death depressed her, and her affliction deepened into paralysis when she fell on the ice. She was also suffering from her husband's desertion at this time. What was novel about her cure in 1866 was that she did it without Quimby's help, on her own, as the result of reading the New Testament—the particular text in which Jesus says that people must have faith if they are to be healed (Matthew 9.2—"Jesus *seeing their faith* said unto the sick . . ."). Her own ministry would not depend on personal suggestion (with or without "manipulation"), as Quimby's had, but on directing people to *read*—not only the gospels, but her explications of those gospels' real meaning.

This was an odd strategy for Eddy to choose, since she was a truly terrible writer. Her poems have entertainment value, but little else. Writing in 1865 to celebrate the slaves' emancipation by the Fourteenth Amendment, she perpetrated this:

> Joy in every belfry bell—
> Joy for the captive! sound it long!
> Ye who have wept four-score can tell
> The holy meaning of their dong.[15]

She was not much better in prose. Writing a paean to Quimby, she took this way of saying he held no seances:

> How, then, can he receive the friendly aid of the disenthralled spirit, while he rejects the faith of the solemn mystic who crosses the threshold of the dark unknown to conjure up from the vasty deep the awestruck spirit of some invisible squaw.[16]

Yet it was her own *reading* that had cured her, and she had an unshakable conviction that this would be the proper procedure for her followers. For years after her 1866 cure, she lived on the move, haunting the shady fringes of the psychic world, teaching Quimbyism while she worked out her own theology on paper. She began with an ambitious project to reveal the "spiritual meaning" behind every passage in the Bible, from Genesis on. She would teach people to read what were in effect the "hieroglyphics" of Scripture.[17] This shows how much she was distancing herself from Quimby. In fact, she was part of the general movement to rescue the Bible from the literalists, who could not cope with scientific challenges. Like Swedenborg, she saw elaborate allegories where others saw primitive history. If her words evanesced into mystical abstracts during this exercise, the same thing had happened to Swedenborg and his imitators. Mark Twain made famous fun of the pretentious Eddy style; but Emerson had already done the same with Swedenborg:[18]

> "What have I to do," asks the impatient reader, "with jasper and sardonyx, beryl and chalcedony; what with arks and passovers, ephahs and ephods; what with lepers and emeralds; what with heave-offerings and unleavened bread; chariots of fire, dragons crowned and horned, behemoth and unicorn?"[19]

Yet even in her idiosyncratic theologizing, Eddy was on the side of the biblical progressives in theology—much as the Victorian mediums (described by Alex Owen) were progressive in their politics. Although she was about to imitate St. Paul in the labor of founding churches, she was undoing his message in her own writings. He put the redemptive death of Jesus at the center of his theology. She could not found her system on death, whose reality she was denying. Paul was too materialistic for her. She spoke of "the life and not-death of our Master—for he never died."[20]

> The material blood of Jesus was no more efficacious to cleanse from sin when it was shed upon "the accursed tree" than when it was flowing in his veins as he went about his Father's business.[21]

She wanted "the spiritual essence of blood"—and of everything else. Like the rationalist celebrants of Jesus, she went to the gospels for an "earlier" picture of the man Jesus before Paul theologized his life.[22] She might seem to differ from a Renan, who eliminated the miracle accounts to reach "the human Jesus," but the difference is only apparent. The cures were *not* miracles in her eyes but the most natural of occurrences. The

Intrusions into the normal order are death, disease, and malice, not cures and health and imperviousness to pain.

After nine years of obscure labor at various writings, Eddy published the first edition of *Science and Health* (1875) around which she could form her church (an ambition Quimby would not have understood). The story of this early church, as of so many others, is one of scandal, conflict, and mutual accusations. Both obstreperous followers and rival leaders challenged Eddy's authority, denounced her as a mere plagiarist of Quimby, and questioned the authenticity of her cures. The undignified scene recalls the travails of Paul's churches:

> You are all saying:
> "I am on Paul's side."
> "I am on Apollo's side."
> "I am on Cephas's side."
> "I am on Christ's side."[23]

Some disciples sued Eddy and she sued back, over money brought in or exchanged by the movement. Others tried to displace her, and would have succeeded had she been less determined or skilled at organizing her resources. Two men who had helped financially in publishing *Science and Health*—George Barry and Daniel Spofford—broke with her when she married Asa Gilbert Eddy in 1877. They felt lowered in her esteem, and tried to get back money they had given her. This so tortured Eddy that she had one of her disciples charge Spofford with witchcraft under ancient Massachusetts statutes. The trial, which appropriately took place in Salem, caused a sensation in 1878. To understand the charges, we need to consider Mrs. Eddy's doctrine of M.A.M. (Malicious Animal Magnetism). If the mind can cure, it can also afflict—that was Quimby's insight into the subconscious of children. Thus "mind crimes" were a danger to which Eddy was constantly alert. She inserted this passage into *Health and Science*: "The peril of Salem witchcraft is not past. . . . Metaphysical Science will show the need there is for laws to restrain mesmerism."[24] When enemies concentrated their wrath on her, she assembled a bodyguard of "watchers" to intercept these emanations. In periods of crisis, she needed twelve watchers bunched around her, cushioning her, creating a healthy mental atmosphere for her to breathe.[25]

Since witches were no longer executed in Massachusetts, the *Newburyport Herald* wondered what punishment for Spofford was being sought by Eddy: "What good the Court can do does not appear, inasmuch as prison walls could not restrain such power."[26] In fact, even execution would not stop Spofford's mind from evil emanations, since Eddy believed the mind outlasts death. The judge dismissed the case, saying the court had no power to control Spofford's thoughts—a theological point Eddy should have agreed with.[27]

Even as Eddy's position grew more secure, there were embarrassments for the church. When her able assistant, Mrs. Josephine Woodbury, announced that she had conceived a child virginally, Eddy had to admit that the power of mind over matter made this—well, conceivable. Only six years later was Mrs. Woodbury finally excommunicated. A wife had taken her to court with the charge that her husband (rather than the Holy Ghost) was treating the miraculous child as his.[28]

It is not surprising that such clashes should occur in the charged atmosphere of a new church. Paul's Corinthian community was full of people suing and denouncing each other—for committing incest, for offering pagan sacrifices. Paul responded with tough assertions of his own authority—and so did Eddy. Her importance is not as a thinker or therapist but as a church leader. She supported her followers not only with a theology but with an ecclesiology—establishing a structure of authority, shared rituals, a communal identity. In this organizational effort, she proved, as even Mark Twain admitted, a genius. In answer to those who said she just took over Quimby's system, he answered:

> Whether she took it or invented it, it was—materially—a sawdust mine when she got it, and she has turned it into a Klondike; its spiritual dock had next to no custom, if any at all: from it she has launched a world religion.[29]

Once she had her Mother Church organized in Boston, her various printing efforts launched (including the prestigious secular paper, the *Christian Science Monitor*), a board of directors set up, all under her firm control, she wisely retired from active directorship of the church. She had invented the whole system of readers, classes, students, practitioners, governors, and a priesthood for the age of science—lay, literate, book-centered. The church members tended to be middle-class, affluent, more responsive to readings than to revival sermons or emotional songs. It is a church that is very American in its makeup, emphasizing individual effort, success, and continual improvement. By withdrawing above the fray, Eddy avoided the personal squabbles that had marred her years of struggle. She let the church structure get used to running itself without her. That is why there was little turmoil when she died.

There is perhaps no better expression of the "healthy-minded" ideal James described than the Eddy system. She took what was a general mood in the America of the last century and turned it into a body of teachable knowledge that could serve as the basis of spiritual discipline for a body of believers. Her work continues to inspire many people who hope to transcend the cultural and psychic cripplings of "diseased thought." This does not, as many think, require the opposition to all medicine. Eddy continued to take morphine for the pains of her old age.[30] The medical practices Eddy opposed in her time often deserved opposition, if not denunciation, especially as they dealt with women. For all her flaws, Mary Eddy has rightly earned the regard of modern feminists. She was not only strong for herself, but for others, and she prayed to a Father-Mother God from her Mother Church. She was a unitarian, not a trinitarian; there was only one God, but it was both male and female—so she changed the Lord's Prayer from a *Pater Noster* to a *Patermater Noster:* "Our Father-Mother God, all-harmonious, Thy kingdom is come." Her motherly yet commanding nature—along with her haunting eyes—was captured in a photograph taken when she was about fifty. While she holds someone's squirming child, she keeps her eyes on the camera. She had given her only child, a son born to her first husband, up for adoption when he was six. Her church was her real child—as those discovered who tried to take it away from her. Then she was a tigress guarding her cub.[31]

Mary Baker Eddy
From Ernest Sutherland Bates and John V. Dittemore, *Mary Baker Eddy: The Truth and the Tradition* (Knopf, 1932).

ANTITYPE

Phineas Parkhurst Quimby

T hose involved with the history of Christian Science tend to be Quimby people or Eddy people. The former think that Eddy stole Quimby's system and passed it off as her own. The latter think that Quimbyites want to reduce everything Eddy accomplished to one simple act of plagiarism. In fact, the two people were so different that their body of work had to be drastically different in aim and method.

This is not to deny the similarities that exist in their stories. Like most mind-healers of the period, they had begun life sickly and run through inadequate remedies on the way to their own health technique. Quimby (born in 1802) was, for the first four decades of his life, the victim of "consumption." The doctors treating him did not, as in Eddy's case, prescribe morphine; but he said they gave him so much calomel that his teeth started falling out.[1] Quimby was a practical man, an inventor who loved experiments, so he experimented on himself. He discovered, for instance, that excitement—as in driving a galloping horse before his chariot—blocked out pain (something boxers know, who do not notice broken bones in their hand or nose or jaw in the scramble of the fight itself).[2] He was intrigued, then, by the mind's ability to affect bodily sensation. This made him react at once to the powers of hypnosis, as demonstrated by Charles Poyen. After meeting Poyen in 1837, Quimby began hypnotizing others. In 1843, he met a young boy so quickly hypnotized, so open to all his suggestions that the lad—Lucius Burkmar— seemed to read Quimby's mind. The two went on tour giving demonstrations of Burkmar's capacity for reading what went on inside others' minds and bodies. Naturally, Quimby tried to use Burkmar to cure his own ailments. Burkmar assured him he could *see* the disintegrating organs in his body and put them back together by manipulation. The "operation" worked—but Quimby was too rational to believe in it. He came to the conclusion that he was *not* sick at all, and Burkmar had just made him *think* of himself as well, on grounds however inadequate. "The disease vanished by the absurdity of the cure."[3] If that was the case, he could think himself into health without Burkmar—which he proceeded to do, not only for himself but for others.

In treating others, Quimby sympathized with them so thoroughly that he sometimes took on their symptoms, becoming a "scapegoat" for their release from pain.[4] His writings were undertaken to explain to himself and the patient what was happening. They were in the nature of laboratory notes made after an experiment.[5] Since he had received even less formal education than Eddy, and read less widely than she did, his notes are disjointed, full of misspellings, even when corrected by Emma Ware, a patient who was devoted to him.[6]

Though Quimby was a successful therapist, he founded no school, elaborated no theoretical system. He had patients rather than followers (Eddy always excepted). In this he resembled any prosperous medical practitioner. In the twentieth century, Émile Coué, the French advocate of "induced autosuggestion," cured people on much the same principles Quimby had—Franklin Roosevelt sought Coué's help to cure his polio.[7] But these individual virtuosos of curing techniques created no body of people practicing their principles.

Quimby was patient-oriented. He worked case by case. This down-to-earth experimental quality is what makes the man appealing. It is what he meant by science. But Eddy was not only or mainly a curer—others were more successful at that, in and out of her movement. When the patient was cured, Quimby was through with him or her. Eddy taught a wisdom that applied to all of life, to the sick *and* to the well. She set out to create a body of followers. She not only trained and disciplined but excommunicated and punished—something very far from Quimby's practice, but remarkably close to St. Paul's. Whatever his other recommendations, Quimby was not really a leader, and least of all a church leader.[8] She was Mother Eddy. He could never have been Father Quimby.

12.

SPORTS LEADER

Carl Stotz

S tar athletes are heroes. Little boys—and some big boys—
want to imitate them. But imitating a hero is not the
same thing as following a leader. The athlete plays to
win, to make money, to be famous, to share his team-
mates' elation—he plays for many motives, but not (at least directly) in
order to be imitated. His fans do not share his own motives—it is not their
own main goal to give him money or increase his fame. And he cannot
share what is their goal: Michael Jordan cannot wish to be more like
Michael Jordan. He already is Michael Jordan.

It is true that some stars have a social impact, based on their own
qualities and the situation they enter. Jackie Robinson, the first African-
American to play in the major leagues, was a symbol of black pride and
progress. Babe Didrikson Zaharias, perhaps the best all-around athlete in
American history, provided similar encouragement to women. Muhammad Ali was a multivalent symbol of black pride, Muslim faith, and
opposition to the Vietnam War. But these forms of influence are not, of
themselves, leadership. Jackie Robinson, so far from leading his fellow
players, had to endure in isolation the rebuffs that came with his influential role.

There are, however, many kinds of leadership "on the field" or "on the
court." Units of a football team—defensive line, defensive backfield,
special teams, and so on—often work better if they recognize some member's inspirational effect. Coaches have to be leaders of their players, and

some—Knute Rockne, Vince Lombardi—become more broadly recognized as advocates of a particular sports ethos.

Owners of teams, on the other hand, are business leaders rather than sports leaders. They market a product. The fact that the customers are fans means that their sales pitch must stress the excellence of a *sports* product. But the skills are essentially commercial, nonetheless.

The difference between a sports star and a sports leader can be nicely illustrated in the collaboration of two men in the 1920s—Bobby Jones and George Herbert Walker. Jones was to golf what Babe Ruth was to baseball—a natural athlete as clearly born to hit golf balls as Ruth was to hit baseballs. In his brief career (he retired at twenty-eight) Jones blazed through every arena of competition. His culminating year was 1930, when he won the "grand slam"—both the U.S. and the British open tournaments and both the U.S. and the British amateur tournaments. Yet Jones was only a part-time golfer, even in his active years—he studied engineering at Georgia Tech, English at Harvard, and law at Emory, passing the bar while winning golf contests. It is plausibly claimed that no other great golfer spent less time at the game than Jones.[1] His losses, when they occurred, came from boredom or from taking risky shots that did not quite come off. The game was almost too easy for him. After retiring, he did a lucrative business in standardizing the golf clubs of the 1930s for the Spalding company, and opened his own course at Augusta, Georgia, which he made the home of the Masters International.[2] He was a successful business leader, turning his fame to profit.

George Herbert Walker, by contrast, took Jones's talent and made it the basis of his own sports leadership. An immensely wealthy investor, Walker had a consuming interest in sports. His two vacation homes, one at Kennebunkport in Maine, were hives of frenzied athletic activities in hunting, fishing, riding, boating, tennis, golf—activities his grandson, George Bush, kept up at the ancestral home in Maine during his presidency. Walker sometimes combined his business and sports interests, buying race horses and tracks and helping finance the reconstruction of Madison Square Garden in 1925. But his devotion to golf was a matter of principle, not profit. He served as the president of the PGA (Professional Golfers' Association) and promoted the game tirelessly. His son-in-law, Prescott Bush, George's father, impressed Walker by his golf prowess—Prescott, too, became a president of the PGA.

Walker saw the teenage Bobby Jones playing inspired golf and felt that America could now take the lead in a sport that had been British by proprietary right of its Scottish inventors. He set up a British-American contest for biennial possession of "the Walker Cup." Every two years, from 1922 to 1930, Jones led the American team to victory over the British.[3]

Walker's advocacy of golf, his ability to mobilize clubs, players, and the public, were in a rich tradition of aristocratic promotion of the gentlemanly sports. America's prep schools and Ivy League colleges had made games the crucible of character. Skill at one of several sports— racing crew, fencing, polo, yachting, golf, tennis—were marks of caste. Groton and Harvard encouraged ferocity like that of Theodore Roosevelt in the pursuit of athletics. The investment firm whose board Walker chaired—Brown Brothers Harriman—took great pride in its members' athletic feats.

> Anyone in 1920 who wanted to spot those who would be "coming men" at Brown Brothers in the years ahead could have done pretty well, it seems, just by picking the top men in the field of sports. When the firm opened its Chicago office on May 15, 1929, the resident manager was Charles A. Garland, who had been a member of one United States Davis Cup team in 1920, and with R. Norris Williams won the doubles championship that year at Wimbledon.[4]

Averell Harriman, senior partner at the firm, had coached the Yale crew that included Dean Acheson among its oarsmen. The firm was proud to acquire a Harvard crew member, Louis Curtis, Jr., who had been on the team that beat the British in the 1914 Henley Regatta.[5]

The class bias in sports was a target of Thorstein Veblen's satire in his 1899 classic, *The Theory of the Leisure Class*. He called athletics the nonproductive after-image of nobles' training for war and the hunt, a conspicuous display of prowess as social distinction.[6] But a more populist interpretation of sport's uses has often been advanced, often with a quasi-religious emphasis on the forging of spiritual qualities through physical contest. This interpretation can call on St. Paul for support:

> As you know, those in a race run, all of them, but only one takes off the prize—and you are runners for a prize. An athlete does everything he can to get into shape—just to win a crumbling wreath [e.g., of olive leaves]. Our wreath will crumble never. So in running, I do not drift from the mark; in boxing, I do not buffet the air. I punch my own body into submission to me.[7]

Other early Christian writers used sports analogies—in fact, Ignatius of Antioch coined the athlete's motto, "The greater the pain, the greater the gain" (*pleiōn kopos, polu kerdos*).[8] So one need not agree with Veblen that all sport reflects the predatory training of social elites. The idea of sports as a self-chastening was expressed by the Hellenistic freed slave, Epictetus—hardly an aristocrat: "Opposition proves the man; so when opposition fronts you, consider that God, like a coach, has matched you with a tough fighter."[9]

Still, if sport need not be the monopoly of the privileged, in nineteenth-century America it tended to be.[10] The great exception was baseball, which arose from an old child's game and became *the* sport for the American masses.[11] But even the privileged sports were freed in time from their social bastions. The gentlemanly roughhousing of prep school and Ivy League football was taken over by an initially disreputable collection of pro teams, in which—at the outset—even social outsiders like the Native American Jim Thorpe and the African-American Paul Robeson could play. Leadership in these efforts was exerted by men like Fritz Pollard, who coached, promoted, and publicized a series of black football and basketball teams.[12] Rube Foster, the star pitcher who went on to establish teams in the black leagues, was another such leader.[13]

But no other sports program in America has affected citizens' lives at so many levels as Little League baseball, which was founded, in the Depression year 1938, by a man who was almost penniless and temporarily out of a job. Carl Stotz had fond memories of his father as a kind of Pied Piper for little baseball fans. Since the father worked for the railroad in Williamsport, Pennsylvania, he had free passes for travel to New York. He would take his two sons to Yankee Stadium, returning the same day. When word of these excursions got around, the children of other railroad employees, using their passes, joined the Stotzes' pilgrimages to see the Yankees when Ruth and Gehrig led that team.[14]

In 1938, when Carl Stotz was twenty-eight, and shifting from job to job in the unsettled conditions of the Depression, he had a young daughter but no sons. He liked playing catch with his two nephews, listening to the boys "broadcast" imaginary games while they threw the ball, using clumsy grown-ups' gloves, occasionally swinging a regulation bat that was far too big for them. Stotz wondered why they could not play a real game, not the delusory one running in their heads. It would have to be a scaled-down version of the grown-ups' game—his nephews were six and eight years old at the time.

He began to imagine what a child-size field would measure. Watching them throw, he adjusted the home-plate-to-first-base distance to keep it within their capacities. Then he experimented with pitching distances. By the time he had created his own imaginary child-size field, he wanted to lay it out upon real ground. He found an unused field, asked around for other boys to play and other men to coach and umpire—then went out begging for money to sponsor his first three teams. Fifty-six companies turned him down before he found one willing to put up the necessary thirty dollars for one team. Even that sum was hard to come by in 1938.

Already, in that first season, Stotz was dreaming of an ambitious boys' league, with its own play-offs, its "World Series," its Hall of Fame, its record books, its All-Stars. He showed a previously unsuspected skill at promotion. He recruited the local sportswriters, who liked the "let's pretend" aspect of covering the league's early games—the papers ran box-score results as for a big-league game. Soon Stotz was speaking at local banquets, praising the educational value of baseball, arguing (like St. Paul) that it builds character. He arranged for an abbreviated exhibition game to be played by his boys before the local minor-league team's scheduled contest. In 1939, he took the boys, wearing their uniforms, to see the World's Fair in New York. Wise to his father's old railroad ways, he had the conductor use the public address system to welcome "the Little Leaguers from Williamsport" at each stop. [15]

Stotz was not only good at formulating his own vision but at conveying it to others. Each summer of his first three seasons, he had to lay out a new field for the teams to play on. The earlier ones were either defective or challenged by other users. The construction of the fields entailed felling trees, draining low spots, filling in with the proper mix of sand and other elements to make for safety and traction. His friends, relatives, and fellow volunteers pitched in, eventually building bleachers, sewing cushions for them, embroidering team names on uniforms. Stotz experimented to find the right bats, a ball slow enough to give runners a chance, shoes that could use harmless rubber cleats. He was a perfectionist on safety and cooperation.

He drew up rules that would let all boys play—in early games, he put four in the outfield rather than have the extra boy sit on the bench. He set up recruiting rules that made sure all team members came from the same school district and fell within the right age brackets. Each team was limited in the number of upper-age players it could field (only five twelve-year-olds at most) and required to have some from the lowest eligible age (at least three ten years old or under). He set up a complicated point system that meant a team spending many points for a desired player would have few left for other "stars." There was a ceiling on the points, unlike the limitless money spent for players in pro ball.

At first, Stotz concentrated on his own school district's league, one of whose teams he coached. The original three teams became four in his second year, and parents from other school districts in Williamsport asked him to set up leagues for them. He was wise enough to realize from the outset that local enthusiasm and cooperation were necessary to make the league work, so he refused to organize these new leagues himself, though he gave advice, encouragement, and discarded equipment to help those who cared to launch their own league. Once other leagues started coming in, of course, the ambition of a play-off between them brought closer Stotz's dream of a "World Series."

The League's growth was stalled by World War II. Coaches and umpires disappeared into the army; uniforms and equipment were hard to get. Even so, the movement spread to other towns in Pennsylvania. Then, after the war, the Little League took off.[16] Returning veterans stepped in as volunteers. Celebrations of reunited families set the stage for a fifties era of "togetherness"—and for a baby boom—that would make Little League a symbol of the Eisenhower years.[17]

With success came problems, especially for a man with Stotz's concept of local initiative. The need for uniform competition meant that he had to deal with the large corporations that could supply this booming market for authorized bats, balls, shoes. Stotz had accepted the post of Little League commissioner; but he still kept his accountant's job with one of the League's original sponsors, and coached one team, until 1948. By then Stotz found himself traveling to coordinate League activities, deal with sponsors, and see to the observance of the League's rules. Late in 1948, the principal sponsor of the League World Series, U.S. Rubber (which made the League's authorized shoes), offered Stotz a full-time salary for his services as League president. Stotz trusted his first backer at U.S. Rubber, an advertising executive named Charles Durban, who would later become chairman of the corporation's board.

By 1951, when the company incorporated the League, Stotz had misgivings about its commercialization.[18] It was becoming big business, with pressure to endorse products, encourage fiercer competition, and make of its World Series a desperately serious thing for preadolescents. In 1952, tension between Stotz and the company led to his replacement as president by Peter D. McGovern. Stotz kept the honorary titles of founder and commissioner. Teams were getting more competitive. The number of players for each was increased from twelve to fifteen, raising for Stotz the specter of the boy who rarely gets onto the field. Coaches were becoming more cutthroat. Eligibility rules were being stretched. In 1955—the year after he made a world tour for the State Department—Stotz resigned in protest over the direction the Little League had taken. The League is bland about the split, but Stotz was bitter.[19]

Stotz, who died in 1992 (he was eighty-two), was a purist, and no doubt hard to please. He admitted that he felt out of place in a big corporation's headquarters. Yet he was the best spokesperson for the Little League, one the company tried to keep on its own terms. He was not good at accepting others' terms. When Ralph Edwards chose him to appear on the TV show "This Is Your Life" in 1955, Stotz refused to go on after learning that the show was sponsored by a cigarette company.[20] Some of his worst fears came true as children were hardened toward a premature professionalism in the Little League play-offs.[21] Perhaps this was inevitable. If kids imitate the major leagues, they come to resemble the major leagues, in bad ways as well as good. But Stotz had led the boys he mobilized for as long as the League maintained his original vision.

And the localism of the League, the volunteer nature of its coaching, always left open the possibility of repeating Stotz's early work with his boys. Little League can bring out the boy in men; but it can also bring out the boy in jaded inner-city youths—as one sees in the account of one Little League year in a Chicago housing project.[22] Every year, all over the world, at least some fathers and sons recapture the fun of playing together—as Carl played with his nephews in those innocent prewar years when he created the League that took baseball back to its origins. It had been, from the outset, a children's game.

Carl Stotz
Courtesy of the Stotz Family

ANTITYPE
Kenesaw Mountain Landis

I f Carl Stotz was a stickler for rules and fairness, Judge Kenesaw Mountain Landis was a tyrant for the rules, a fierce legal enforcer in his twenty-four years as commissioner of baseball. Landis has often been credited with saving baseball at a point of crisis, and many would consider him an obvious example of sports leadership. But we have to ask this book's recurrent questions. Who were followers to this leader, and what was their joint goal? Carl Stotz's followers were the boys, parents, volunteer coaches and umpires, sponsors, and community fans who all wanted to give boys a cooperative and enjoyable experience of scaled-down baseball. It is hard to say who Landis's followers were. Many obeyed him—even the free spirit Babe Ruth had to accept a suspension from Landis. But he was, in his own mind, a judge dealing with criminals, or at least delinquents. We do not say that a convict "follows" a judge to the scaffold, just because he has been sentenced by the judge.

Were the baseball teams' owners the followers of Landis? They certainly did support his position (much of the time) for their own good; but that good was a commercial one, and the owners obviously considered Landis a necessary evil. They could not make money from baseball so long as the public thought it was tainted. They submitted to Landis's autocratic ways just as racehorse owners submit to drug tests for their thoroughbreds. The owners do not consider a doctor administering the drug test their leader.

Landis was called on to restore baseball after the scandal of the Black Sox's fraudulent 1919 World Series. What made him useful was an image he had created of cantankerous integrity, one the public admired in a jocular way. Landis was a person of limited sympathies and limitless certainties. He was named for the Civil War battle site where his father lost a leg, and he spent his life turning deficiencies into advantages. He dropped out of high school because he felt the need to get going in life.

After work as a reporter and court stenographer, he picked up a law degree at Chicago's Union Law School (later merged with Northwestern Law School)—the same place where William Jennings Bryan acquired his law degree. It was not a seedbed of scholars.

When Walter Gresham, a Union Army veteran who had served with Landis's father, was appointed secretary of state by President Grover Cleveland in 1892, Landis went to Washington with him as his secretary. Despite this work for a Democratic administration, Landis was an active Republican. Illinois pols recommended him to Theodore Roosevelt for appointment as a federal judge. On the bench, Landis's high-handed and colorful ways made for many headlines, and for many reversals of his decisions on appeal. Even his most famous decision—the record-breaking fine of $29 million levied on Standard Oil for railroad kickbacks—was voided. But the public loved it when Landis brought John D. Rockefeller into court and grilled him personally.

During World War I, Landis handed out sedition sentences to radicals, most of them reversed, but all of them applauded by bellicose patriots. Landis was considered a man who spoke his mind, a kind of cracker-barrel Solomon, ready to do justice. Heywood Broun said of Landis: "His career typifies the heights to which dramatic talent may carry a man in America if only he has the foresight not to go on the stage."[1]

By happy chance, Landis had made some decisions that pleased baseball owners. In 1915, he quashed the effort of a third league, the Federal League, to join the two existing leagues. In a wage arbitration of 1921, he defended the right of employers to set whatever wages they would. Besides, he was a Chicago Cubs fan, who found ways of escaping the bench at game time.

The panic over the 1919 Black Sox scandal hit baseball just as it was blossoming toward the euphoria of the 1920s. Babe Ruth was taking the game into a new dimension of superhuman feats. In 1920 he would lift his record for home runs from twenty-nine to fifty-four. The baseball goose was ready to lay golden eggs, and along had come this goose-killing crime of the Black Sox. Desperate remedies were proposed. The most favored seemed to be "the Lasker plan" (named for its proposer, Chicago businessman Albert Lasker)—a three-man board with unlimited power to police baseball practices and punish offenders. Many celebrated persons had their names floated as candidates for this board. But the head of the American League (Ban Johnson) fought the plan. Fearing that he would jeopardize baseball's recovery, some of his own teams rebelled and threatened to join the National League in support of the plan. A rush to get the board in place led to Landis's selection as its head, with the two other members to be named later.[2] The relief caused by Landis's appointment, and the flair with which he took charge, made people accept the single "czar" as not only sufficient, but as preferable to a divided authority. It was a time friendly to autocrats. The postwar dizziness of diplacements and moral shifts, the premonitory noise of "the roaring twenties," made people long for a little old-fashioned chastising. The movies went through a re- markably similar process at just this time: death at a scandalous party given by the silent comedian Fatty Arbuckle made Hollywood appoint a "morals cop" named Will Hays to frown at cinema laxities. In the FBI, panic over a "red menace" lifted a puritanical young bureaucrat named J. Edgar Hoover to the role of national monitor with few limit on his power.

At times it appeared that Judge Landis had *no* limit on his hectoring, blustering authority as baseball commissioner. He put on his office door the simple word BASEBALL.[3] (*Le baseball, c'est moi.*) The man so often overruled on the bench found himself in a position where no stand he took was reversible.[4] He reveled in this power, making owners and players quake. He not only pursued team members who made any bets, but expelled from the game any owners who did (William D. Cox of the Phillies).[5] One of the few points on which he had to yield was surren- dering his federal judgeship. For two years he tried to retain it while drawing $50,000 as the baseball despot. Only after a semicomic motion for his impeachment in Congress did he step down from the federal office. He had more power in baseball, anyway.

Landis's effect on the game was positive—more so than that of the Hays office on movies; more so, in the long run, than Hoover's despotic power at the FBI. But drug testing is also beneficial in horse races. Landis's self-dramatizing "war on crime" was not an exercise in public education. Adopting the policy "Never apologize, never explain," he worked behind closed doors, issuing no statements, giving no press conferences. The owners needed him—besides, he was a whip to wield against their play- ers. The players had to pretend they had nothing to fear from keeping him. The fans liked the idea that their credulity was lodged safely in his hands. He was, some of the time, a healthy check on excesses, and, all of the time, a useful public relations gimmick. The game got some gadfly prodding, the public got blanket assurances, the people who renewed his term year after year got casual blandishments. It was, as Heywood Broun recognized, a wonderful show. But leadership had nothing to do with it.

13.
ARTISTIC LEADER

Martha Graham

A n artist can be successful, important, and influential without being a leader. The artist's aim is to give aesthetic satisfaction to an audience. Absorption of that satisfaction does not, of itself, move the audience to some further goal, much less to one shared with the artist. The artist's desire is to perfect the artifact, to *give* such pleasure. Other goals—like professional advancement or monetary reward—are even more private to himself or herself, not shared with the audience.

One might argue that some artists have ulterior objectives, outside the aesthetic work considered in itself, that can be shared with the audience. In Bach's sacred music, perhaps he wanted others to praise God along with him. If so, he was to that extent a preacher as well as an artist. Yet if a person is profoundly moved and satisfied by a Bach cantata, without any belief in God or desire to praise Him, we do not think the work has failed of its purpose. Its essential work is the same as that of a secular cantata by Bach—to give aesthetic pleasure. In fact, the basic similarity of Bach's sacred and secular music is seen from his willingness to use the same arias and choruses in the one or in the other.

Some national anthems are used to heighten patriotic feeling. We call that propaganda, and feel it is at least partly at odds with genuine art. Yet there *are* artists who are also leaders—those who attract followers precisely to advance their art as part of a cause. Turner was an artist whose concern was the deepening of his painting's truth to nature. But John

Ruskin, when he defended the works of Turner in his own artistic prose, was the leader of a movement. His aim, shared with a large group of followers, was to change the ideals of "modern" art, to make artists and the public alter their behavior and standards.

Another Victorian example of the artist as leader was William Morris, who not only designed artifacts—stained-glass windows, wallpaper, chairs, books—but carried on a campaign to instill craftsmanship among workers, taste among buyers, and a sense of material furnishings as reflective of social values. His followers included not only the hundred or so workers he employed in his design school, but the socialists he felt were the only true friends of responsible workmanship. He worked for the return to a medieval guild system, precisely to improve *art* as well as society.[1]

An illustration of the difference between the artist as such and the artistic leader can be seen in the Los Angeles dance school, founded in 1915, called Denishawn, from the names of its married partners, Ruth St. Denis and Ted Shawn. St. Denis was an impressionistic dancer who had toured the world giving dance concerts or working in dramatic productions (especially those put on by David Belasco). Shawn was a less successful dancer who wanted to use St. Denis's fame to found a school codifying her largely improvisational methods. Students, financial supporters, and audiences would be treated less as mere consumers of art than as subscribers to an embattled new form of art.[2]

St. Denis was not enthusiastic about teaching. She was untaught herself, and skeptical about work on technique. But she gave in to her husband out of a hope that she could instill attitudes toward the body, toward psychic preparation for the dance, that she had acquired from various mysticisms. Between them the two succeeded in drawing to Los Angeles a corps of young disciples who wanted to make nonballet forms of dance aesthetically serious and technically professional. Some of these dancers developed the form beyond anything Denishawn's founders could conceive. Two schools especially went on to create modern dance for the twentieth century. One was founded by Doris Humphrey and Charles Weidman. The other, the more important, was founded by Martha Graham and Louis Horst. These veterans of Denishawn took different legacies from that school's partners. From St. Denis they took a sense of the body as a sacred thing, whose energies must be summoned individually from within (by contrast with the imposition of ballet disciplines from without). From Shawn they took the sense of social mobilization for the acceptance of their new ideal.

Martha Graham, born in 1893, came late to the dance. After graduating from high school in Santa Barbara, California, she spent three years in an acting school. She was twenty-three by the time she enrolled at Denishawn (in 1916), older and less trained than the other students, her body out of shape and her appearance below St. Denis's high standards of exotic beauty. She was small but not delicate, so she was not allowed to do the Japanese dances her height would otherwise have consigned her to. Instead, St. Denis bound her breasts and presented her as a galumphing boy dancer.[3]

In the days before there was an audience for modern dance, or a system of private and public grants for experimental work, it was hard to keep Denishawn solvent. St. Denis would have let the school fail if it could not support itself, but Shawn had the zeal of a promoter, and he sent his dancers out to get what money they could from work on vaudeville cards, from dance instruction in department stores, from occasional movie appearances. The young Martha Graham can be seen briefly whirling like a dervish in Cecil B. De Mille's *Male and Female* (1919).[4] Charles Weidman, another young Denishawn star, picked up some money as an extra in D. W. Griffith's *Orphans of the Storm* (1922). Griffith sent his actresses to Denishawn for lessons in graceful movement.[5]

The tensions between the partners drove Graham from Denishawn in 1924. (Graham sided with the partner who continued to snub her, St. Denis, while becoming increasingly contemptuous of Shawn, who had promoted her in the troupe.) Her vaudeville appearances for Denishawn enabled Graham to get a steady job in the continuing Broadway review *Greenwich Village Follies*. She did fake-oriental dances, in a company that included other talented youngsters, like comedian Joe E. Brown and composer Cole Porter. After two years of this commercial routine, Graham was happy to accept some assignments to teach dance, in the hope that she could begin to forge her personal style. She taught for a year at the newly founded Eastman School of Music in Rochester, New York.[6]

Teaching part-time dancers in Rochester increased Graham's desire to perform with a thoroughly trained troupe of her own. She was already thirty-three years old and she felt the need to show the world what her extraordinary body could do while it was still in its prime. She called upon an associate (and lover) from Denishawn days, Louis Horst, to help her open a dance studio in New York. Horst had been the "musical director" of Denishawn, playing the piano for school exercises and public performances. A sophisticated arranger and composer with fresh ideas on the relation of music to dance, Horst, eleven years Graham's senior, had spotted the genius of this pupil caught in the flailing scarves of the Denishawn premises. He was glad to join her penniless crusade to remake the whole dance vocabulary.[7]

At first, only the most zealous disciples would train with Graham, submitting to her fierce regimen of basic exercises repeated endlessly. Her few students were all female, and they had to train by night, since they supported themselves as waitresses and department-store clerks by day. Horst, who taught music and dance in other places to earn the money Graham could not pay him, ended his own tiring days in the even more tiring routines of her studio. Graham herself had to make outside appearances for money—she danced the victim's role in the American premiere of Stravinsky's *Rite of Spring* (1930) conducted by Leopold Stokowski and choreographed by Léonide Massine.

Graham hired halls that were "dark" on Sunday to put on her first experimental performances, attracting an early band of followers and promoters, including the *New York Times*'s first dance critic, John Martin. Horst helped advance the cause by founding the first journal of modern dance, *Dance Observer*, in the midst of the Depression, 1933. (Winthrop Sargeant, Graham's brother-in-law, helped finance the magazine.) Throughout the thirties, Graham's daring ideas came to the attention of the New York avant-garde, drawing to her other artists who wanted to be part of this movement. She had designed her own costumes, at the outset, and relied primarily on lighting to define the spaces she moved through. But then she found her perfect set designer in the Japanese-American sculptor Isamu Noguchi, who shared her interest in oriental mysticism. Noguchi claimed that his work sculpted the space surrounding itself, and that charged space is what Graham's dances breathed. Graham danced with the sculptures as so many living partners. Altogether Noguchi created thirty-five sets for her performances.[8]

What made Graham's dance so startlingly new? Ballet fights the earth, touches down on it charily with pointed toe, skims over its surface, leaps or is lifted to be free of it. Folk dances weave choral patterns over the surface of the earth. Graham's dance rose out of the earth, in a chthonic surge. She trained her dancers on the ground. Her basic exercise sat a woman directly on her pelvis, with bent legs swung out and back in a swastika-wheel.[9] The torso, held upright against the tilt natural to this position, was worked forward and backward, returning to earth. The body was contracted and expanded in exaggerated gulps of air. She wanted all the spectators, no matter where they sat in the theater, to see her dancers' diaphragms working. The breathing process, the most fundamental bodily rhythm, became the basis of her dance, overriding all metronomes. The body's desperate need for air was made emblematic of all its urgent drives, its assertions of the will to live.[10] There was a visceral power in the moves she worked out from this core. She told her dancers to develop Pelvic Truth, and to "breath from the vagina."[11] She made the body writhe with primordial sexuality. "I won't have virgins in my company."[12]

Graham cultivated a high seriousness. Her devotees were initiates in the mysteries. She was never a "pal" to her dancers. In fact, satirists made frowning, grunts, and dark clothes the symbols of modern dance. In the political cartoons of Jules Feiffer, the modern dancer's black leotard stands for all of modernity's pained introspection.

But much of that began to change when at last Graham admitted male dancers to her company. At first, she had trained only women, since she was working out her own body's potentialities, and all she was interested in was showing that to other women. It was said that a male watching her lead her first dancers in these exercises might suffer from vagina envy. In performance Graham pitted one or two women soloists against all-female choruses making ritual motions. But her important dance clinics, given in the summer on the campuses of Bennington College and Connecticut College, brought her male students for whom she had to choreograph different moves.[13] Her women now surged up from the earth toward male dancers (most of them over six feet tall). She began to admit some of the ballet movement she had excluded so rigorously while working out her own earthbound style.[14] She created for Merce Cunningham and Paul Taylor leaps that would later be executed by Rudolph Nureyev and Mikhail Baryshnikov, when they joined Graham's team for performances late in her life.

Erick Hawkins was the male who most affected Graham's choreography. Hawkins, who had been trained in ballet by George Balanchine, brought a raw animal force to his dancing, and Graham fell deeply in love with this man sixteen years her junior. Her dances with him in the 1940s took on a playfulness and variety they had previously lacked, though Hawkins was not yet as good as he thought himself, and Graham scheduled some inferior material just because it highlighted him. In time

Hawkins tried to move up to the position of full partner with Graham in running the company. He did this by marrying Graham, repeating the tactic Ted Shawn had used to establish the Denishawn partnership. Graham had observed the sad dynamics of that pairing, and resolved not to let the pattern repeat itself in her own life. But love blinded her, at least for a while. Her first love, nonetheless, was for her company, and she would not let Hawkins take even part of that away from her. Her amazing body was at last giving out as she entered the 1950s—a problem exacerbated by some physical scuffles with Hawkins, on and off the stage.[15] On a tour to France and England, Graham's knee collapsed and she had to cancel the tour. Hawkins left her in England. The marriage was over in 1951.

At the age of fifty-eight (she was claiming only forty-some of those years), Graham knitted her body back together, against all odds, and continued creating new dances for new partners. She was portraying now the vengeful Greek and biblical heroines—Medea, Phaedra, Jocasta, Clytemnestra, Judith, Herodias. Her classical dances helped along the 1950s revival of interest in Greek myth, an interest that extended through all the arts.

The incredibly prolonged career of Graham was made possible by her endless training, and by the tailoring of her every move to her special physique. Her twirling backward fall looked death-defying, yet it came from the tension her torso could sustain in lowering herself—it looked as if she were supported by an invisible dancer's hand under her waist. The control of her body made other dancers gasp at what looked like impossible moves. Agnes De Mille records one such reaction:

> It was in *Dithyrambic* that I first saw Martha perform the astonishing feat of squatting on one foot, the heel on the floor, the other foot extended in the air straight before her, and in one count rise to a standing position on the strength of the single supporting thigh and leg. "Holy God!" I said aloud. I have never seen another dancer capable of doing this.[16]

When her body finally did give out—in her seventies!—there was some question whether even dancers trained in her school could replicate her amazing roles. But a number of fine replacements were ready, including Pearl Lang, who was called by one critic "the supreme interpreter of the poetic Graham roles."[17] (Lang would later have a brief moment of odd fame when it was learned she gave dance lessons to the rock star Madonna.)

After Graham ceased dancing, she lingered on as a celebrity, receiving endless honors and accolades. Her place in the history of modern art was secure. She had stamped her style on the visual arts as well as on dance and music. Noguchi sculpted her striking head twice. Her sense of style affected not only costumes and set designs, but fashions outside the theater. She showed how the body should be draped to express its vitality. She had a sense of basic materials that was almost spiritual: "Never be afraid of material," she said to the dancers who helped her sew costumes; "the material knows when you are frightened and will not help."[18]

Musicians were pleased to compose for her. Paul Hindemith gave her the music for *Hérodiade,* Aaron Copland that for *Appalachian Spring.* Others who collaborated with her were Darius Milhaud, Samuel Barber, Gian Carlo Menotti, Edgar Varèse, Norman Dello Joio. Her dances fit the angular rhythms and irregular tonalities of twentieth-century music.

She affected dance of all sorts, from ballet to Broadway. Agnes De Mille, a trailblazer in the choreographing of Broadway musicals, pays generous tribute to Graham's influence.[19] Dancers she had trained performed in various musicals—Merce Cunningham in Kurt Weill's *One Touch of Venus,* Pearl Lang in *Carousel,* Stuart Hodes in *Paint Your Wagon.*

Graham also influenced actors who were not dancers. During the years when she helped train performers of all sorts at New York's Neighborhood Playhouse School, she showed aspiring actors how to weight their movements with significance. She sent people to the zoo to watch how panthers move. Richard Boone, one of her pupils, attributed his coiled-spring stance as a gunfighter on the TV show "Have Gun, Will Travel" to the time he spent, under Graham's instruction, observing a cat's poise and spring.[20] Katharine Cornell, Graham's close friend and financial patron, urged other actresses to study the Graham method of speaking with the body.

Graham succeeded in merging the two energies that tugged against each other in the Denishawn company where she began. Ruth St. Denis was an artist whose sole concern was her own expressive dance performances. Ted Shawn was a leader who wanted to take the cause of new dance forms to other people. His effort was crippled by two things, his own lack of creativity, which meant that he did not *have* a radically new dance style to spread, and a proselytizing urgency that could descend to mere commercial peddling. He was more an entrepreneur than an artistic leader. If I were considering him as my principal figure here, I would have to put him in the category of a salesperson, the category Ross Perot exemplifies in this book.[21]

Martha Graham had to show some entrepreneurial skills—raising funds, attracting patrons, cultivating dance critics, organizing clinics that paid her and drew talent she could recruit for her company. But she refused many offers to cash in on her name, her company's skills, or the growing commercial viability of modern dance. As an artistic leader, she promoted the cause of modern dance in ways that would not subvert its serious aspirations. She was called the high priestess of a cult. That was the only way she could keep herself from becoming the shill for a product (which was what she considered Ted Shawn).

Graham was an artist fully of her time and place. Her moves were both modern and American—Paul Taylor calls modern dance "the one art form other than jazz that can be called truly American."[22] In order to establish a dance with independent roots, Graham had initially to resist the disciplines of ballet. This led to hostility from the Russian emigrés who had largely dominated serious dance in the early part of this century. Graham clashed with Massine while dancing in Stravinsky's *Rite of Spring*. When she lectured on modern dance at the New School, in 1931, Michel Fokine, who had brought the traditions of Diaghilev's company to America, heckled and jeered from the audience, until she imperiously demanded that he leave.[23] George Balanchine, who was innovating within the ballet tradition, was long hostile to Graham—though he opened the way toward reconciliation when he asked Graham's company to perform with his in 1959.[24] By then, her indigenous art was defined enough to coexist with ballet.

Graham had led the way in dance as an integrator of Oriental and African-American dancers into her troupe. Her mystical concepts had made her a respectful student of Oriental thought, and her modernity made her responsive to jazz rhythms. She wanted to have Native American dancers—she went almost annually to observe dance festivals in New Mexico, and Erick Hawkins claimed that his birth on the Colorado-New Mexico border gave him spiritual descent from Native Americans.

Though she was asserting a clearly American identity in dance, nativeness was not a goal in itself. Like all artistic leaders, she had to respect and protect her art while seeking her social goals. The artistic leader's instrument of leadership is precisely his or her artifact—that is what distinguishes artistic from other forms of leadership. Ruskin advances the

Martha Graham, 32, 1931 —*Imogen Cunningham*

cause of Turnerian art with a prose as artful, gorgeous, and true to nature as the paintings it describes. Morris advances the cause of brotherly craftsmanship with stunningly beautiful wallpaper and bookbinding. And Graham's instrument for advancing the cause of an original and American form of dance was her finely tuned body, its beautiful lines daringly exposed in her youth. It is a body as perfectly wrought as a Keats sonnet.[25]

ANTITYPE
Madonna

M artha Graham was twenty-three when she went to the Denishawn dance school, and she had received no prior training in dance. Madonna Louise Veronica Ciccone was twenty when she enrolled for instruction with Pearl Lang, a star of the Graham company who was teaching the Graham method in 1978. Ms. Ciccone had been studying dance for years—first in high school, with a teacher who took on her training as a full-time job, so impressed was he by her talent, and then at the University of Michigan, where she received a dance scholarship. After two years of study on the Ann Arbor campus, she sought out Lang in New York. Lang had given a dance demonstration at the University of Michigan, and she was a judge for Alvin Ailey's backup dancers at the American Dance Theater. After winning a berth on Ailey's third team, Ciccone began lessons with Lang.[1]

But the laborious training Lang had learned from Graham was not for this impatient Italian-American. She might be expected to like the earthiness of the Graham floor exercises, but she had in fact learned more from bump-and-grind dancers of the go-go school (who inspired serious dance patterns in Bob Fosse) than from primitive myth. Reducing her long name to its first element (which had also been her mother's name), Ciccone became Madonna in a series of small rock groups (including one called Modern Dance). She tried her hand as a drummer before becoming a singer and composer. At all these various tasks she was no better than many an aspiring male or female dancer or drummer or singer or composer. But, packaged together with her aggressive showmanship-salesmanship, these accumulating half-skills made for a combination that the rock culture apotheosizes—the outsize icon that can serve as a centerpiece in the frenetic mass ritual of a rock concert. Madonna's models were sexually explicit yet ambiguous display items like Michael Jackson, Prince, and Boy George (though she could direct savage comments at some of these idols).

Anthropologists of the new are possessively learned about such cultural phenomena. They seem as odd to most Americans as Trobriand Island customs did to cultural detectives trudging to that "primitive" locale. In the cult of an Elvis, fame seems to elicit devotion of a quasi-religious intensity. A scholarly industry has grown up around Madonna, wrapping her vivid theatrical gestures in dense thickets of learned ignorance:

> A second more abstract argument for the MP [Madonna Phenomenon] as subversive, to which I now turn, enables a level of discourse in which we can understand the conflicting discursive constitutions of Madonna, including her own, as they function not only politically but also in terms of gender as a sign system not linked to identity.[2]

We have been offered a whole series of Madonnas as the carriers of Higher Meaning. She undermines feminism with her little-girl "boy toy" image, or she advances feminism with a tough take-charge control of her act and her life. She is destroying patriarchal authority. She is enshrining capitalist consumerism by her self-commodification.[3] She is a weapon lesbians can use in breaking down gender fixity.[4] When she goes on a diet, she is submitting to a cultural tyranny that demands thinness in women.[5] When she uses religion, she is superficially mocking it but actually—according to the Reverend Andrew Greeley—restoring a sense of the sacred.[6]

Martha Graham came along before social criticism had acquired its clanking rebarbative armor. Theorists might have read wild meanings into her new art, as they do into Madonna's. In fact, there are some points of comparison between them. Both use a combination of visual arts, costume, and music to pose and drape and undrape their bodies. Madonna's treatment of her traveling company, in the 1991 documentary film *Truth or Dare*, resembles (a little) Graham's concern with her disciples' training. Madonna calls her dancers "my children"—though she also tells the camera that her children are "emotionally crippled," not a thing most mothers would want to advertise to the world. Madonna teases her gay men dancers by frolicking with them nude in her bed, pushing them away from her bared breasts with a maternal pout: "It's not time for feeding." She says, "I wouldn't hire a fag that hates women."

The sex Madonna flouts is curiously unseductive. What Marjorie Rosen wrote of Mae West could as well be said of Madonna: "In the mouths of Harlow or Crawford, her delicious provocations might indeed have seemed indecent."[7] Madonna fans have not acted on the subversive values scholars find in their idol. Her audiences have been notably well behaved, with little evidence of the alcohol and drug abuse found at other rock stars' concerts. No matter how naughty her words or gestures, there is an irrefragable innocence about her. It is hard for anyone but a Jesse Helms to take her sins very seriously. Of course, we think the same thing of Mae West now, though the censors went after her far more energetically than they have gone after Madonna. West was banned from radio. The Hays office posted a guard on the set of her movie *Belle of the Nineties* to make sure she did not improvise words or gestures not contained in the script cleared by the censors.[8]

West had studied her own walk while writing a play about female impersonators.[9] Madonna's high school dance teacher, Christopher Flynn, a homosexual, took her to gay bars and discothèques, where much of her camp aesthetic was formed.[10] As Madonna infantilized her dancers in *Truth or Dare*, she gives her fans a child's ogle at sex, treating it as something grotesque that grown-ups do. Parker Tyler, the pioneer film critic, found a similarly infantilizing effect in Mae West's sexuality.[11] W. C. Fields, the bumpkinish con man and professional antiadult, was her perfect foil in *My Little Chickadee*. Tyler hints that West's handling of him was the closest she came on screen to humoring a child.[12]

The childish delight in saying provocative things gives a weightlessness to Madonna's sacrilege. When she says that she likes crucifixes "because there is a naked man on them," we do not expect her fans to run out and desecrate churches.[13] That would be as naive as to expect, with Father Greeley, that her fans will experience "God hunger" from watching Madonna wear a cassock. Madonna is not leading a crusade. She is an entertainer. Her artistic goal has often been stated: she wants to "entertain myself" and "to fuck with people"—mainly with their minds.[14] Shock is to her what counterpoint was to Bach or tonality to Debussy; it is the medium in which she creates.

She is an artist, then, but not an artistic leader. To what goal would she be leading her followers? The early Madonna fans dressed like her; but it was not Madonna's goal to make young teenagers wear their bras outside their sweaters. This imitation of a celebrity is simply an emblem of fandom. It plays "follow the leader" in the sense that a parlor game relies on imitation. When Clark Gable appeared without an undershirt in the movie *It Happened One Night*, sales of undershirts fell off. When President John Kennedy gave up wearing hats, so did many other men. That just shows that men can be as starstruck as squealing teenage girls. But those who *followed* Kennedy to his real political *goals* did not do so by taking off their hats.

As a performer, Madonna has certain ploys and disciplines, which give her audience aesthetic-kinetic satisfaction. As a businesswoman, she has been shrewd and resourceful. She has versatility. Acting in certain movies (*Desperately Seeking Susan* and A *League of Their Own*), she has proved herself a skillful comedienne. But, unlike Graham, she has not formed a school, advanced a new art form, campaigned to win converts to this cause. Graham not only performed a dance but preached an aesthetic. This does not displace the supremacy of the artist in the act of creation. Bach did not promote the cause of his art, he just exemplified it. But if we want to understand *leadership* in the arts, we must go to Graham, not Madonna.

14.
RHETORICAL LEADER

Martin Luther King, Jr.

Most leadership training includes some instruction in public speaking. Executives are rehearsed for their television appearances. Politicians have voice and debate coaches. Roger Ailes became an important advisor to Presidents Nixon, Reagan, and Bush because of his training as a TV producer.[1]

Yet there is a profound distrust of prepared speech—of rhetoric itself—in human nature, and more particularly in American culture. We glorify the "strong silent types" who do things instead of talking about them, the John Waynes, the Gary Coopers, whose eloquence runs to "Yup" and "Nope." Only spontaneous expression, it is felt, can be authentic. We shy from the studied performance, the elaborately crafted statement, the "slick" answer. So true is this that William Safire, the former presidential speechwriter, advised politicians to make deliberate mistakes in order to seem less "programmed." (Those who heed him will, of course, be *programming* their unprogrammed errors.)

Even the ancient Greeks, who invented the rhetorical tricks we have inherited, contrasted actions with words (*erga* with *logoi*) and distrusted their own glib demagogues. Plato, that superb stylist, presents a picture of Socrates forever calling his own words unstudied. Cicero, the orator supreme, wrote a long dialogue in which a great speaker maintains that natural instinct is all a person needs for expressing his thought—as opposed to the long training Cicero himself received under Greek tutelage.[2]

Clearly one *can* be a leader—even a great one—without being a great speaker. George Washington was no orator. Nonetheless, if mobilizing others toward a goal is the task of leaders, it would be odd if words were not useful, at times, for such mobilization. Washington used speechwriters—Jonathan Trumbull, Jr., David Humphreys, Alexander Hamilton, James Madison—who were thoroughly trained in classical rhetoric. Other presidents—Jefferson, Lincoln, Wilson—were skilled rhetoricians themselves; and though Jefferson was too diffident to deliver his words effectively, Lincoln and Wilson actually enhanced theirs in performance.

In fact, it is impossible to imagine our national history without the strong impact of orators. The colonial period rang with sermons that stirred people to repentance, witch-hunting, or war. Jonathan Edwards and other masters of the jeremiad could move their audiences more deeply than Demosthenes ever swayed Athens with his eloquence. In the colonial South, the most influential colony was Virginia, famed for its orators, led by Patrick Henry and Richard Henry Lee. When the Constitution was being debated, Patrick Henry, Harry Lee, John Marshall, and James Madison made the Virginia ratifying convention a feast of oratory.

In the nineteenth century, America remained an arena of great speechifying. Henry Clay, Daniel Webster, John Calhoun, and Edward Everett were outstanding figures in an outstanding field. In the pulpit, on the lecture circuit, at chautauquas, at revivals, lecturers were everywhere. Populists at the turn of the century supported and imitated William Jennings Bryan. In the thirties, social discontent was voiced or exploited by Huey Long, Father Coughlin, Elizabeth Flynn, and others. The world was being torn apart by orators (Hitler, Mussolini) and put together again by other orators (Churchill, Roosevelt).

Some think that the great days of rhetoric are over, the victim of radio, TV, accelerated changes, a shorter attention span, an emphasis on visual rather than oral image making. Yet speaking ability has been important in the modern careers of people as different as Ronald Reagan, Clare Boothe Luce, Fulton Sheen, Mario Cuomo, Jesse Jackson, George Wallace, William Buckley, Ann Richards, Louis Farrakhan, and Billy Graham.

It is true that oratory is no longer the central skill in politics, as it was in Greece or Rome. It is not even as central as it was in the nineteenth century, when the ability to harangue large crowds for hours, or to answer on one's feet in lengthy debates, was the main ritual of political contest. Lincoln and Douglas debated each other in eight three-hour matches.

They could not have held the audience if they had not been able to project their voices, articulate their words, and vary their rhythms. People tire early of what they must strain to hear. Lincoln's carrying tenor voice was a great political asset. The husky-throated Bill Clinton could never have competed on the circuit with Lincoln or Douglas. He would be like a postmicrophone crooner up against Al Jolson, who belted his songs out to huge crowds with no artificial amplification.

The sheer physical demand of oratory in antiquity led to an athletic regimen. Attic speakers to the Assembly on the Pnyx had to be heard by their fellow legislators numbering in the thousands (6,000 for a plenary session).[3] Only the clear-voiced and the clearheaded had a chance to win others to their view—which led to specialization in various styles of speaking and forms of argument.[4] The tale of Demosthenes' ability to make himself understood, even with pebbles in his mouth, shows how important was clarity of diction in such a setting.[5]

The prestige of the *rhetor* continued into Roman times, when his skills were the basis of diplomatic, legal, military, and administrative careers in late antiquity. The orator's education was the glue that held together the diverse and unruly parts of the Western and Eastern empires.[6] The orator's life was a discipline undertaken with all the seriousness of a semireligious vocation.

> One needs a grounded knowledge of the most varied things, so as not to rattle off meaningless words for others to mock at. One needs to shape one's discourse, not only culling but collocating words effectively. One needs to read others' motives, to the very depths of human nature, since tickling or soothing anxieties is the test of a speaker's impact and technique. One should have at hand, as well, poise and the play of wit, an educated bearing, swift short ways of deflecting others' challenges or launching one's own, along with an understated gracefulness and sophistication. . . And do I have to mention the delivery itself—how the body is controlled, its gestures, facial expressions, vocal inflexions and modulations? Or need I emphasize the memory, where all of this is filed away? Unless this stands guard over the material collected and elaborated, the material will evaporate, no matter how precious it was in itself.[7]

It seems unlikely that we could find in our time any such exalted attitude toward public speaking. Nonetheless, the ideal does live on, in one place—the pulpit. And especially in the pulpits of black churches. Even more especially, in Southern Baptist churches.

The pulpit has shaped American speech more than any other factor. Even politics echoes the themes of sacred eloquence, as William Jennings Bryan demonstrated. A large number of political leaders were the sons of ministers, or studied theology themselves. In recent times, seminary-trained candidates for the presidency have included George McGovern, Gary Hart, Pat Robertson, Jesse Jackson, Al Gore. Church schools or church attendance have left their mark on the speaking habits of Catholics like Mario Cuomo and Bill Buckley. The public rhetoric young Americans were most regularly exposed to came, in the past, from hearing Sunday sermons. For many evangelicals, both black and white, that meant hearing several sermons on Sunday, and some on weekdays. As an eleven-year-old, Martin Luther King, Jr., wrote to his parents (absent at a National Baptist Convention):

> We had good church services all day today. No one joined the church but Rev. Edward brought too [two] good sermon[s]. Mather Holleys funral was today and Rev. Sims and Rev. C. S. Jackson preached the funral[8]

When Dr. King rose, on later occasions, to deliver a homily, he had thousands of sermons echoing in his head, going back to his earliest childhood memories. Learning and preaching and learning-to-preach were all one thing for a man of his upbringing. The preacher's art held his community together, just as rhetoric had held together the societies of late antiquity.

In no other form of schooling—not even in law schools or schools of education—is the learning of a body of material so intimately linked with the re-presenting of that material as in ministerial programs. At Crozer Theological Seminary, where King did his first postgraduate work, he took thirty-five courses, and eleven of them were related to preaching or singing the gospel. They included:

Preaching Ministry of the Church
Public Speaking
Preparation of the Sermon
Practice Preaching
Preaching Problems
Conduct of Church Services
The Minister's Use of Radio[9]

If the acquisition of learning is subordinated to the dissemination of gospel wisdom in most seminaries, it has always been a *special* mark of the black preacher. He was, for a long time, the main repository of the community's wisdom. The same was true of Catholic priests when they were dealing with congregations of immigrants who were illiterate or ignorant of English.

The black preacher, even the illiterate preacher of slave days, had an oral lore and a scriptural knowledge absorbed from hymns and sermons, if not from the written text itself. Harriet Tubman was eloquent in speech and song, though she could neither read nor write. In the 1840s, Willis Williams, the freed slave of a plantation owner, William N. Williams, preached to his former owner, demonstrating the special status of Christian ministers.[10] Willis Williams was Dr. King's great-grandfather. He had twin children called Adam and Eve. Adam, better known later by his initials, A. D., rose in the community by developing even further the privileged status of his father. Willis Williams had been semiliterate. A. D. Williams waged a long, painful campaign to become a master of the word as well as a servant of the Word. Another minister tutored him to the level of the third-grade reader, but when A. D. went to Atlanta, an urban milieu where his preaching skills looked primitive, he studied for years at the Atlanta Baptist College (later to become Morehouse College), beginning all over again with elementary English. He was thirty-four years old before he received his college preaching certificate.[11]

This A. D. Williams, King's grandfather, had a dogged determination. He took a forlorn congregation of thirteen members, with no church to meet in, and built it into Atlanta's most prestigious and influential African-American church. When his daughter was in the high school run by his old Bible college, she met a rural student who had come to Atlanta to become educated in the ministry, Mike King (later renamed Martin Luther King). King had some schooling, but he still could not write at age fifteen. As a minister in his late twenties, he completed preparatory school and tried to enroll at Morehouse College; but the standards had risen since A. D. Williams studied there, and King was twice turned down because he could not pass the entrance examinations. By now, however, he was the son-in-law of A. D. Williams, who saw promise in this stubborn plodder. King was finally accepted because of his father-in-law's influence; but his troubles were not over. He twice flunked introductory English, and eked out a passing grade only in a last-chance summer school session. Mike King succeeded A. D. Williams as the pastor of Ebenezer Baptist Church, and built upon his father-in-law's influence. His son, destined to be a fourth-generation preacher, sought higher levels of education, going north to earn a doctorate. It was an ascent that somewhat intimidated his father, yet it was a continuation of the urge that had made grown men keep learning, as a way of mastering the art that was their main credential. For Martin junior to go from his fine grounding in the Atlanta University Laboratory School to Boston College's doctoral program was not as large a leap forward as it had been for the son of Willis Williams to go from illiteracy to the fluency and mastery of language he displayed before his congregation.

The entire discipline of these men's lives issued in the eloquence they kept refining for pulpit use. The sermon might have folk roots, but it was an art form in continual process of refinement, its practitioners skilled critics of each other, improvers of the common store of themes and tropes. Improvisation as a tradition made the great sermonizers resemble jazz artists or blues interpreters. The sermon verges always on music, picking up on the singing that preceded it and looking forward to the hymn that will follow. In a volume of the recorded Riverside History of Classic Jazz, a 1926 sermon illustrates this beautifully. The Rev. J. M. Gates of New York recites the words of a spiritual, announcing that the congregation is going to sing the song. Then, while he explicates and paraphrases the hymn, parishioners hum snatches of it, unable to wait, the tension mounting. At last he sings out the first verse, joined by the congregation. Then he plays verbal variations on the thought, in phrases of similar length and intonation, building up to the second verse.

This interpenetration of song and sermon goes back to fourth-century Milan, to St. Ambrose. We find it in the sermons of St. Augustine, delivered before his volatile North African audiences. It is not suprising that A. D. Williams, Mike King, and Martin junior were all singers before they became preachers, performers in church choirs and *a capella* groups. Their sermons had very strong musical features—refrains, like those in the blues; syncopated variations on the refrain; phrases punctuated by cries from the worshipers; quiet overtures, crescendos and accelerandos, recapitulating codas. Listen to the way Dr. King varies a refrain like "I have a dream," linking it to the prior sentence, shifting the emphasis back to "I," finding a new pitch for "dream" when he adds "today" to the end of the phrase.

The sermon, like jazz, is capable of the utmost sophistication in what it can incorporate. Dr. King presented his higher studies in the North as somehow at war with the fundamentalism and emotionalism of southern religion. But Keith D. Miller has discovered the real meaning of King's higher education: though King liked to refer to theologians like Reinhold Niebuhr and Paul Tillich, the readings that left their traces on King's own later writings were *sermons* that he read in the seminary. Some authors of these sermons were well known (like Harry Emerson Fosdick) but others are quite obscure today (like J. Wallace Hamilton or Thomas Butterick).[12] The more abstract theologians affected King's thought only to the extent that those men's ideas had been absorbed by the white *preachers* King read and imitated. Only in sermon form did religious thought inspire King. He did his school exercises, as a jazz musician might perform his scales at a classical musical conservatory; but he came alive only when the classical devices were put in a jazz idiom.

King up North was acquiring credentials to help his preaching. He was not interested in or capable of scholarship for its own sake.[13] He acquired the doctorate much as he collected, and rolled around in his mouth, "big words" for their use in impressing others. This was part of the "educated manner" that (Cicero tells us) the orator uses to give greater authority to his words. In that sense, the whole *persona* forged in order to win an audience can be considered a branch of rhetoric. Black ministers—like all ministers—try to preserve their moral authority by a dignified bearing. Martin King, as a "PK" (preacher's kid), had it instilled in him from youth that he should be a model of responsible appearance. His language was always elevated. Even as an eleven-year-old, he wrote to his father in these terms: "When you are idle and [have] nothing to do with your time sit down and write me a few lines."[14] This studied deference was carried into the concerns of adolescence:

> If I were a minute late to class, I was almost morally conscious of it and sure that everyone noticed it. Rather than be thought of as always laughing, I'm afraid I was grimly serious for a time. I had a tendency to overdress, to keep my room spotless, my shoes perfectly shined and my clothes immaculately pressed.[15]

Such concern for appearance raises the objection some people have to all forms of rhetoric—the constant striving for effect. Rhetoric, in this view, is totally artificial, manipulative, hypocritical. It adds to, ornaments, or disguises the truth—dresses it up, though truth's body is best seen naked.

But being on one's best behavior—linguistic behavior as well as other kinds—is not a sign of falsehood in itself. There is nothing more authentic than our desire, our need, to impress others whom we respect, love, or feel responsible for. Parents who did not want to improve their own lives in order to be responsible toward their children would be quite *un*natural parents—and pastors have that motive for helping their congregations at large.

Rhetoric is unnatural, but so is speech. Inarticulate cries of rage or loss are "sincere" but uninformative. Language uses conventional signs to express subtler feelings behind the undifferentiated yells. And *heightened* language intensifies this reportage on our internal condition. We say to everyone "Good morning," yet that expresses little of our different feelings for each of the persons greeted. It would be truer to our feelings if we hailed a lover with a sonnet, a child with a deft little sermon, an employer with an expression of allegiance, and so on—but most of us are not energetic enough, mentally, to be thus truthful.[16] We hide the truth under uniform and misleading conventions: "Good morning" or "Hello" or "Too bad." When deeply felt moments arrive—a death, a birth, a national catastrophe—we can only say "I don't know what to say."

The pulpit orator is trained to *know* what to say to grieving or joyous congregations, to live up to the demands of the moment. His or her training uses artifice to reach the truth, to be adequate to the situation, to respond to and elevate the audience's feelings. The test is pragmatic. As Cicero said, "The *effect* the orator intended is in the *affect* of the audience, and only popular reaction and approval can test that."[17]

Martin King, like Cicero's ideal orator, marshaled all his resources—his learning, vocal exercises, physical bearing, memorization—to the effective address of his chosen audience. He tried to lift others up, and found himself lifted up in the process. He literally talked himself into useful kinds of trouble. Like many prophets in the Bible, King did not aspire to the kind of leadership he finally undertook. He would gladly have fled the task, like Jonah. But the task pursued him.

King's oratory urged others on to heroic tasks—and where they went he had to follow. His voice wielded him rather than vice versa. Reluctant to go to jail, he was shamed into going there after so many young people responded to his speeches and found themselves in danger. King had, progressively, to face imprisonment, threats, a stabbing, blackmail, FBI harassment, and a growing certitude that he would be murdered. All these pressures drove him deeper into his own religious motivation—back, that is, into the meaning of his own words. As one says, "Physician, cure theyself," he was forced to be the preacher who inspired himself.[18]

Cicero, it is interesting to note, followed a similar course. Vacillating for much of his life, eager to avoid dangerous confrontation, he had sung the praise of liberty so often, urging others to resist despotism, that he finally talked himself into the brave defiance of Mark Antony in the "Philippic" speeches that cost him his life. The orator's first test is his ability to create heroes in response to his call. The orator's final test is his ability to create heroism in himself to match what he has been preaching. Here the artificial *becomes* the true in the most complete way. Leaders and followers prod *each other* toward their shared goal.

All of Martin King's rhetorical exercises were marshaling him along the way to death. All his borrowings brought him to the point where he could not borrow the courage that made the words truly his. That is the drama that lies behind his greatest oration. We can take that speech apart, trace its elements to several sources. But putting it all together meant putting together his own life, as a pledge of the weight he placed on his own words.

The most famous of his perorations comes from another man, from Archibald Carey, a black preacher who said, in 1952:

> From every mountainside, let freedom ring. Not only from the Green Mountains of Vermont and New Hampshire; not only from the Catskills of New York; but from the Ozarks in Arkansas, or from the Stone Mountains in Georgia, from the Blue Ridge Mountains of Virginia . . . from every mountainside, let freedom ring![19]

What is important about the passage is not where King got it but what he did with it. This was only one of the many strands he wove into the greatest American speech given since Lincoln's time.

The speech, delivered at Washington's Lincoln Memorial, picks up where the Gettysburg Address left off: "Fivescore years ago . . ."[20] As Lincoln harked back to the Declaration of Independence, telling Americans to live up to their ancient commitment, King goes back to the Gettysburg Address and, through that, to the Declaration, establishing a lineage for his claims. Lincoln used the Declaration to effect emancipation: "But one hundred years later, the Negro still is not free." King turns "Fivescore years ago" into a refrain, "One hundred years later . . ."

> *One hundred years later*, the Negro is still anguished in the corners of American society and finds himself in exile in his own land.

He has already begun to create the moral geography that will lead to the climactic "every mountaintop." Here are people crippled, islanded, "in the corners"—marginalized, off the map of American prosperity and rights. Before he ends the speech, he will march these people right across the map, up to its highest peaks.

Lincoln issued a promissory note by the act of emancipation. King has come back to Lincoln's memorial to pronounce that note "marked 'insufficient funds.' " The supposedly freed people were given a bad check, but "we refuse to believe that there are insufficient funds in the great vaults of opportunity of this nation."

And after all this time, after these empty promises, the blacks are still asked to wait. Here King overlays his moral map with a moral calendar based on "the fierce urgency of *now*":

> *Now is the time* to make real the promises of democracy.
> *Now is the time* to rise from the dark and desolate valley of segregation to the sunlit path of racial justice.

Already phrases are sounding that will come back with greater weight. The "sunlit path" is picked up and developed in contrast with the cant phrase of the day ("long hot summer") and with Shakespeare's "winter of our discontent": "This sweltering summer of the Negro's legitimate discontent will not pass. . . ." We hear of "the bright day of justice," the "warm threshold" of justice.

Yet King tempers the urgency of demand with the moral restraint of nonviolence. "We must forever conduct our struggle on the *high plane* of dignity and discipline . . . rise to the *majestic heights* of meeting physical force with soul force." This does not mean there will be any turning back, however. When others ask, "When will you be satisfied?" the answer must come back, again and again:

> *We can never be satisfied* as long as the Negro is the victim of the unspeakable horrors of police brutality. . .

The struggle of a whole people is reenacted as King climbs this catalogue of indignities, cresting at last on the verse from the prophet Amos (24.5):

> No, *we are not satisfied* and we *will not be satisfied* until justice rolls down like waters and righteousness like a mighty stream.

The King James bible was the basis of black pulpit eloquence, its archaic forms and strong rhythm. In this phrase King dwelt on the strong spondaic syllables *rolls down*, then fell off on the dactylic-trochaic ripple of "righteousness like a mighty stream."

King then turned to the activists who were wearied by prison and by beatings, and said they must keep on this path of redemptive suffering:

> *Go back* to Mississippi.
> *Go back* to Alabama . . .

One cannot stay in "the valley of despair." The heights are still there for the climbing.

His assigned time was running out, but the crowd had warmed up and was urging him on. He began to ad lib from a refrain he had used elsewhere; but it is tied here to the Declaration with which he had begun. His is a dream "deeply rooted in the American dream":

> *I have a dream* that one day [here launching again into the rolling King James words, into Isaiah 40.4–5] every hill and mountain shall be made low, the rough places shall be made plain, and the crooked places shall be made straight and the glory of the Lord will be revealed and all flesh shall see it together.

The last phrases were almost sung, in the preacher's exalted tones. Then King returned to his written text, on the faith to go forward:

> *With this faith* we will be able to hew out of the mountain of despair a stone of hope [drawing on Daniel 2.35, "the stone that smote the image became a great mountain"] . . .
> *With this faith* we will be able to work together, to pray together, to struggle together, to go to jail together, to stand up for freedom together, knowing that we will be free one day.

The quickening together-phrases elicited a rolling and growing applause—this was where the text was to end. But King knew he had carried the crowd to a plateau, not the pinnacle; so he used, once again, the Archibald Carey variation on "My Country 'Tis of Thee." Carey had delivered this patriotic appeal at the Republican National Convention of 1952, where Dwight Eisenhower was making some overtures to black voters. Carey said that patriotic songs talk of "liberty." King had several times, in his speech, asked the country to live up to its creed, to the Declaration, the Gettysburg Address, the Emancipation Proclamation. Unlike some protesters of the 1960s, he was not willing to cede the patriotic high ground to those who were distorting the message of the national symbols. The flag was his flag. The land was his land.

Lincoln, bringing unwelcome demands for equality, returned Americans to something familiar, to the Declaration Americans warmly celebrate every Fourth of July. He braced people to face the new by reminding them of old ties and commitments, identifying their own earlier voice with the new message he brought. He reassured them that they were being true to themselves, not giving in to others. They were listening to the better angels of their nature. In the same way, King came before the nation, not as an outsider shoving in with threats of force. He had sneaked around to the back places of the American heart. He was singing its song to the country, asking how people can drive away black demands without disavowing what is best in their own history, symbols, and emblems of pride. "*My* country . . ." is the one blacks had fought for; the flag was one they had carried into overseas engagements. How could they come back home and *not* feel that its every mountain was theirs to be proud of, too? The whole speech's yearning toward heights reaches its climax as King lingers out the theme Carey first sounded. First King travels across the country, leaping from peak to peak, as the fires on mountaintops passed the message of Troy's fall in Aeschylus's *Agamemnon*, a list of great names unrolled and savored.

So *let freedom ring* from the prodigious hilltops of New Hampshire . . .

And from the mountains of New York, the Alleghenies of Pennsylvania, the Rockies of Colorado, the slopes of California. Having taken a purely scenic trip across the country, King then makes the tourist itinerary yield to moral geography, to a landscape of the heart, where landmarks of human commitment are contended for:

But not only that.
Let freedom ring from Stone Mountain of Georgia.
Let freedom ring from Lookout Mountain of Tennessee.
Let freedom ring from every mountain and molehill of Mississippi, from *every* mountainside, *let freedom ring.*

The Peaceable Kingdom of the Branch—*Edward Hicks*
Yale University Art Gallery, Gift of Robert W. Carle

This working out of a passage borrowed from another preacher has resonances, in King's use of it, not felt in the original. It picks up on other mountain language in the speech—the heights from which Amos's waters of justice roll down, the mountain yielding up a divine rock in Daniel, the mountains turned into a royal progress route in Isaiah. There is a moral language of mountains in Scripture that a preacher like King appealed to naturally, just as St. Augustine had in his sermons. The mountains are signs of God's steadiness in the Psalms (36.5–6). Prophets are summoned to mountaintops (Isaiah 40.9). God reigns on his holy mount (Psalm 43.3). The preacher has a repertoire of charged symbols for calling up the emotions of his audience. He does not use logic, any more than Lincoln did in his great speeches. Lincoln spoke of a miraculous conception ("brought forth on this continent") and a "rebirth" in language also taken from Scripture.

King wove together the best from national, patriotic, biblical, and song literature. He ended with a folk spiritual, after beginning with national documents, and every step he took in the motion from one to the other brought out their essential identity. He sang with many voices one song, of national pride and shame, loss and gain, struggle and transcendence. The dream he had, of all sitting down together, with linked hands, with linked hearts, is the apocalyptic dream of peace that Edward Hicks painted over and over. Hicks created a moral landscape, using American topography as symbols. He, too, borrowed from others, especially from Benjamin West's painting *Penn's Treaty with the Indians*, a founding compact Hicks equated with the Isaiah text on the lion that couches with the lamb, or on the little child who will lead them. In an 1825 version of this dream, Hicks makes the Natural Bridge of Virginia, Jefferson's favorite American landscape, form an arch in the sky like a rainbow of peace over the figures of Penn and the Indians. This is a striking visual equivalent of King's greatest speech.

ANTITYPE
Robert   Parris   Moses

N ot all orators live up to the measure of their own words.
There were many fine preachers in the civil rights movement whose later lives have not been an inspiration. The
artificiality of rhetoric can be used to hide the truth. That is why some felt
there was something false even to Dr. King's rhetoric. These people
admired Robert Parris Moses more than the showier Reverend King.
Moses inspired, but not by giving speeches. He was not only nonrhetor-
ical but antirhetorical in his attitude toward the civil rights movement.

Bob Moses was descended from a prominent African-American
preacher, but his own father was deprived of an education, and made sure
that his son received a fine one.[1] After a scholarship to Hamilton College
in New York, Moses went to Harvard's graduate school of philosophy.
Forced to take care of his ailing father, Moses left Harvard to teach high
school mathematics. He had gone through a period of evangelical proselytizing before he became interested in eastern mysticism. He was so
quiet that King's Southern Christian Leadership Conference did not know
what to do with him when he went to Atlanta as a volunteer during his
summer break from teaching. But Moses found things to do, and these
were so off-the-beaten-track, even for the SCLC, that he was considered
an oddity, perhaps a Communist provocateur, perhaps an FBI plant.

Moses went where even the SCLC had not dared, yet, to go—into the
rural enclaves of the most desperately deprived blacks of Mississippi. He
organized voters there in 1963 and 1964, as part of the breakaway Student
Nonviolent Coordinating Committee. Moses became famous for his serenity under blows in terrorized McComb County. Among the hotheads
of SNCC, he was the imperturbable saint—jailed, shot at, undefeated.
He helped bring the alternate slate of delegates to the Democratic National Convention—the Mississippi Freedom Democratic Party. He was
so self-effacing that he tried to disown his own achievements. When King
and others were preparing their speeches at the March on Washington,

Moses was quietly picketing the Justice Department with a sign that quoted St. Augustine: WHEN THERE IS NO JUSTICE, WHAT IS THE STATE BUT A ROBBER BAND ENLARGED? When some found biblical force in the name Moses, he dropped it and started using his mother's maiden name, Parris, as his last name. When Moses was drafted, in 1966, to fight in a Vietnam War he opposed, he fled to Canada, where he lived under a different name. After two years there, he went to Tanzania for eight years. In 1976 he returned to America, where his interest in the educational problems of young blacks led him to develop an algebra program based on dramatic methods. Helped by a MacArthur Foundation "genius grant," he spread his effective algebra program from school to school.

The force of personality, conviction, and example made Moses a great leader in the days of worst danger for the civil rights movement. But those who contrasted him with King, as the real thing to the spurious, did honor to neither man. There are tasks that rhetoric can perform, just as there are tasks that only a quieter act of witnessing can accomplish. Lincoln was no Harriet Tubman, and vice versa. But they were working toward the same goal, and helping each other get there. The antitype to rhetorical leadership can supplement it but not entirely replace it.

15.

OPPORTUNISTIC LEADER

—•—

Cesare Borgia

My book may, to this point, have encouraged a misconception—that good leaders lead people only to the good. The people so far treated have been admirable (or certainly acceptable). Some might cavil at Napoleon, or at Ross Perot—but in their leadership, narrowly considered here, Napoleon *was* good at war, as Perot was good at business.

Yet there have been great leaders who took people toward destruction, of others or themselves or both. Hitler. Nero. Stalin. Some would like to sanitize the term "leader" by distinguishing it from words like demagogue or dictator or autocrat. "Bad leaders" trick others, impose their will, leave others no choice. James MacGregor Burns says that autocrats cannot *not* be followed, so they are not leaders.[1] But Hume reminds us that even the head of a police state cannot impose his single will by force. His police outnumber him; he must *persuade* them to oppress the people.[2] St. Augustine says that the leader of a gang of thieves must keep good order in the gang, observing equity in matters like the division of spoils: "Even robbers, in order to *disturb* the peace of others with ruthless efficiency, take care to *maintain* peace among themselves."[3]

The evil leader cannot treat his followers evilly. He may rob outsiders, to enrich the insiders. If he robs *everyone*, he has no followers—and will soon have no life. St. Augustine says that no one can, even if he wants to, kill *everyone else*. And with everyone a man cannot kill, he must establish at least "some workable semblance of concord" (*qualiscumque umbra pacis*)—which involves persuasion at the barter level: "I'll leave you alone if you leave me alone." If, going farther, the evil one wants to *lead* others in order to get his way, he must promise them some goods beyond being left alone: "Follow me, and I will make you rich!" It will do no good, in such a case, to say, "Follow me and I will make *me* (but not *you*) rich."[4]

So even the immoral leader, insofar as he is a *leader*, advances the good of his followers. Hitler claims to be giving back to Germans what the Versailles peace settlement deprived them of. Nero claims to be giving Rome the cultural values of Greece. Stalin claims to be carrying forward the workers' interests around the world. The evil man is followed for the good he convinces followers he can lead them to. Nothing could better prove the dialectial nature of leadership—the *structural* importance of the followers' will. They must see their own stake in the goal to which they are being mobilized.

No one grasped these truths more incisively than Niccolò Machiavelli (1469–1527), who has become the symbol of evil leadership. His manual on one-man rule (*Il Principe*) was considered such a devil's guide to power that Richard III's worst boast is that he will teach that evil teacher new tricks. He will "set the murderous Machiavel to school."[5] But Machiavelli was a neutral analyst of the dynamics of power. He studied what works. He did not promote evil for its own sake, though he saw how evil acts can *work* in the accruing of power. He knows, as well, that often they do *not* work—that in many cases "honesty is the best policy." He is for "the best policy," not for honesty as such. He would agree with St. Augustine that policy sometimes requires truth in dealing with others— the equity not even a robber chieftain can do without.

Machiavelli's dark legend has been extended to the leader who most fascinated him, his contemporary, Cesare Borgia. Which may make it startling to find what Machiavelli considers the firmest basis for Borgia's leadership: the equitable administration of law in his realm (the Romagna). That point is obscured, neglected, or denied in most treatments of the two men. Yet Machiavelli's importance for all later discussion of leadership makes it necessary to trace exactly what intrigued Machiavelli in the young leader he observed close up.

The Borgia family has come to typify the dark side of the Italian Renaissance, though it was a Spanish family, not an Italian one. Rodrigo Borja, when he became Pope Alexander VI—in 1492, the year of other Spanish achievements, including Columbus's voyage to the Americas—

brought bullfighting into the Vatican. He spoke Spanish in his family circle, and called his most famous son César. Like his sister Lucrez (Lucrezia Borgia), César had a fair-haired northern Italian mother. But he was raised in his father's Spanish ways. He was an acrobatic horse tumbler and bullfighter. He became the cardinal of Valencia at the age of seventeen. (His father had held the same Spanish see at a more advanced age.) Later, when he abandoned his clerical career (he had never been ordained a priest), he married into the French title of duc de Valentinos. In both capacities—as ecclesiastical ruler and secular heir— the Italians called him the Valens-Man, Valentino.

He is hard to pin down, even in so simple a matter as giving him a name. He was in a constant state of becoming, never fixed in one role, not famous for any specific achievement. As a cleric, he might have risen to be pope, like his father and his great-uncle, Alfonso de Borja (Calixtus III). As a warrior, he might have founded a unitary new Italian state. As the custodian of his father's political machine, he might have been a kingmaker in the negotiations that brought a successor to the chair of Peter after Alexander's death. He accomplished none of these things, leading some historians to ask why he has received so much attention.

But Machiavelli was as good a judge as any when it came to political talent. As a learned Florentine diplomat, he had no reason to love or admire the papal policy of his time. Pope Alexander, when he failed to make a fellow Spaniard, the king of Naples, subordinate to his schemes, helped call in a foreign power (France) to conquer the Neapolitans—a great offense in the eyes of Machiavelli (*Discourses* 1.12). Why, then, was Machiavelli so taken by this Pope's illegitimate son?

He found in Valentino the best embodiment of the polar struggle between male mastery (*virtù*) and female Luck (Fortuna).[6] The personified Fortuna was a gambler's "Lady Luck" in Machiavelli's eyes, a dangerous ally but an implacable enemy:

> Better to be headlong (*impetuoso*) than to be civil with her. Luck is female, and must be kept in her place with punches and kicks. She will more often let such treatment conquer her than she will yield to men of cooler behavior. That is why, like any woman, she dotes on young men, who are less civil, more savage, and reckless enough to subdue her.[7]

Those words are full of male swagger, but they betray an uneasy awareness of the woman's power. It is conceded, for instance, that even when

Luck favors the bold, *she* is in the controlling position. She "often *lets* herself be conquered"—*si lascia piu vincere.* Earlier in this chapter (25) Luck's distinctive power was presented in a simile descended from Homer's description of the way Zeus wipes out a whole country *that has been ill ruled:*

> I compare her to one of those obliterative rivers that, when angry, overwhelm the fields, obliterating trees and buildings, picking up whole parts of the countryside and depositing them elsewhere, so that everyone runs before the waters, yielding to their headlong force (*impeto*), with no means at all of resistance.[8]

If one foresees Luck's anger, one can build dikes and dams to control the raging waters. (Machiavelli, a Florentine, is thinking of spring spates in the Arno.) Yet no one can foresee all the tricks of Luck. What if she uses earthquake instead of flood the next time she gets angry? Even with foresight and youthful assertiveness, one can hope—at most—to get the better of Luck only about half the time. And, once again, Machiavelli sees the outcome as a matter of Luck's *concession,* not her *impotence:*

> I think it may be true that Luck keeps herself supreme over about half our actions, but yields control of the other half—well maybe less—to us.

She yields (*lascia governare*), but she keeps the edge by letting man win *almost* half the time (half, or a little less, *o poco meno*).

Machiavelli's heroes resort to desperate measures because they are facing such cruel odds. One must take every inch of available advantage, to compensate for the blows Luck will surely deal out. On the other hand, because Luck is so whimsically reversible, one should not give up, even when beaten flat, because another turn of the wheel may lift one back up to prosperity. Luck "moves through thwart unknowable ways" (*Discourses* 2.29). Machiavelli's contemporaries cowered before the astrological signs that dot the Vatican chamber's ceiling painted by Pinturrichio for Pope Alexander. Machiavelli called this extreme fear of Luck an insult to Christian belief in free will. Yet by our standards he gives the will very straitened quarters for movement. Human beings, in his view, are hemmed in on all sides, by incalculable accidents as well as by celestial malignity. Machiavelli had seen governments fall almost as soon as they were installed, and great men humbled. A prophet like Savonarola is burned. The powerful Medici are hounded from Florence (twice in Machiavelli's lifetime). Popes chase princes from their fortresses and are chased in turn. His Italy was of a friable texture. It fell apart at the strong man's touch—and then the strong man fell apart.

In such a situation, one must strike quick and hard to have any impact at all. Machiavelli's advice tends always to extremes. Despite his constant invocation of antiquity, he despised the "golden mean" praised by Aristotle and the Stoics. Better to be struck down gloriously by Luck than to be silently overwhelmed by her. Stun your subjects, he told princes, with extravagant kindness or severity, but get their attention.[9] Even if one wanted to hold a "middle course," Luck moves so swiftly, so inexplicably, it is impossible to find or keep to such a delusive "middle way" (*via del mezzo*).[10] As in a storm at sea, you must let the sails go or tighten them hard—you cannot keep them half-filled all the time.

It is easy to see why a man with these views would be awestruck by "Valentino." That bastard warrior—baffled in his early clerical days, rejected as a suitor for the king of Naples's daughter because of his illegitimacy, marked as a Spanish outsider (even called a secret Jew) in Italy—took a commission from his father the pope to bring the semi-independent papal holdings of the Romagna back into submission to the Vatican. Setting out late in 1499, Valentino quickly captured, or accepted the surrender of, former papal realms to the east of the Appenines, and proclaimed himself the duke of Romagna. Then he began to move up the peninsula into territories allied to Venice or Florence.

Those nervous city-states sent emissaries to sound out his intentions, and Machiavelli was a member of the Florentine delegation hastily dispatched in the summer of 1502. Even before these diplomats reached Valentino's headquarters, they received word that the town of Urbino had been snatched from its complacent ruler by a combination of ruse and rapid maneuver. Machiavelli, who was critical of his own republic's passivity, praised the decisiveness of this coup in a letter sent back to Florence before he arrived at Valentino's camp:

> This kind of victory is based entirely on this Lord's foresight (*prudentia*) since, starting seven miles from Camerino, stopping neither for food nor drink, he reached Cagli, thirty-five miles distant, while Camerino was besieged by the direction of his couriers. Your lordships [of the Florentine Council of Ten] should be alert to a maneuver of this sort, and to a swiftness linked with the utmost success (*faelicità*).[11]

Machiavelli was clearly disposed to admire this man, though he had never met him. The reality did not disappoint him. Valentino was a creature of mystery who kept himself aloof, often not appearing in the daytime. He received the Florentine emissaries late in the night, and instantly took the offensive. Though he had been working with those who wanted to restore the ousted Medici to Florence, he said that any suspicion of his intentions was a sign of *Florence's* high-handed ways. "You treat me like an assassin!"[12] He professed a desire for friendship, but not of the distrustful sort the Florentines exhibited.

> In any case, pay close attention to this—close! I do not intend to continue on these terms. If you do not want me as a friend, I will truly be your enemy.[13]

For two hours, he kept these men rocked back on their heels trying to defend a city that was more threatened than threatening. No wonder they alerted their superiors to this twenty-six-year-old's effrontery.

> This is a lord of much flash and grandness, so spirited in war that he treats lightly the greatest undertakings. To gain glory and realms, he never rests, ignoring fatigue and peril. He arrives here before anyone knows he left there. He has won over his soldiers; he has collected the best there are in Italy. These things make him victorious and formidable, linked as they are with Luck's continuing regard.[14]

The duke gave Bishop Soderini, the head of Machiavelli's legation, a four-day ultimatum for Florence to sign a treaty with him. Soderini dispatched Machiavelli to argue for that in Florence—to no avail. The city continued to stall. That closed Machiavelli's first brief exposure to Valentino—two intense days of diplomatic push and shove in the middle of June 1502.

But late in September of that year the Florentines heard of a rebellion brewing among Valentino's allies, who had met at Magione to plan his overthrow. Machiavelli was sent back to Valentino (then stationed at Imola), to impart news of these developments, hoping to drive a wedge between the duke and his troublesome anti-Florentine friends. At Imola, he found the duke, who had formerly stunned him with accusations, ready to smother him in a diplomatic embrace. Valentino wanted more than good news and assurances from Florence. He demanded *troops*. He said he was pinned down, unable to rely on his former allies, waiting for French and Swiss reinforcements. If he got no help soon, he might have to come to terms with the rebels rather than punish them. Machiavelli was under orders to make friendly overtures but no firm commitment to Valentino. He tried to persuade his superiors to seize the occasion, quickly, and make common cause with Valentino.[15] But he had to do this indirectly, since he was being criticized for trying to make policy rather than relay intelligence.[16] At one point, Machiavelli even invented a surrogate, an unnamed friend in Valentino's entourage, to raise the arguments he could not make directly.[17]

Machiavelli stressed that Valentino, despite his setbacks, had many resources left, and that Florence would not be needed at a later stage, when reinforcements came to the duke. The duke told him: "If they [the Florentines] do not act now, I am through with them. Not if I were in water to my chin would I consider their friendship any more."[18] Machiavelli became more insistent with his superiors as Valentino negotiated a truce with the rebels, seeming to welcome them back—though the duke kept up warlike preparations even as he talked of peace.[19] If the Florentine Council did not mean to act now, Machiavelli said, then it should recall him—it was embarrassing to face Valentino day after day with nothing new to offer him.[20] Finally, the duke and his inner circle made themselves unavailable to Machiavelli. The truce with the rebels had reached the ratification stage. Machiavelli got hold of a text of the peace terms and sent it to Florence (on November 10).[21]

Valentino's policy was by turns to take Machiavelli into his confidence and shut him out, leaving the diplomat confused—and deceived. On November 20, Machiavelli wrote:

> Everyone is puzzled by the military preparations going forward as peace terms are being concluded, especially considering the faith that is being pledged now. . . . It is not believed that faith will be violated once a promise is made.[22]

Machiavelli finds it hard to believe that the duke would simply forgive those who plotted against him.[23] On the other hand, maybe his setbacks have made Valentino "less accustomed to getting his own way, recognizing that Luck will not let him win every time."[24]

Machiavelli's reaction is just the one Valentino was trying to create in his rebellious associates. His success at fooling even Machiavelli—who was near at hand and watching the duke, day after day, like a hawk—

explains some of the admiration expressed for Valentino in *Il Principe*. The two enjoyed fencing with each other, but Machiavelli was the one left in the dark after most of their exchanges.[25]

On December 10, Valentino, after his long pause at Imola, moved quickly—to Forlì, then to Cesena. Machiavelli followed as soon as he could make arrangements. He warned his superiors that they might have thrust the man back into the company of their enemies.[26] But the more Machiavelli studied the duke, the less could he predict his actions:

> As I have often written to your Lordships, this lord is very secretive, and I think no one but himself knows what he will do. His highest aides have often assured me that he never reveals his plans until he issues an order, and that is as late as possible, when the thing has to be done, and not otherwise.[27]

That was written the day after Christmas, when Valentino gave his subjects a grisly Christmas present, the exposed body of his hated Spanish henchman Ramíro Lorqua, decapitated in the public square of Cesena. Machiavelli was certain that this meant something, but he was not certain what: "The reason for his deed is not well understood, unless the ruler merely wished to show how he can make or unmake a man at will, according to the man's deserts." Machiavelli clearly felt there was more behind this move than an imperious demonstration of will. To sacrifice the unpopular instrument of his rule was a bid for approval: Valentino was revealing a wish to rely on his new subjects, not on the fellow Spaniard who came with him. But why was the move made so suddenly, just at this moment?

Some people have believed that the loyal follower was turning *dis*loyal—that Ramíro had been in communication with the rebels of the Magione conspiracy.[28] But Valentino was trying to lull those conspirators—something he could hardly achieve by killing their own man (if he was their man). It seems, rather, that by killing the "hardliner" in his camp, the duke was indicating a wish to compromise. In fact, this savage sudden act, so far from being impulsive, sent signals to all the people Valentino was trying to impress—the Italians of the Romagna, the Magione faction, the French allies (for whom Valentino expressed his need by giving up on the Spanish mercenary), and—even—Machiavelli himself. The Florentine was clearly impressed by the deed, which he carefully says was merited by Ramíro. (The duke treated him according to his deserts, *secondo e' meriti*.)

Valentino had now made his truce with the rebels, whom he dispatched to seize the city of Sinigaglia. He arrived to congratulate the victors, who were elated at their conquest—then imprisoned them in the city they had won. This coup Machiavelli reported from the scene, since Valentino had hinted that there would be something worth reporting on at Sinigaglia. The two leading figures of the Magione conspiracy were strangled the night of their arrest—New Year's Eve—and Valentino saw in the New Year talking tranquilly to Machiavelli of the great service he had just performed for *Florence!* This, he revealed, is why he wanted Machiavelli to witness the countercoup:

> Afterward, at about the second hour of the night, he called me to him, and with all the ease in the world expressed his gratification at this success, saying he had told me something of it—but not all—the day before. Which was true.[29]

Valentino spread out before him all the good that would come of this act. He had, at one stroke, strengthened relations with France, removed the causes of division within Italy, and—above all—removed the threat of pro-Medici activists against Florence. Unfortunately, the detailed first letter in which Machiavelli reported this conversation is lost. But we can deduce some of its content from the literary account Machiavelli wrote shortly after, his "Description of Duke Valentino's Method in Killing Vitellozzi Vitelli, Oliverotto da Fermo, Signor Pagolo, and the Duke of Gravina Orsini."

Some date this essay considerably later, thinking it a sketch for incorporation into Machiavelli's *History of Florence*.[30] They notice apparent inconsistencies between the dispatches to his superiors and the "Description." In the dispatches, for instance, he presented the duke as full of confidence and strength in early October; but the "Description" says he was a man "full of fear" at that moment (*pieno di paura*). Actually, Valentino, after making his first intended impression of strength on Machiavelli, had begun revealing some of his real grounds for concern. After two weeks, he confided:

> When you first came here, I did not speak so frankly about the parlous condition of my realm, realizing that Urbino had rebelled, that I could not know what was holding firm. All my affairs were uncertain, in such newly established realms. I did not want your superiors to think that I made

empty promises out of my great apprehension (*timore grande*). But now that I have no more worries, deeds will back up promises.[31]

Thus, when his principals wrote to Machiavelli about Valentino's weaknesses, he could honestly say that he had reported some of these.[32] And he would point out more—including the threat posed by the pope's age and uncertain health.[33] Already in November of 1502, Machiavelli realized that the loss of the pope's resources would put his son, Valentino, to the supreme test.

There is no real contradiction between the dispatches and the "Description," except that what was revealed only gradually in the dispatches is seen from the inside, as it were, in the "Description"—thanks, no doubt, to the revelations made in that New Year's Eve conversation where Valentino revealed the far-reaching goals he had been working toward in this period of great trial.[34] He had begun at a point of maximum vulnerability, as the "Description" claims—so he had to hide his condition with a bluster of confidence that Machiavelli briefly fell for. But as he got stronger, he began to portray himself as weaker—dispersing reinforcements as they arrived, to hide his strength. Only if the rebels thought he was forced back to them by need would they trust his overtures. Machiavelli had watched this process in an initial puzzlement—close to Valentino, but unable to penetrate his inmost secrets. When the logic of the whole process was revealed to him at last, the daily orchestration of effects that had been necessary to pull it off dazzled Machiavelli.

The next time Machiavelli met Valentino, it was in a situation entirely overshadowed by the event he had foreseen as a potential catastrophe for Valentino—the death of the duke's father, the pope. This occurred on August 18, 1503, seven and a half months after the coup at Sinigaglia. Valentino had spent the interval trying to solidify his holdings—against, mainly, Venetian opposition. Not only was the death of Alexander VI a blow; Valentino himself, who was in the Vatican at the time, almost died of the same illness, probably a form of malaria. (Rumor, which connected all Borgia deaths with poison, claimed that they poisoned themselves, by accident or design or a combination of the two.)[35] Thus the crisis for Valentino, one that was bound to occur at Alexander's death, was made far more testing by his own immobilization. Nonetheless, the pope elected in September—Pius III—was backed by the French, who were still allied with Valentino; so he seemed to have survived. But Pius, an old man chosen as a compromise to serve while opposing factions in the clergy jockeyed for power, was dead within a month of his installation; and Valentino, still convalescing from his scrape with death, was farther removed from the shadow of his father's influence. Cardinal Giuliano della Rovere, excluded from Rome under Alexander, had stayed in the city since the conclave that elected Pius, actively working for his own election when Pius should die. He was on top of a situation that Valentino had been absent from, first while sick and then while touring the Romagna in his earliest days of recovery.

Machiavelli found a different duke in Rome from the one he had watched, for months, at Imola. Since Machiavelli had missed the first conclave, which elected Pius III, he had not seen Valentino when he was at death's door. Over a month later, the duke was not ill in any obvious ways, but he was subtly drained of the confidence he had displayed in Machiavelli's earlier dealings with him. Surprisingly, given his earlier sympathy with Valentino at the moment of his triumph, Machiavelli displays more contempt for his fallen condition than sympathy with it.

Some of this change in tone may come from the demands of his audience. Machiavelli is, after all, writing private correspondence for the use of his republic, and there is every reason to think the Florentine foreign office (the Council of Ten) had expressed displeasure at his pro-Valentino dispatches of the preceding year.[36] There is also the fact that Valentino was pitted against another political genius this time: Giuliano della Rovere, shortly to become Pope Julius II, one of the towering figures of the Renaissance. Even on short acquaintance with della Rovere, Machiavelli wrote with a professional's admiration for a politician who had established such trust in his word that, when he did betray it, he could afford to wait until the highest stakes were at issue.[37]

Machiavelli thought it the ultimate imbecility for Valentino to take the word of this inveterate family enemy. When Valentino saw he could not prevent the election of Giuliano, he tried to join him, making the maximum use of his assets, some of which the pope would clearly need in his earliest days of rule. Valentino had the support of the Spanish bishops his father had created. He was also in league, now, with the Spanish rulers of Naples and Sicily. He still had some money his father had left him, along with a dwindling but still formidable army, and some castles held by his loyalists in the Romagna.

These last items were his best cards. The new pope needed those old papal territories, and even the historian Francesco Guicciardini—who would shortly be governing the Romagna at the behest of Pope Julius—admitted that Valentino (for whom he never shared Machiavelli's enthusiasm) had established himself as a ruler worthy of his subject's loyalty:

> The Romagna was inclined to devotion to Valentino because it had learned from experience how much more tolerable it had been for that region to serve all together under a single powerful lord than for each of those cities to remain under a particular prince, who could not defend them because of his weakness or benefit them because of his poverty, but rather was bound to oppress them inasmuch as his small revenues were insufficient for his support. The Romagnoli also remembered that as a result of Valentino's authority and greatness and because of the honest administration of justice, that country had remained at peace and been spared the factional conflicts which had previously vexed them continually and frequently resulted in assassinations. Valentino's measures had served to make the people feel kindly disposed toward him, and similarly he had won many of them over by giving them benefits, by distributing money among troops, government officials and magistrates (both of his domain and of the Church), and helping ecclesiastics in matters which would be beneficial to his father: whence neither the example of the other states where everyone was rebelling, nor the memory of their former lords, estranged them from Valentino.[38]

A man so entrenched in the area Pope Julius needed could not be dismissed at once; but Machiavelli was sure that Julius would betray and destroy Valentino as rapidly as possible. When he saw Valentino refusing to admit this to himself, he was scathing in his judgment:

> The Duke lets himself be rapt up by his lively self-assurance—he believes that the word of another is to be relied on, though his own never was.[39]

> Behold how his sins have led him, step by step, toward his humiliation [*penitenza*]—which may God turn to good.[40]

This pious note was struck again, shortly after Valentino's fall, in the rhymes Machiavelli wrote on Florence's recent history:

> Alexander, by heaven killed,
> Left his son's reign askew,
> with rot and fissures filled. . . .

> The new Pope fed his [Valentino's] mind—
> The misleading Duke misled,
> Deceived by his own kind.[41]

Some have found it surprising that Machiavelli, after this harsh judgment on Valentino's fall, would "rehabilitate" the man in *Il Principe*, written twelve years after that fall. It is true that the later book takes into account the famous illness Machiavelli had not witnessed. It has even been alleged that he uses that illness as an excuse for his hero, exaggerating its impact. But even Guicciardini describes the duke's sickness as a near escape from death.[42]

A better sense of what Machiavelli is up to is provided if we note the restrictions he put on his commendation of Valentino:

> Taking *all* the Duke's actions into account, I would not know how to correct him anywhere. Rather, as I said, would I offer him as the man to be imitated by *all those who have risen suddenly, aided by Luck and others' armies.* . . . Anyone, therefore, who finds it *necessary* to secure *a new one-man rule* against enemies, to recruit allies, to conquer by power or trickery, to become loved and feared by subjects, to be followed and obeyed by troops, to get rid of those who would (or should) challenge him, to replace settled ways with new measures, to be harsh *and* generous to others, to get rid of rebellious troops and create loyal ones, to keep on good terms with kings and other princes (so that they are happy to join or slow to resist him)—such a man can find no more immediate [*freschi*] examples of them all than this man's actions.[43]

That last sentence is a brief biography of Valentino, and it comes down, in terms of practical recommendations, to saying that the man who judges it *necessary* to do all the things Valentino did—should do so!

Actually, the situation is even more circumscribed than one can tell from these isolated sentences. Valentino is one example of a severely restricted type, "the new *principe*"—the *initiator* of a *one-man* realm.[44] Founding any state is a heroic task in the humanist tradition Machiavelli speaks from and for. State founders (*conditores imperiorum*) were the first heroes Plutarch considered in his *Parallel Lives*, the highest benefactors of mankind according to Francis Bacon.[45] Founding a *republic* is so superhuman a task that it takes an almost saintly self-abnegation, according to Machiavelli's *Discourses*. Initiating one-man rule is not quite that hard, though its results are less stable. In focusing on this latter situation, Machiavelli says that a man who sets up the primacy by his own efforts (*virtù*), without Luck's help, has a better chance of holding on to it, because he put in place some of his means for ruling in the process of working his way up. (To that extent, his "new" realm is not entirely new—those subdued as he rose are already settled into their role by the time he finishes his rise.) But a man suddenly swept to the top by Luck has not acquired friends along the way, or defeated challengers: he must do all this at once, *de novo*. It is an almost impossible assignment. Only the unstable political conditions of Italy in Machiavelli's time made it seem necessary to offer advice for a job no one should have to undertake in the first place. This is the supremely trying role Machiavelli gives to Valentino—not one that many can or should aspire to.

It is quite wrong to say that Valentino is a model ruler for Machiavelli, whose ideal state was a republic. His preferred founders were of the self-abnegating type Plutarch proposed in the persons of Solon, Lycurgus, or Numa. In praising such moral exemplars, Guicciardini argued, Machiavelli "the immoralist" was too naively moral.[46] But Machiavelli, like every humanist, knew that all forms of government, and especially the pure forms, fall. Thus, when the republic he had served fell in 1512, defeated in its experiment at government without the strong hand of a Medici "boss," Machiavelli studied the problem of making a one-man rule comparatively stable and successful.

Since Machiavelli dedicated *Il Principe* to the grandson of Lorenzo Medici, after trying to keep the Medici from returning to Florence during the republican period, he is accused of opportunism—though some suspect he is being satirical: having seen the failure of his favored moral realm, he describes what follows as *necessarily* immoral![47] But, aside from basic plausibility, these interpretations labor under a false distinction that intrudes far more widely into the discussion of Machiavelli—the belief that the author sequestered his thinking into a "moral part" (expounded in the *Discourses*) devoted to republics, and an "immoral part" devoted to one-man rule.

It is true that Machiavelli prefers republics as better governments in themselves: they spread *virtù* around, while one-man rule monopolizes it. But republics have their own faults—the squabbles that lead to anarchy (as in the disorder of the Romagna before Valentino brought it *buon governo*). And, even in one-man rule, the most satisfying fame a man can aspire to is the reputation of a good lawgiver, or reformer, or protector of the people. In terms of mere ambition and glory, this is an effective motive.

Truly a *principe* who seeks worldly glory ought to wish for power over a corrupt city, not to complete its ruin like Caesar but to repristinate it like Romulus. Truly the heavens offer no greater chance for reputation, nor can man desire a greater.[48]

Thus neither form has a monopoly on good government. Each has its crises—those in a republic arising from rudderless debility, those in a one-man regime from resistance to the ruler's will.

When all is said, and when Valentino's very special circumstances are recognized, the question again arises: why so much fuss about a minor adventurer who failed? Garrett Mattingly takes Machiavelli's fascination with Valentino as a sign of the author's essential shallowness.[49] But the real shallowness is in those who think Machiavelli was, either straightforwardly or satirically, offering Valentino as a model for general emulation. Why should anyone want to imitate a man who, though he made no correctable mistakes, was a failure at the age of twenty-seven (and dead at thirty-one), leaving no permanent legacy behind him but an accumulation of hatreds and dark rumors?

Nor can Machiavelli be said to recommend the forming of new states. In general, he agrees with Plutarch, and with such later interpreters of Plutarch as Montesquieu and Rousseau, that the best chance for founding a state is confined to the infancy of a race, when morals have not been too much corrupted. Usually *nuovo* has a pejorative air in Machiavelli, as other words for the new (*neos, kainos, novus*) did in his classical sources—it meant "crude, raw, harsh, unmellowed by time, custom, or ancestral prerogative." It was often a synonym for "illegitimacy," and thus for "instability"—the great curses of the time.[50]

One will not get far in understanding Machiavelli's concentration on Valentino unless one can accept the fact that this "pragmatic" author is drawn to the romance of failure. Luck "piles on" at the end of Valentino's short career. *Una estraordinaria ed estrema malignità di Fortuna* combines (1) Alexander's death, (2) Valentino's illness, (3) the early death of Pius III, and (4) the opposed *virtù* of Giuliano. Luck had set Valentino up in the first place, by making him not only a *nuovo principe*, but one of the most unstable kind, who had risen by the arms of others, not his own *virtù*. What Machiavelli sees in Valentino is the extreme case (and he was drawn to extremes) of man's unequal struggle with Luck. Only his amazing *virtù* let him stay in the ring with her for his two years of rapid accomplishment. His desperate measures were brilliant because of the odds against him. Admittedly, this is not a case study for understanding ordinary political life. On the other hand, what is extreme about Valentino is important, in reduced measure, to the life of all rulers or leaders—a need to cope with the unexpected. Machiavelli's claim that Luck governs a little over half of human affairs is not restricted to extraordinary blows from the Lady but covers all the difficult affairs of state. Foreign enemies, divided subjects, rival leaders—all these interact to produce new threats every day. Willingness to run this intimidating obstacle course is itself a form of *virtù*, of courage to face the unforeseen.

This sense of everyday crisis is what makes Machiavelli use his dramatic either-or-technique, a technique so pronounced, especially in *Il Principe*, that it can easily be satirized. Everything is sorted into rhetorical opposites.

> "There are two kinds of men," he seems often to be saying, "thin men and fat. Now if your enemy is a fat man . . ."[51]

Guicciardini made one of the shrewdest criticisms of Machiavelli when he said that choice cannot be reduced to such stark terms. When Machiavelli proposes the paradox, for instance, that weaker generals should take the offense while stronger ones *await* attack, Guicciardini said that many factors would have to be weighed before this could be considered a rational choice—the terrain involved, the economic conditions of each side, the prior maneuvers or engagements, the state of third powers and their likelihood of intervening, etc.[52]

Machiavelli could answer that he isolates certain aspects of political and military activity for consideration *in themselves*—i.e., with the assumption that other things are equal, or not affecting the choice under study. Much of Machiavelli's considerable claim to have made a science of politics is his creation of "laboratory experiments." Reinserting the isolated choice into the web of reality will of course call for considering other matters (themselves the object of similar "laboratory treatment") with which they become connected again.

Yet this is not the whole of the matter. Though Machiavelli begins each thought experiment with a stark choice to be made (either/or), that choice immediately entails a new one, which entails a new one, and so on. Each branch of the original fork ramifies into new branches, each with its own thicket of twigs. The testing that Machiavelli envisions is like the shooting range for certain military trainees, where benign and hostile figures pop up and one must shoot rapidly at the right one—only to have two more figures appear. An endless series of "kills" keeps one in the game only so long as the enemy is being shot. Even one shot at the wrong person means that one has lost the game.

What makes Machiavelli's advice so practical is his insistent preaching of the truth that nothing stays the same in the volatile mix of passions, pride, and physical shortages that make up the ruler-ruled relationship. One should always expect new turnings of Luck's interconnected wheels.[53] This prevents one from resting in whatever power is gained, mistaking it for a fixed *thing* instead of a *process* in precarious equipoise. One is always on the defensive in Machiavelli's scheme, expecting trouble from any or all directions, *reacting* to adversity. Even Valentino's most daring initiative was taken in response to the conspiracy of Magione meant to overthrow *him*.

If one is to avoid disconnected improvisations to ad hoc threats, one must achieve a defensive *strategy* of interconnected moves—must build a system of dikes and dams to contain probable inundation by Luck's torrents (to use the Homeric simile). It is surprising how few commentators have noticed that the most important and recurring strategy recommended by Machiavelli is—currying the favor of one's subjects. Valentino's last and best prop, after all, was the loyalty of those in the Romagna whom he had *governed well*.

In his discussions of warfare, a condition he considered interchangeable with politics (as it mainly was in his day), Machiavelli stresses again and again the limited use of mere natural advantages—terrain, money, artillery, fortresses. None of these can be of any help without *men* willing to use them. The ardor and loyalty of the troops must be won by engaging their affections and gratitude. In discussions of his war writings, this is usually reduced to questions of troop "morale." But it belongs in a larger framework of Machiavelli's concern that subjects' loyalties be those of a *citizenry*, not a mercenary band. Machiavelli thought a republic had more opportunities to engage that kind of loyalty—but for that very reason the *principe* should strive all the harder to win his subjects' esteem and support. Otherwise he is forever trying to control a mob rather than mustering an army:

No one can be strong or safe who holds his state on a basis of mercenary support, since mercenaries are divided, greedy, and undisciplined; disloyal, boastful among themselves, skulking before the enemy. They have no fear of God, nor trust from men. They prevent conquest only when there are no foes. In peace, you are *their* prey; in war, you are the *enemy's*. The reason for this is that they have no real regard (*amore*) for you, or any other reason for staying in the field than their wages—which are never high enough to make them face death for you. [54]

Those words are from *Il Principe*, not from the *Discourses*—destroying the idea that only republican leaders must solicit their subjects' love. When considering the subject of fortresses in *Il Principe*, Machiavelli says that forts used against one's own subjects are dangerous—for who will man them *except* the subjects?

The best fortress possible is not to be hated by your subjects. No matter how many fortresses you have, if your people hate you, forts will not save you. . . . I would condemn anyone who, because he trusts in his fortifications, discounts the hatred of his people. [55]

These are not passing remarks but a continuing concern. In chapter 10 of *Il Principe*, Machiavelli admits that forts can be useful at times, but only so long as one has "loving" (loyal) troops to bear the hardships of a siege inside them. Otherwise, the troops will turn the forts over to their assailants.

It is no easy prospect to attack a ruler whose land is vigorous and who is not hated by his people. [56]

So a *principe* who has a strong city, and who has not made himself hated, is proof against assault—or if assailants come, they will be humiliated. [57]

In the *Discourses*, Machiavelli says that even a good fortification system should be distrusted—it can corrupt a ruler, lulling him into less reliance on the citizenry, making him careless about nurturing loyalties:

Fortresses, one must admit, are raised for protection from foes or from subjects—in the first case, they are unnecessary, in the second they do positive harm. Let us begin with the second case, with the positive harm they do. I posit it that a *principe* or a republic fearful of subjects, as if they might rebel, would *not* be fearful but for the subjects' hatred; and that hatred would not exist but for the ruler's misbehavior; and that would not exist but for the ruler's belief that he can hold the subjects down with force, or else from his inability as a governor; and one thing that can make a ruler believe in his power to hold the subjects down is his imposition on them of fortresses—so the mistreatment of subjects that causes their hatred is linked to the possession of such fortresses. And where that is the case, the fortresses are more harmful, by a great deal, than protective—precisely, as I have said, because *they encourage reckless and abusive behavior toward subjects.*[58]

The importance of having grateful subjects is so central to Machiavelli's system that—other things being equal—a ruler should favor the lesser of two competing powers when an alliance with one or other is to be struck. The weaker side will be more grateful (and less able to go it alone in the future).[59] Honest treatment of one's own subjects is good policy—though ruse and fraud are preferable to brainless malice against a foe.[60] Machiavelli's famous maxims of realpolitik are less shocking when read in context than when quoted as single sentences or paragraphs. He says, for instance, that a ruler who *must* choose the one or the other—to be feared or to be loved—should prefer fear. But this is qualified, later in the same chapter, with the words:

Nonetheless a *principe* should *so* make himself feared that, even if he wins no love, he avoids being hated, since being feared does not necessarily entail being hated; and he can always manage to combine the two if he does not prey on citizens or subjects' property—or on their women.[61]

For the same reason, one should not try to conquer territory whose inhabitants will be too hostile to be ruled.[62] If one tries to do this, the refractory nature of the subjects will make them more a drain on the victor's power than an accretion to it. Conquest of territories one cannot hold is a form of self-defeat (*Discourses* 2.19).

Machiavelli's awareness of all the limits on one-man rule (*principato*) resembles Clausewitz's understanding of war's limits. The role of *Friktion* in the one corresponds to that of Fortuna in the other. But *Friktion* is a constant. Fortuna shifts and veers. *Friktion* grinds down, constantly, both sides engaged in war. Fortuna can favor now one side, now another. Machiavelli's is a more fickle and dramatic world, and his *principe* is even more desperate than Clausewitz's general in his struggle against the odds. Nonetheless, both general and *principe* depend on followers—on the troops' morale, on the subjects' loyalty. Machiavelli can recommend tricky or even treacherous dealings with a foe, an ally, a rival state, a diplomatic partner; but subjects should be betrayed once at most, and only to put one in a better position to please them afterward. One cannot go out alone to duel with Fortuna. More than the robber captain needs his band, the *principe* needs for others to be engaged with him in his projects. He must, at some level, be good enough, to enough of his followers, to bind their loyalty. If this occurs, the followers can actually take delight in his false dealings with others.

The charm of the rogue leader is undeniable. The Boston mayor James Curley held and ran for office from jail—but his Irish constituents felt sure that, however much he robbed the rest of mankind, he had genuinely at heart the interests of the Irish. Given that condition, a consummate thief, an outrageous breaker of convention, an artist in crime, can exhibit the qualities that drew Machiavelli to Valentino.

We know Valentino mainly from Machiavelli's word portrait of him. Though Valentino hired Leonardo da Vinci to work on his fortifications in the Romagna, no portrait—not even a sketch—has survived of this Renaissance patron. But something of the heroic fire in Valentino can be seen in the images of Renaissance leaders.[63] The sense of an unending, eventually losing, battle with Fortuna is best caught in Titian's *Allegory of Time* (1565). Machiavelli said the *principe* must combine the qualities of the lion and the fox.[64] Titian is even more Machiavellian than Machiavelli when he shows man with a dog's eagerness in youth, a lion's boldness in maturity, a fox's slyness in age. The light that shines from the right hits the youth full in the face, in a partly blinding glow. It models the mature man's features, making shadow serve, like experience, to round the face out. The old man's features—Titian's, at the time he painted this—are dark except for a bit of light still reaching his forehead, the last bit of wisdom and skill he can deploy against the night.[65] The idea that Machiavelli admired villains and urged villainy on rulers is wrong but understandable. He did sympathize with those in power, and understood that they need all the ferocity and wiliness they can muster. His tone is not that of Shakespeare's cackling Richard. It is more subtle in its sense of tragedy.

An Allegory of Time—*Titian*
The National Gallery, London.

ANTITYPE
Piero Soderini

One scholar has suggested that Machiavelli learned the skills of a ruler by serving a man, Piero Soderini, who lacked those skills.[1] Machiavelli was a trusted diplomat and militia organizer during Soderini's tenure as the most powerful official in Florence—he was even called Soderini's "mannikin" (*mannerino*).[2] Soderini is a convenient antitype to Valentino—though one odd link between them is the role Pope Julius II played in bringing both men down.[3]

Soderini was given a power base that, in Machiavelli's opinion, should have been expanded. His title was standard-bearer of justice—*Gonfaloniere della giustizia*. The standard-bearer was the head of the Signoria, the executive committee of state, but he had only one vote in that committee (out of nine), and the office was short-lived (only two months) until the Great Council appointed Soderini (in 1502) standard-bearer for life. The business of state, split among a number of boards and committees, was hard to carry on without a greater measure of continuity. Soderini, a shrewd manager of finances, kept up a dogged campaign to regain for Florence the rebellious city of Pisa, and he prosecuted a vigorously pro-French policy that made Julius II put Florence under an ecclesiastical ban.

Soderini was put in by the aristocrats to strengthen their control of the state, but he refused to serve them abjectly. Machiavelli admired him for his integrity, but says he was mistaken not to win *some* factions to his side. Soderini hoped to play a neutral role as arbiter in the fierce squabbles of Florentine political life. He thought, according to Machiavelli, that he could adjudicate such conflicts from a position above them. He would not play parties against each other by joining one or another at key junctures: nor would he increase his own officers' power to counter the power of his foes.

This restraint was wise and moral. Evil, however, should not be given free rein out of a concern for one's own virtuous position, when that position will itself be easily crushed by the evil.[4]

Soderini undermined his own values by refusing to use harsh measures to defend them in the political arena—just as the Dominican friar Savonarola had when he presented himself to Florence as a moral "prophet unarmed."[5]

Machiavelli admired Soderini as a man but not as a leader. He admired Valentino as a leader but not as a man. The politician is caught between these two poles. Is it impossible to combine the best of these opposed ideals? In some circumstances, no doubt it is. Nonetheless, Machiavelli hoped for such rare combinations of morality and *virtù*, and thought he glimpsed them in the heroes of antiquity.

16.
SAINTLY LEADERSHIP

Dorothy Day

E very major culture known to us has honored persons held to be sacred. Some of these people are wonder-workers, who have supernatural powers—seers and sacred healers. Some have liberating exemptions—they seem less dependent on their bodies or on physical comfort than the rest of us are. The most spectacular exemption is demonstrated by martyrs—they escape the need to live. This awes those less willing to sacrifice themselves for some value beyond life itself. William James observed the phenomenon:

> No matter what a man's frailties otherwise may be, if he be willing to risk death, and still more if he suffer it heroically, in the service he has chosen, the fact consecrates him forever. Inferior to ourselves in this way or that, if yet we cling to life, and he is able "to fling it away like a flower," as caring nothing for it, we account him in the deepest way our born superior. Each of us in his own person feels that a high-hearted indifference to life would expiate all his shortcomings. [1]

Not even martyrdom is enough of itself to make the slain hero a *leader*. Some martyrs were not leaders before they died for their beliefs. Their posthumous influence does not create followership, though admiration may cause emulation. Other people may lead lives that are slow martyrdoms—"witnessings," as the word means in Greek—by devotion to a cause beyond most worldly cares. They, too, are not necessarily leaders. The Catholic Church may canonize reclusive saints, giving them an influence on the believers who pray to them. But the cultist who wears a hair shirt in honor of St. Thomas More is, in terms of mere psychological mechanics, like the fan who refuses to wear an undershirt because Clark Gable wore none in the movie *It Happened One Night*. Some saints can be "holy" without having any earthly influence recognized outside the circle of such admirers. As William James said of Teresa of Avila:

> In the main her idea of religion seems to have been that of an endless amatory flirtation—if one may say so without irreverence—between the devotee and the deity; and apart from helping younger nuns to go in this direction by the inspiration of her example and instruction, there is absolutely no human use in her, or sign of any general human interest.[2]

This is what many people think of as "the saint," holy perhaps, as idiots are in some cultures, but of little *use* as a leader in the rougher world of human needs.

Yet there are other saints who do earthly work as well as bear heavenly witness. They usually put the heavenly witness first in their own minds; but the world honors them for services performed here below. To continue quoting James:

> When we are in need of assistance, we can count upon the saint lending his hand with more certainty than we can count upon any other person.[3]

One does not have to be a Catholic to honor Mother Teresa for her mobilization of care and nursing and feeding operations among the poor. Ruskin called such people "working saints"—to be distinguished from the kind who "with their cloudy outlines disguise, or with their impossible virtue deaden, human response."[4]

What sets the saint apart from others who perform useful services is that the saint looks beyond the service performed, toward some *transcendent* goal or reward. Even the godless do not equate Mother Teresa with the United Way. When the saint performs the world's work, it is done as a donkey draws a cart, by turning his back on it. To see that this is a separate type of leadership, we have to distinguish it from mere wonder-working or good-doing in themselves. The charismatic leader, like King David, performs divine deeds—but David was not a moral saint, even to his ardent followers. The philanthropist *does* good, but one can doubt whether he or she *is* good in any superlative way. The saint, by contrast, draws followers for what he or she is as well as for what he or she does. The hint of higher possibilities in life, of a larger sphere of aspiration, is what James found in such leaders:

> The world is not yet with them, so they often seem in the midst of the world's affairs to be preposterous. Yet they are the impregnators of the world, unifiers and animators of potentialities of goodness which, but for them, would lie forever dormant.[5]

Such people are "outsize," for better or worse, escaping the boundaries that hold the rest of us constrained by self-regard, convention, or fear. The protection against their challenge is to dismiss them as outstandingly crazy. Most saints met that response at some point. Dorothy Day, the founder of the Catholic Worker Movement, found it in her own home, in her father's nagging contempt for what she had become. He wrote in 1937, when his daughter was forty years old:

> Dorothy, the oldest girl [of his five children], is the nut of the family. When she came out of the university she was a Communist. Now she's a Catholic crusader. She owns and runs a Catholic paper and skyhooks all over the country, delivering lectures. She has one girl in a Catholic school and is separated from her [common-law] husband. You'll probably hear of her if you have any Catholic friends. She was in Miami last winter and lived with [cousins] Clem and Kate. I wouldn't have her around me.[6]

Day was hurt by her father's rejection of her, which was unwavering from the time she joined the Socialist Party in her teens. She obviously admired her father, a dour Irish writer who worked on novels and plays but made his living as a racetrack journalist. All three of his sons followed him into journalism—as did Dorothy. His daughter was the only one for whom he expressed no pride or support.

This was not because of any noisy rebellion in the girl's past. She was always quiet and accommodating; but from infancy she kept a certain space between herself and others. This went oddly along with a desire to observe people close up. As a child, she used to walk strange neighborhoods, wondering what the people who lived there thought. She would go into churches, to see how people behaved there. One of her vivid early memories was of the San Francisco earthquake in 1904, when she was eight—not only of her wheeled little bed rolling about on the floor, but of an influx of strangers brought together in a community of disaster. She observed her mother, for the first time, giving clothes to those whose homes had perished in the quake.[7]

After the quake, her family moved from the San Francisco area to Chicago, where Dorothy grew up taking long walks along Lake Michigan. All her life she sought the shores of lakes and oceans, which she found conducive to meditation. Later on, she would reserve serious thinking for rides on the Staten Island ferry. At seventeen, she won a writing scholarship to the University of Illinois in Urbana, where she quickly searched out campus radicals—perhaps in part because they were the most exotic parts of the student body. She always went to "other neighborhoods" of the mind, to observe different lives, discontented with what was at hand. She was reading Dostoyevsky, and thought he might be causing her discontent. "Maybe if I stayed away from books more this restlessness would pass," she wrote to a friend.[8]

Her best friend at the university was Rayna Simons, a radiant Jewish rebel who ended her short life in Moscow. When Day's family moved to New York after her sophomore year in Urbana (1916), Dorothy went along, ready to plunge into radical journalism—not, as her father no doubt informed her, a remunerative part of the profession. As soon as she had income from the socialist publication *Call*, she moved out of the family home and took her own apartment. She joined the Industrial Workers of the World and worked for the Anti-Conscription League.

Since radical journalism was underpaid, it was dependent on (and open to) cheap labor. When she moved to *The Masses*, edited by Max Eastman and Floyd Dell, Day was the dependable one, ready to make up the magazine when others were off making speeches. She was sometimes the editor in chief because she was the only editor on the premises. She learned every aspect of getting a journal out on a shoestring, a skill that would be important when she launched the *Catholic Worker* sixteen years later.

The magazines she worked for sent her to cover slums, strikes, and radical meetings. She interviewed Trotsky during his New York visit. She went to Washington with those opposing World War I. But her most important trip to Washington was not undertaken as a journalist, and it led to her first imprisonment. She went with a friend, Peggy Baird (the poet Hart Crane's best woman friend), to join suffragist demonstrations outside Woodrow Wilson's White House. Day was not a suffragist—like Mother Jones, she thought of the vote as a reformist measure, not a radical one. But she was ready to protest the treatment of suffragists in jail. She was arrested with others. When bail was put up for them, they went out and got arrested again. On the third arrest, they were sentenced to thirty days in jail. Day went on a hunger strike with the other women thrown into the Occoquan Work House. Authorities were force-feeding the hunger strikers, afraid that some prominent women (such as Alice Paul) might die on their premises. On the sixth day of the strike, the fasters were put in a hospital for intravenous feeding. On the tenth day, the strikers won all their demands and were sent back to prison for the rest of their sentence.

Returned to the jail with ordinary prisoners, Day was stunned by the raw sexuality of the women. When the prisoners bathed in communal tubs on Saturday night, preparing for their Sunday visits from men, "I saw sex at its crudest and was ashamed that I should be stirred by it."[9] The debility caused by her fast had sent the twenty-year-old Day into a black depression, out of which she began to pray (which she still considered a form of weakness). Returned to the prison, she tried to forget her "lapse" into faith.[10]

Back in New York, she was an uncooperative government witness against her colleagues on *The Masses*, which had been closed for seditious libel during the war. She acquired a new circle of friends, more literary than political, which included the writers Malcolm Cowley (soon to be Peggy Baird's husband), Max Bodenheim, Mike Gold, Kenneth Burke, Allen Tate, Hart Crane, and—most important to her—Eugene O'Neill. Tate, a Southern agrarian, praised life in the country—the agrarians had picked up some ideas from the Catholic "distributist" movement in England, a movement that would later claim Day as one of its victims. But at this point, she warmed more to O'Neill the playwright—to his mysticism about the sea, to his maudlin recitals of Catholic poetry when he was drinking with Day and others in their Village hangout (Jimmy Wallace's bar).

For months Day drank through the night, then wandered out at dawn to stop by churches that were just opening. Though she did not realize it at the time, she was absorbing O'Neill's Catholicism, from which he was still wriggling himself free. One night, as they were drinking together, a despondent Village friend, Louis Holladay, took a phial from his pocket and swallowed most of its contents. When he went into grotesque convulsions, O'Neill and others left, presumably not wanting to get involved in a police investigation of drug use. Day held the thrashing man in her arms till he died, then took the phial so the police would not find it, and went to tell O'Neill what had happened.[11]

Day had fallen in love with various men, especially those who seemed, like O'Neill, "doomed."[12] But now she became deeply infatuated with a tough-guy journalist, Lionel Moise, who had awed the young Hemingway when they both worked at the *Kansas City Star*. Day met him when Moise had drunk and brawled himself out of newspapers into an orderly's job at the hospital where Day was doing wartime nursing. Drawn before to sensitive "boys," she was swept away by Moise, ten years her senior, because "You are hard—I fell in love with you because you are hard."[13] The infatuation was recorded in Day's only published novel, which has come in for some justified feminist criticism.[14] Day even nursed Moise's other lovers, after he had dropped her, when these women got into drug or police troubles. This led to her second imprisonment. Having pursued Moise to Chicago, Day went with a woman, a recovering drug addict in love with Moise, to a house rented by IWW union men. When Chicago police raided the place, they arrested the two women as visiting prostitutes.

This experience in jail was totally different from Day's earlier one, which she had shared with high-minded (and middle-class) suffragists. Day was struck by the way the prostitutes protected each other from the police—another community formed in disaster, like that created by the earthquake. She was strip-searched and investigated for venereal disease, and the humiliation formed a bond with the victims of official callousness. When she ran her own "hospitality houses" later, she made no demands on those who came for food or shelter.

Earlier, while she was still in New York with Moise, she had told him she was pregnant, and he ordered her to get an abortion. She did; but when she returned from it, he had left her. Suffering from her rejection, she married on the rebound a rich suitor and went abroad with him, where she spent most of a year in Sicily writing the novel about her affair with Moise (*The Eleventh Virgin*). Some have treated Day's later contrition over her early life as a saintly exaggeration of remorse. They think she felt guilty mainly for sexual affairs; but the one truly disgraceful act of her life was having *legal* sex, with her own husband. She used the man she married, and she clearly had the spiritual discernment to see that such exploitation of others is deserving of remorse.[15]

She had left her husband by the time she returned to America in 1921 (they were divorced a few years later). She continued her work as a journalist—for the *Liberator* in Chicago, then the *Item* in New Orleans (where she wrote a series on taxi dancers after becoming one). With money derived from the sale of movie rights to her novel, she bought a cottage on the beach of Staten Island, where she lived with her new lover Forster Batterham (Kenneth Burke's brother-in-law), by whom she had a daughter, Tamar. Batterham, a marine biologist who loved the sea, shared many of Day's tastes, but was tone-deaf to religion. Their time by the sea was happy, despite her nagging sense of something beyond the beauty of the moment. The same emotions, stirred by the waves, that nurtured her love for Batterham were driving her away from him, toward faith. She recalled their life together as her peak of worldly content.

> Sometimes he went out to dig bait if there were a low tide and the moon was up. He stayed out late on the pier fishing, and came in smelling of seaweed and salt air; getting into bed, cold with the chill November air, he held me close to him in silence. . . . I loved him for the odds and ends I had to fish out of his sweater pockets and for the sand and shells he brought in with his fishing. I loved his lean cold body as he got into bed smelling of the sea, and I loved his integrity and stubborn pride.[16]

William James describes conversion as the breaking in on the conscious mind of connections long growing in the subconscious.[17] The crisis for Day was the birth of her child, the sense of responsibility for another's soul that this brought home to her. She wanted Tamar baptized. It was done, in July of 1927. But Day could not be baptized herself, the priests told her, unless she either married Batterham or left him. Batterham was opposed in principle to marriage. She had to leave. She was baptized, five months after her daughter.

In order to support herself and her child, Day began writing for Catholic periodicals, principally *Commonweal*, and wrote a play on which the Pathé Motion Picture Company took an option. After frustrating months as a dialogue writer in Hollywood, she spent seven months in Mexico, writing on workers' conditions for *Commonweal*. Back in New York, she lived by freelance writing and secretarial work for Catholic organizations. Her social conscience was still active, so she went to Washington with the Hunger Strikers March that picketed President Hoover's White House. She noticed, once more, the absence of any Catholic leaders in the march, and went alone to pray at the Catholic Shrine of the Immaculate Conception in Washington. Day had not been able to put together her social concerns and her new faith. She seemed to have reached a dead end, sundered from her radical friends, unimportant to the Catholic community she had joined. She prayed desperately for guidance.

When she returned to her New York apartment, the answer to her prayers, a quietly forceful bum, was sitting at the kitchen table lecturing her sister-in-law. Peter Maurin, an autodidact obsessed with ideas, had led a vagabond life since his birth in France in 1877. He lived as a teacher and laborer, haunting churches and libraries, haranguing anyone he met. [18] Much of this country would become briefly infatuated with Maurin's secular equivalent, the "teamster philosopher" Eric Hoffer, in the 1950s. But Maurin filled a permanent need for Dorothy Day from the time they met in 1932.

If their encounter had occurred in the Middle Ages, Giotto might have painted it as another meeting of St. Francis of Assisi with St. Clare. Only this Clare outshone her Francis: Day was more vivid and commanding than Maurin—though without Maurin, her great work would never have been launched. Day, as a convert, had no standing, not even in her own eyes, with the cautious officialdom of her church. Priests assured her that the way things are is the way they always were and had to be. Maurin knew better. Formed in a French lay tradition, he had read and pondered Catholic theology and philosophy for decades—he could supply Day with apt quotes from St. Thomas or the papal encyclicals. But he also believed that the gospel was not being preached to the poor because church officials showed so little love for them.

It took a while for Day to realize what Maurin meant for her. Most people thought him a bore, and so did she at first. She tried to get rid of him, but he never took a hint, or even a rebuke; he just kept talking. He put his truths in maxim form, breaking up his sentences into didactically recitable breath-units. Day would later print them stichically in the *Catholic Worker* as "Easy Essays"—not a title Maurin liked. He thought them hard and deep.

Maurin was old enough to be Day's father (he looked older than the twenty years that separated them), and in the deepest sense he became the only father she ever had, her "father in the faith." He had something to pass on to her. She could rebel against this father, more than against her biological one—but the breaks were brief and soon healed.

The first fight occurred over their first project together, their newspaper. Maurin believed that the Christian gospel called urgently for three things—intellectual renewal through a worker's publication, houses of Christian "hospitality" (he rejected the condescending term "charity" for performing a *duty* to the poor), and a return to life on the land.

This last point meant little to Day at the outset—though she liked to read and write by the seashore, she was basically an urban person. Farms would later plague her life, Maurin's evil gift to her. But the first two items on his list appealed to her instantly. She would feed and clothe the poor, and her work on "little papers" of the left had prepared her to put out a Catholic publication. She did not, yet, have the money to buy food or shelter for others, but she could start a paper with only the cost of the first issue—something kept to a minimum by use of the press at the Paulist Fathers house where she had worked.

Despite the enthusiasm Day and her friends poured into the newspaper, Maurin grew morose as the dummy took shape on her kitchen table. Too much secular protest, he thought (too many ideas not his own). "Everybody's paper is nobody's paper." He disappeared from the house. At last, when she no longer wanted to, Day had found a way to get rid of him. On May 1, 1933, in the depth of the Depression, Day and three others went to Union Square, thronged with Communists celebrating May Day, to distribute (for a penny a copy) the *Catholic Worker*.

Maurin returned, after the paper had appeared, and insisted that his name be taken off the list of editors. He would be responsible only for articles he wrote and signed himself. He thought the paper "too political." His own form of personalism maintained that worldly institutions could be undermined by love—they should not be confronted on their own terms. Maurin opposed labor organizations if they resorted to intimidation. "Strikes do not strike me," he would intone (he often mistook a pun for an argument).

Day held firm in this conflict. She was not going to renounce the radical activities she had seen as vehicles of love, not departures from it. But the two were united on the need for hospitality houses, which they soon opened in Greenwich Village and in Harlem. And after they had the money to purchase a farm, Day yielded to Maurin's insistence that a "green revolution" was the proper Christian response to industrial oppression. Maurin's farm ideals were a mixture of Peter Kropotkin's back-to-the-land movement in Russia and the Catholic "distributism' invoked by Southern agrarians like Tate.

The paper proved to be a good fund-raiser for the hospitality houses, shelters made especially important by the Depression. Day touched a need in Catholics that was not filled by official church "charities"—to go out to the poor, live with them, share their lot. Those who could not do this in person sent their money. Soon the New York houses were feeding hundreds of people out of work; then, with the purchase of more space, housing them as well. A dozen other cities set up Catholic Worker houses in imitation of the original.

The Workers lived with the poor, but kept up a daily discipline of prayer, reading, and spiritual instruction. At first, this meant listening to Maurin's droning of his maxims. But soon sympathetic priests, professors, and theologians were helping out at the soup line and then holding seminars on the role of the church in the world. The movement was watched anxiously by Catholic authorities, who assigned Day a diocesan "advisor" to warn her against any doctrinal or disciplinary infractions. Yet Day stayed almost magically exempt from ecclesiastical admonishment. This was partly because she rarely took a confrontational stance with the church (as opposed to her blithe defiance of secular authority). Catholic Workers picketed and agitated when dealing with corporations or the government. With the church, they usually stuck to Maurin's tactic of undermining with love. Day no doubt felt the convert's lingering sense that she had come into the church as a guest. Born Catholics are often readier to tear down any parts of the old homestead that displease them.

But the deeper reason for her remarkable exemption was the response, inside her church and outside it, to Day's obvious sincerity, both in her religious faith and her earthly concerns.[19] This was a woman who fed the poor, not with a handout, but by handing over her life to them. Yet she was also a woman who went to mass every day, and confession weekly, and wrote as much about the spiritual life as about the condition of the poor. As a radical believer, she was a nuisance to some authorities; if they had made her a martyr, she would have been a disaster for them. So, when the Catholic authorities in America favored Franco during the Spanish Civil War, the *Catholic Worker* opposed him with impunity. At the height of the Cold War, Day wrote sympathetically of Marx and Lenin as lovers of the poor—yet when dockworkers struck, Irish cops refused to arrest Catholic Worker picketers.[20]

It was a hard life that Catholic Workers lived, which accounts for the generally rapid turnover of volunteers. Day seemed to bear all the crises with serenity, though her journals show how tomented she was by disagreements among her associates, violence in the hospitality houses, breakdowns (human and mechanical) on the farms. The hospitality houses, since they put no conditions on acceptance of those seeking help, were always coping with drunkards, the mentally ill, the sexually predacious. Day, who treasured her books, her private time with music on the radio, found that others took her belongings, broke in on her privacy with squabbles, demanded that she hear each complaint of workers or guests in the house. Alcoholic priests, or those unhappy with their vocations, had a dreary tendency to seek her out as the solver of their problems.

The farms had been intended by Maurin as permanent family communes; but those who married began to think of the needs of their children, demanding ownership of the fields they worked—Day at last had to decree that only single people could live on the farms, which made for a transitory, unskilled population.

People came to work with her for a while, then left, taking whatever part of the experience they could use in later life. A whole generation of teachers, journalists, and social workers was formed by her—John Cogley, Michael Harrington, Robert Coles, Ed Marciniak, and others. But she felt some of their departures as defections—Harrington left the Catholic Church to become a socialist, Cogley left the pacifist community to become a soldier.

Cogley was part of a great defection that occurred in World War II—young Catholic Workers joining the military despite Day's effort to set up centers for Catholic conscientious objectors. Few heeded her call. War fever closed some hospitality houses, and shrank the numbers at those that survived.

As usual, Day survived the troubles and decline. In the 1950s, the Catholic Workers opposed nuclear arming and McCarthyism with a wave of fasts, picketings, and protests. New houses were founded across the nation, and Day traveled to them constantly, raising money for them, calling on them to make retreats and deepen their prayer life (as hers was deepening at the time).

The sixties brought into the Worker houses a new kind of radical, one that Day found disconcerting largely for generational reasons. She had been daringly sympathetic, in her earlier years, to prostitutes and drunkards. Nearing seventy, she could not feel the same empathy with lesbians or drug users. She had been jailed often for her antinuclear demonstrations, and the lesbianism of the women's prison disgusted her. But she fought her judgmental attitude with a saint's resolve to love everyone. Once she went to jail with the attractive actress Judith Malina Beck

Dorothy Day
Marquette University, Memorial Library Archives

(cofounder of the Living Theater). When the inmates crowded sala-ciously around Beck, reaching to fondle her, Day brusquely demanded of the authorities that Beck be put in her cell. Then she tortured herself with second thoughts: "I found it hard to excuse myself for my own immediate harsh reaction. It is all very well to hate the sin and love the sinner in theory, but it is hard to do in practice. . . . Jesus is this Jackie who is making advances [to Beck]."[21]

Despite all her efforts at sympathy, she felt obliged to "stomp" (in their words) the sixties activists living promiscuously and using drugs in the New York Catholic Worker house. She also withdrew her name from the letterhead of the activists' Catholic Peace Fellowship. This caused a rift in the Catholic left that respected figures like Thomas Merton, the Trap-pist monk, and Daniel Berrigan, the Jesuit priest, labored to close.[22] Day remained loving toward the leaders of the Catholic Peace Fellowship, but she had never questioned her church's stand on things like contraception, abortion, homosexuality, the celibate clergy, or the male priesthood. Her combination of theological conservatism with social radicalism had pro-tected her from being silenced by the church.

Her views were not taken on merely tactical grounds. In fact, her journals are full of prayers to help her avoid doing things for effect, "posing," looking for approval or acclaim. This is the paradox of saintly leaders. This kind of leader is the least accommodating to followers. The ancient prophet must deliver the message God gives him, whether it has any effect or not. There is no absolutism like that of the saints. They must please their God, not their followers—but, paradoxically, that is what draws followers. It was her spiritual intensity that made Day a mentor to several generations of people concerned with the poor. She still fills that role, since the *Catholic Worker* has never suspended publication, and hospitality houses continue to feed and clothe the needy long after her death. The *Catholic Worker* has been read by several generations of young Catholics in seminaries and convents, where it deepened a com-mitment to the poor.

It was as a living mystery that Day looked back on the world from the margins where she chose to live and work. She was called "elfin" in her Greenwich Village days, more radical than anyone in the way she asked for and gave love. Her wondering gaze was caught in an early picture by John Spier, which more than any other image suggests the continuity between her early radicalism and her later dedication.

ANTITYPE

Ammon Hennacy

I n the 1950s, Ammon Hennacy succeeded to the role played formerly by Peter Maurin (who died in 1949)—he was the second-most commanding figure in the movement, second only to Dorothy Day. He thought, for a while, he would make the role permanent by marrying Day—he even became a Catholic to please her. But they were both in their sixties; and Day, though she admitted she was "a reluctant celibate," knew that Hennacy had never in his life settled for just one woman. She admired him for his dedication to the cause of peace, but she was shrewdly aware of his vulnerability to "frilly" girls.[1]

Hennacy could not have been more different from Maurin. He was four years younger than Day—Maurin had been twenty years older. Maurin was a prayerful and quietly insistent talker who did not like intimidation of others or political confrontation. Hennacy was a boisterous activist who engaged in what would be called, in the sixties, "street theater." Indeed, he led the way for many sixties activists. When he climbed over the fence of a military base to deface weapons, he created a form of protest the Berrigan brothers would pursue for years.

Hennacy called himself "a one-man revolution," as Abbie Hoffman would later boast, "The revolution is where my boots hit." He was a rhetorically bellicose pacifist. When a bystander asked him on the picket line, "Do you think you can change the world?" he answered "No, but I'm damn sure that it can't change me!"[2] When he first met Day, he told her he thought Catholic Workers were wishy-washy: "He didn't think our people there [they had met in Milwaukee] had much gumption. None of them had ever been in jail."[3] Day, of course, had been to jail—but that was back in the twenties. Eventually, Hennacy had Day going to jail regularly as part of his antinuclear protests.

Hennacy had admired radical women from the time when, as a teenager in the Midwest (and already a member of the Industrial Workers of the World), he had driven Mother Jones in a horse and buggy to a meeting with West Virginia miners. Mother Jones was still going to jail in what she claimed were her eighties (though she exaggerated her age by at least six years).[4] Thanks to Hennacy, Day would still be going to jail in her seventies (with the striking farmworkers of Cesar Chavez).

It is hard, at first, to see how Day and Hennacy could have worked together so closely for seven years. She was merciless on any tendency of her own toward boastfulness. Hennacy was all boast:

> Characteristically, he pasted all the [newspaper] stories about himself into two or three large scrapbooks which he would take out and give to visitors [to the hospitality house].[5]

Maurin had insisted that everyone should choose his or her own way to serve. Hennacy, the self-professed anarchist, told others exactly how they ought to do everything:

> Someone who is always right, who points out that he knows how to eat, to fast, to sleep, to meet each problem of the day, can also be irksome.[6]

Yet there were some points of common experience and ideals. Like Maurin, Hennacy not only sympathized with workers but had lived much of his life by manual labor, supporting his proselytizing this way. He began his association with the *Catholic Worker* by writing a chronicle of his work experience in a column called "At Hard Labor." Like Day, he had undergone a moment of despair in prison, asked for a Bible, and begun to pray. This was in the Atlanta Federal Penitentiary, where he spent a year and seven months of World War I for refusing military service. (He tried to prod the government into jailing him for resisting the draft in World War II, but he was too old to be drafted anyway.)

Hennacy was a breath of fresh air in the Catholic Worker establishment of the fifties. In a place where more people talked about the dignity of work than actually performed it, he was the first to pitch in on any job that needed doing. He brought discipline to the newspaper's files and production schedule. He had enormous energy. At a time when so much of the federal budget was going to the production of nuclear weapons, he prodded Catholic Workers into imitating his refusal to pay federal taxes.

By updating the concern for peace in the nuclear age, and going out onto the streets to protest, Hennacy equipped the *Catholic Worker* to be part of the sixties. He forced growth on Day and her older associates. As he happily admitted, "I love my enemies, but I'm hell on my friends."[7] This kind of hell Day was happy to suffer, this creative irritation, which did her and all around her good.

But Hennacy was too vain to be a team player for long. It is a tribute to Dorothy Day's moral authority over him that he could stem his restlessness for the seven years he spent with her in New York. In the late fifties, he took a young and pretty Catholic Worker with him to Salt Lake City, where he opened Joe Hill House for the poor. He continued his flamboyant protests and died, as he would have wished, on a picket line. It was 1970, he was seventy-seven years old, and he was protesting the death penalty.[8]

Though he was a brave man who dramatized his sincerely held beliefs, Hennacy was too idiosyncratic to be a real leader. The only time he had a following of any size was when he allied himself with the Catholic Workers. Even among them, there was a rather condescending attitude toward Hennacy's "showboating." It does not invalidate his efforts that he was clearly having so much *fun* at them. There was a certain gaiety even to the stigmatic Francis of Assisi. But Hennacy had no moral *weight* comparable to Day's. No one, even those who disagreed with her, condescended to Day. She shed a radiance from all she did, the kind William James noticed in saintly leaders. The contrast between Day and Hennacy was adumbrated in these words:

> Their [the saints'] sense of mystery in things, their passion, their goodness, irradiate about them and enlarge their outlines while they soften them. They are like pictures with an atmosphere and background; and, placed alongside of them, the strong men of this world and no other seem as dry as sticks, as hard and crude as blocks of stones or brickbats.[9]

Hennacy was a brickbat thrown at the warfare state. Dorothy Day was, as Peter Maurin had hoped, undermining it with love.

Conclusion

I fear that some readers may have opened my book, as they do so many others on the subject, with this question: "How am I to become a leader?" It is an incomplete question. Leader of *whom?* Going *where?* Dr. King would, in any case, have been an impressive preacher, a respected pastor, pampered by his congregation—a leader in that sense. But at a moment in history, he identified a different range of potential followers; lifted up his voice for them; was carried forward, by them, to goals he had not foreseen, but which he ended up pursuing with them. What differentiated him from a successful preacher like, say, Robert Schuller, was a different set of followers and a different goal. How, then, should one become a leader? By finding the right followers and the right goal. One of the two is no good without the other. And they must be right for you and for the historical moment.

But what if one has the followers and the goal, yet is unable to mobilize the former toward the latter? Perhaps one is not meant to be a leader. Not everyone is. That does not consign one to second-class humanity. Hume the original thinker (who has exercised *influence* in history, not *leadership*) was a more important figure than Hume the intellectual leader, with his popular political writings. Roger Smith would have been better off if he had stayed in his office of financial planning, from which he influenced the fortune of General Motors in a benign way, rather than moved up to an office that called for leadership as well as influence.

Other leaders proved inadequate because they were more enamored of their own *image* of leadership than of the followers *or* the goal—General McClellan clearly illustrates that; as, to a lesser degree, do Ammon Hennacy, Adlai Stevenson, or Stephen Douglas. This does not mean leaders must be entirely selfless. Ambition is a useful—often a necessary—fuel for driving the leader. But if it makes him or her blind to the followers' needs and desires, then those cannot be addressed in such a way that they end up mobilized toward the goal. Stevenson preferred losing with grace (and not too much effort) to accomplishing the political projects he praised so mellifluously (in other people's words).

Some of the antitypes I have chosen were great leaders themselves—but not great in the category being considered. Cromwell was a fine leader of men, though he could not lead them to the republican goals he enunciated for them. Robert Moses was a great civil rights leader, though he was not the *rhetorical* leader that Dr. King was.

Some should lead. Others should follow. My book has missed its object if the role of the follower is made somehow less worthy than that of the leader. Dr. King's greatness is genuine, but not entirely his. Hundreds of men, women, and children marched, sang, and protested with him. They were beaten for it, knocked down with hoses, attacked by dogs, thrown into jail, threatened with bombs, killed with bombs, killed with guns, killed with clubs. The heroes were not all leaders. But they were all heroes.

Some of the civil rights leaders were less than heroic. Some were showboaters, backbiters, people more flawed than the ones they marshaled forward. Flawed leaders are as common as noble followers. But the goal was what mattered, to enough of them, to make them risk insult, harm, and their very lives marching toward their goal. It was a joint achievement, as all social accomplishments must be. And once they had reached their goal, being there was more important than sorting out each person's different role in getting them there.

Circumstance is important, if unpredictable. Many get their chance to lead by accident. Angelo Roncalli was chosen pope late in his life, and not because great things were expected of him—quite the opposite. Without realizing it himself, he had prepared well for this unexpected office—he was a good bishop before he was a good pope. But his impact would not have been felt if a body of followers had not also, without knowing it, been preparing themselves in ways that made them respond to him. The ecumenical and liturgical and biblical study groups within

Catholicism had set up a kind of covert activity, in seminaries and parishes, that John XXIII summoned out into the daylight. In that sense, Dorothy Day, affecting so many young Catholic leaders in America, was training them to be followers of John XXIII when he came along. In the same way, Harriet Tubman's missions in the 1850s helped prepare the ground for Lincoln's efforts in the 1860s.

Both Washington and Napoleon needed great revolutions to make them great leaders—different as their actions were (because their revolutions differed so greatly). What would Roosevelt have been without the Depression and World War II? Of course, the leader must not only be given his or her historical moment, but must be able to see that it is a critical time. For this, a sense of history is required. Washington grasped earlier than anyone—even Hamilton—the fact that armed withdrawal from the British Empire would remake the colonies engaged in this secession. He recognized how many forces were opposed to national union, which alone (he believed) could make the former colonies masters of their own situation. With this in mind, he acted throughout the Revolution and after as if setting precedents for a national system of legal responsibility to the American people as a whole. Washington was not a bookish student of history, but he had eagerly absorbed everything he could of the imperial British navy's and army's action on his continent. His sense of a classical past was derived from symbolic formulations like Addison's Roman play, *Cato*, and from the arguments of Madison at the constitutional convention.

Pope John XXIII was a man saturated in the church history of councils (especially the one attended by his hero, Charles Borromeo). Martin King had lived the African-American story of enslavement and deliverance encoded in spirituals, biblical extracts, and sermons. Dorothy Day was not freed for her own original work until Peter Maurin brought her the lore of Catholicism's past. She could not circumvent ecclesiastical obstacles until he convinced her that this had happened regularly in church history. The saints, he knew, stride through barriers, even church barriers. Napoleon was an avid reader of Plutarch, who described the different ways great men reacted to the different cultural situations of Greece and Rome.

Napoleon did not directly imitate any known leader from Plutarch, though his sense of any leader's possibilities and problems no doubt grew by reading the book. Pope John *did* imitate specific acts of Charles Borromeo—especially his parish visitations and clerical synods—but different circumstances made him less authoritarian than Borromeo could be (perhaps had to be) in the sixteenth century. A sense of history can tell one when *not* to imitate historical models.

Washington followed the *ideals* of Cato, as presented to him in an Enlightenment context. It was a very eighteenth-century Cato he became, a man of his time, one who would not have the same opportunity for austere leadership in our own less formal and more egalitarian period. No American politician can directly imitate him today. No one person, past or present, has the "secret" for becoming a leader, or even for fostering leaders. A sense of diverse opportunities is one of the best lessons that can be taken from a study of great leaders in their incommunicable historical moments.

Well, but how about *non*great leaders? Most people will not lead revolutions, reform a church, conquer an enemy nation. The basic tools of leadership are available in small arenas as well as large. To lead a PTA meeting well, one must still have a firm grasp on the goal—improvement of the particular school in its particular troubles—and a sense of the parents' and teachers' needs and aspirations. A Napoleon would be a poor leader of PTA meetings; but Lincoln would be a superb one. And a person who could never be a Lincoln on the national stage can have something like his success at the PTA level.

The mystery of leadership and followership goes on all around us—and within us. We are all in some measure leaders *and* followers—as we are, most of us, alternately parents and children, employers and employees, teachers and taught. Integration of our leading and led selves is one of the goals we seek when we look at exemplary cases of leadership and following. Tell me who your admired leaders are, and you have bared your soul.

Appendix
CHOOSING THE TYPES

———

I n choosing the examples of leadership, I was not looking for the greatest or best leaders but those who can be seen, at some point in their career, exemplifying a distinctive kind of leadership. Some of my instances exemplified other kinds of leadership at other times. Washington, for instance, was a military leader before he became a constitutional leader. Napoleon became a lawmaker after his early military feats. I concentrate only on Washington's later and Napoleon's earlier roles for the purposes of my analysis.

A number of distinguished people were leaders in overlapping areas. The physicist J. Robert Oppenheimer was mentioned in chapter 4. He went from intellectual leader to diplomatic leader (at Los Alamos) to moral leader (opposing nuclear proliferation). I could have used him in any of three chapters included here; but he did not seem as clear an exemplar, of any of the three types, as the people I chose—Socrates for intellectual leader, Andrew Young for diplomatic leader, Dorothy Day for moral leader.

Some great leaders I excluded because they exercised leadership in two or more areas simultaneously (not in different phases, as Oppenheimer did). St. Paul and Martin Luther were intellectual leaders and church leaders in ways that were, for each of them, intimately connected. That made them less useful for defining one aspect of their leadership in isolation. Socrates was an intellectual leader but not a church leader.

Mary Eddy was a church leader but not an intellectual leader. Her thought is important to believers but not to thinkers in general. Napoleon was several kinds of leader—a charismatic one when he set up a new empire—but his military success can best be studied in the early campaigns where he was *only* a commanding officer.

In order to fix the separate types as distinct, I tried to find for each a thinker who analyzed that type. This not only helped define the boundaries separating these samples, but allowed me to bring to bear on the subject some of the most important work done on leadership in the past. The thinkers chosen are all mentioned in the appropriate chapter, but I list them here to show how wide a range of speculation leadership has prompted.

1. Franklin Roosevelt: Bagehot on staying engaged with the electorate.
2. Harriet Tubman: Thoreau on refusal to compromise radical principle.
3. Eleanor Roosevelt: Shaw on reformers from the social elite.
4. Andrew Young: Castiglione on the service of a courtier.
5. Napoleon: Clausewitz on the nature of war.
6. King David: Weber on charismatic leadership.
7. Ross Perot: Veblen on salesmanship.
8. John XXIII: Chesterton on renewing traditions.
9. George Washington: Rousseau on the contitutional lawgiver.
10. Socrates: St. Augustine on teaching as learning.
11. Mary Baker Eddy: Alex Owen on women's spiritual control in the nineteenth century.
12. Carl Stotz: St. Paul on sport as a spiritual discipline.
13. Martha Graham: William Morris on art as a social cause.
14. Martin Luther King: Cicero on the orator's life.
15. Cesare Borgia: Machiavelli on "the new *principe.*"
16. Dorothy Day: William James on the power of sanctity.

Of these sixteen thinkers, I suppose that three—Machiavelli, Max Weber, and Clausewitz—were the most original and influential in their writings on leadership. But precisely because they have had such broad effect—because they are so often cited or referred to, even by people who have not read them, or read them closely—their views have been the ones most often stretched or misapplied. Machiavelli's objectivity has been reduced to simple amoralism, Weber's charismatic structure of authority has become simple personal glamour, and Clausewitz's military philosophy has been flattened into sheer militarism. It is important to get these figures right, both because they are so central to thought in this area and because it is so easy to get them wrong. That is why I have matched the opinions of these three with a specific person that each of them used, himself, as an example of his theories. This has taken me to comparatively distant social contexts that have to be spelled out more carefully than are those closer to us in place and time (or both). Socrates also takes us farther afield than do most of my examples—but I thought it important to get him right as well, since we so often hear people claiming to use a "Socratic method" in the area of intellectual leadership.

For the rest, I tend to use figures from our own (American) past or present—eleven of the sixteen cases. I suppose it would have emphasized more dramatically the theme of this book—that leadership is tempered by specific social context (both the goals conceivable and the followers available in a concrete situation)—to take exotic instances (like the Syrian holy men referred to in the Introduction). But that would have tested both my readers' patience and the limits of my own knowledge. I am ignorant of the forms of leadership in more distant cultures; and though I do not propose any leader here for direct imitation, the relevance of some leaders will be more immediately apparent if their social context is more familiar. But that does not preclude others from supplying, in their own reading, leaders they are familiar with, to test the generalizations made about specific kinds of leadership. In fact, I hope readers will be sending me their own lists of alternative examples—and additions of whole new categories of leadership that did not occur to me.

I did consider many different examples for each of my chapters, and could have substituted, say, Lee Iacocca for Ross Perot, Beverly Sills for Martha Graham, Jane Addams for Dorothy Day, Voltaire for Socrates, and so on. My choices did not reflect a "win" for one person over the other. I simply felt I could put the case for the chosen exemplar more compendiously than for any rivals. The people were chosen less for intrinsic merit than for didactic usefulness.

I did not strictly limit my choices to the dead, though only two of my chapters have living subjects. The shape and point of a career are more easily grasped when it has been concluded. That is why even the living subjects, Ross Perot and Andrew Young, are considered in terms of episodes in their lives largely closed now—Perot's prepolitical rise in the business world, Young's diplomatic activity for Dr. King. Though I interviewed Perot and Young, I do not feel their exemplary effect is more vivid than that of people I merely saw and did not interview (Dorothy Day and Martin King), or even of historical characters I could not have met. The aim was not fully rounded biography in any of these cases, but a focus on the acts or events that illustrate the relevant form of leadership.

Finally, since so much of leadership is the projection of an image that will appeal to followers, I have chosen illustrations that convey the relevant concept of leadership for each person—sometimes symbolic images, as for John XXIII or Martin King.

Notes

INTRODUCTION

1. Thucydides, *History of the Peloponnesian War* 2.65.8.
2. Aristotle gave a very different picture of Pericles, expressly denying Thucydides' claim that he was above truckling to the democracy. See John J. Keaney, *The Composition of Aristotle's 'Athenaion Politeia'* (Oxford University Press, 1992), pp. 58–62, 139–40; and W. Robert Connor, *The New Politicians of Fifth Century Athens* (Hackett Publishing Co., 1992), pp. 119–28. Xenophon has Pericles' son complain of the way Athenians tear down their great men (*Memorabilia* 3.5.15–17).
3. *Henry IV, Part One* 3.1.50–53.
4. Abraham Lincoln, *Speeches and Writings*, ed. Don E. Fehrenbacher (Library of America, 1989), vol. 1, p. 636.
5. Peter Brown, *Society and the Holy in Late Antiquity* (University of California Press, 1982), pp. 103–65.
6. Jefferson held that "some preparation seems necessary to qualify the body of a nation for self government" (letter to Joseph Priestly, November 29, 1802).
7. G. K. Chesterton, *What I Saw in America* (Dodd, Mead, 1922), p. 217.
8. David Hume, "Of the First Principles of Government," in *Essays Moral, Political, and Literary*, ed. Eugene F. Miller (Liberty Classics, 1985), pp. 32–41.
9. Cult "leaders," though they begin with certain skills and acts of leadership, often end up relying on "brainwashing" techniques that suspend the fol-

lowers' wills. Charles Manson's druggie acolytes murder people in an *acte gratuit* that was less their shared goal with the leader than his demonstration of absolute control over them, even in aimless (goalless) acts. Jim Jones's devotees, obediently committing suicide on his command, had become incapable of independent determinations. This resembles hypnotism more than leadership.

10. James MacGregor Burns, *Leadership* (Harper & Row, 1978), p. 18. Burns, it is true, goes on to say that leadership accomplishes goals "mutually held by *both* leaders and followers" (p. 18); but he did not include that note in his italicized and repeated definition—for a good reason. One of his two major types of leadership, the "transactional," is defined this way: "Such leadership occurs when one person takes the initiative in making contact with others for the purpose of an exchange of valued things" (p. 19). This is barter, not leadership, as his own examples show. In fact, his analyses of leaders show that he works from a definition of leadership as *uncoercive influence over people*.

11. Hesiod, *Works and Days*, 273–77.

1. ELECTORAL LEADER: FRANKLIN D. ROOSEVELT

1. Thucydides, *History of the Peloponnesian War* 2.65.9.
2. John F. Kennedy, *Profiles in Courage* (Harper & Brothers, 1955), p. 4. Kennedy celebrates "individual conscience in a sea of popular rule," islands of *resistance* to the voters (p. 244).
3. Walter Bagehot, *The Collected Works*, ed. Norman St. John-Stevas (Harvard University Press, 1968), vol. 3, pp. 245–46. This is the best essay I know on the nature of democratic leadership.
4. Richard E. Neustadt, *Presidential Power* (Wiley, 1980), pp. 118–19. This was the book, in its 1960 edition, that John F. Kennedy studied, along with his aides, in preparing for his administration. William Leuchtenburg describes how Roosevelt set the standard for all later presidents in his book *In the Shadow of FDR* (Cornell University Press, 1993).
5. Neustadt, op. cit., pp. 118–19.
6. Richard Hofstadter, *The American Political Tradition* (Vintage, 1948), p. 316. Hofstadter called his chapter on Roosevelt "The Patrician as Opportunist."
7. Ibid., pp. 316–17.
8. Ibid., p. 343.
9. Geoffrey C. Ward, *A First-Class Temperament* (Harper Perennial, 1989), pp. 651–52.

10. Hugh Gregory Gallagher, *FDR's Splendid Deception* (Dodd, Mead, 1985), pp. 102–3.
11. Ward, op. cit., pp. 782–83.
12. Ibid., p. 749.
13. Gallagher, op. cit., pp. 87, 115.
14. Ibid., p. 195.
15. Before this, a delegation had traveled after the convention to the candidate's hometown, to make the formal offer of the nomination.
16. Even his admiring biographer, Douglas Southall Freeman, thought Washington was too careful of his image when it came to taking the bold step of attending the Philadelphia constitutional convention. See Freeman, *George Washington*, vol. 6, pp. 82–87.
17. Roosevelt seems to have lost, for a while, his feel for limits during the heady reelection landslide of 1936—the first postpolio race he had run without his trusted aide and truth-teller Louis Howe. See now Kenneth S. Davis, *FDR: Into the Storm* (Random House, 1993), chaps. 1–3.
18. Denis Diderot, *The Paradox of Acting*, trans. Walter Herries Pollock (Hill & Wang, 1957).
19. Ward, op. cit., pp. 760–61.
20. James Roosevelt, *My Parents* (Playboy Press, 1976), pp. 209–10.
21. Gallagher, op. cit., pp. 53–54.
22. Ibid., p. 172.
23. Ibid.

Antitype: Adlai Stevenson

1. As a student at Harvard, Franklin used his ties with Theodore (who was then the vice president) to get a news story that helped make him the editor of the *Harvard Crimson*. Cf. Geoffrey Ward, *Before the Trumpet* (Harper & Row, 1985), pp. 232–33.
2. For Marguerite (Missy) LeHand as the closest confidante of Roosevelt in the depths of his struggle with polio, see Geoffrey Ward, *A First-Class Temperament* (Harper Perennial, 1989), pp. 678–79. For Dorothy Fosdick as the source of information and advisors to Stevenson (including Bob Tufts, who wrote Stevenson's foreign-policy material in the 1952 campaign), see John Bartlow Martin, *Adlai Stevenson of Illinois* (Anchor Books, 1977), pp. 474–79, 531–32.
3. Martin, op. cit., pp. 265–80.
4. Stevenson in later life signed love letters to various women "Adpai" and "Addlepate" (Martin, op. cit., pp. 493, 531, 608). Roosevelt used nick-

names for others as a means of controlling them. Stevenson made up names for himself in the cute poses of a suitor.

5. For Schlesinger's opinion, see Martin, op. cit., p. 642. As a twelve-year-old, Stevenson killed a young girl, Ruth Merwin, while playing with a .22 rifle he thought unloaded. Stevenson never spoke of the incident, even to intimates. It was dug out of old newspapers when he ran for president. Ibid., pp. 42–45.

6. Ibid., p. 640. For Stevenson's refusal to court voters, even sympathetic ones, see Jacob Arvey's comments on his relations with Jewish voters (ibid., p. 630).

7. Ibid., p. 642.

8. Even after eight years of Eisenhower as president, Richard Neustadt found Ike's appeal a mystery: "The striking thing about our national elections in the Fifties was not Eisenhower's personal popularity; it was the genuine approval of his candidacy by informed Americans whom [sic] one might have supposed would know better." *Presidential Power* (1960; Wiley, 1980), p. 142.

9. That Eisenhower understood power and leadership better than Stevenson emerges from Fred I. Greenstein's fine study, *The Hidden-Hand Presidency: Eisenhower as Leader* (Basic Books, 1982).

10. Alistair Cooke, *Six Men* (Alfred A. Knopf, 1977), pp. 140–41.

11. Martin, op. cit., pp. 851–52.

12. Ibid., pp. 847–48.

13. Ibid., p. 826. The secretary-general of the U.N., Dag Hammarskjöld, said, "That man will be ruined by the dowagers" (Cooke, op. cit., p. 136).

14. Some admirers of Pericles in Athens mocked his intellectually inferior replacement, Cleon, as a demagogue, somewhat as Stevenson's followers mocked Eisenhower. But M. I. Finley argues powerfully that "demagogues—I use the word in a neutral sense—were a structural element in the Athenian political system." *Democracy, Ancient and Modern*, rev. ed. (Rutgers University Press, 1985), p. 69.

2. RADICAL LEADER: HARRIET TUBMAN

1. See *The Autobiography of Mother Jones*, ed. Mary Field Parton (Charles H. Kerr & Co., 1925), p. 202: "I [as a woman] have never had a vote, and I have raised hell all over this country. You don't need a vote to raise hell. You need conviction and a voice." Mary Jones (c. 1830–1930) was a United Mine Workers organizer and freelance agitator with a genius for publicizing the plight of mineworkers. She once led a march of miners' children to President Theodore Roosevelt's vacation home.

2. Henry David Thoreau, "Civil Disobedience," in *Walden and Civil Disobedience*, ed. Owen Thomas (Norton 1966), pp. 228–29, 233.
3. Ibid., p. 233.
4. The materials for Tubman's life are meager. Since she was illiterate, she left no documents of her own. Her work for the Underground Railroad was of the sort that made record keeping too dangerous for those collaborating with her. The main source—apart from incidental newspaper references and a few testimonials issued to raise funds for her in later life—is the series of interviews conducted by Sarah N. Bradford for her hastily assembled book of 1869, *Scenes in the Life of Harriet Tubman* (W. J. Moses of Auburn, New York). Bradford rushed her book out before leaving for Europe. She rearranged and slightly expanded it in 1897 as *Harriet: The Moses of Her People* (Geo. R. Lockwood & Son). Bradford admired Tubman's courage and idealism but was condescending to her cultural forms of expression. Tubman's account of her own concussion is in Bradford, *Scenes*, pp. 13, 73, and *Harriet*, p. 15.
5. The funeral is described in Bradford, *Harriet*, pp. 104–5. Bradford's attempts to reproduce Tubman's dialect reflect conventions of dialect reportage closer to minstrel shows than to Mark Twain's precise observation of Negro speech. Some, like Earl Conrad (see n. 16 below), try to clear up Tubman's speech, to give it more dignity. But it is absurd to make the uneducated slave woman speak standard modern English. A sympathetic stenographer at a speech she gave to abolitionists said he could not reproduce her words, though they were stirring (*The Liberator*, July 8, 1858). Tubman herself admitted that the speech of African-Americans from other regions was difficult or impossible for her to decipher: "Why, dey language down dar in de far south is jus' as different from ours in Maryland as you can think. Dey laughed when dey heard me talk, an' I could not understand dem, no how" (*Harriet*, p. 103). Bradford's phonetic system is internally inconsistent (e.g., "could not" in the preceding sentence but "couldn't" elsewhere) and illogical; but, unfortunately, we cannot correct her from a better observer of Tubman's speech. I correct the absurd use of "false" forms where the sounds are identical (I give, e.g., "dead" for "ded," or "somewheres" for "somewhere's"). As Stephen Leacock pointed out, "false" printing of an identical sound is a reporter's attempt to show the speaker was not speaking "correctly" even where there is no difference between correct and incorrect sounds. All of Bradford's transcriptions must be read with a realization of their inadequacy. My own corrections are minimal, for consistency (Bradford would use "frens" and "friens" in the same speech, "think" and "tink"), and for less erratic punctuation. Tubman lived well into the recording era, and it is a tragedy

of African-American history that no one recorded her telling her story—and singing her songs.

6. Tubman constantly used Buckra for White Man, distinguishing Sesh (secessionist) Buckra from Yankee Buckra. The term came from Nigeria (Backra, master) by way of the West Indies. Cf. Eric Partridge, *A Dictionary of Slang and Unconventional English*, 7th ed. (Macmillan, 1970), p. 101.
7. Bradford, *Harriet*, p. 29.
8. Ibid., pp. 30–31.
9. Bradford, *Scenes*, p. 110, and *Harriet*, pp. 81–82.
10. Bradford, *Scenes*, p. 36, and *Harriet*, p. 79.
11. For songs as part of a slave signal system, see Lawrence W. Levine, *Black Culture and Black Consciousness: Afro-American Folk Thought from Slavery to Freedom* (Oxford, University Press, 1977), p. 52.
12. Bradford, *Harriet*, p. 103.
13. Ibid., pp. 66–70.
14. Bradford, *Scenes*, p. 25, and *Harriet*, p. 33. Earl Conrad, in his biography, quotes a cleaned-up version of Tubman's threat, derived from one of her nephews: "Move [on] or die" (*Harriet Tubman* [Associate Publishers, 1943], p. 63). But there is no evidence that Bradford misreported Tubman's words, except by faulty phonetic transcription. Conrad presents Bradford's information as accurate in most cases. His well-meant efforts at gentrifying Tubman are matched, in his work, by the uncritical inclusion of diverse materials to pad out a meagerly attested story.
15. Stephen Oates, *To Purge This Land with Blood* (Harper & Row, 1970), p. 242.
16. Conrad (*Harriet Tubman*, p. 232) accepts Bradford's estimate that Tubman made nineteen expeditions south to rescue three hundred slaves—though he hedges his bet by saying it might have been as few as fifteen raids and two hundred rescued. Bradford reached her number by taking Tubman's own claim of *eleven* trips as the ones undertaken only from *Canada*—there must have been some earlier rescues. Since Tubman seems to have escaped in 1849, that would have meant about two trips a year, in the 1850s, though there is evidence that she worked in the summer to finance a major effort in the winter (when slaves were more confined but less well guarded). Her trips were carefully planned, and did not run on a commuter schedule. In 1859 she claimed only eight trips, according to her admirer Thomas Wentworth Higginson (Jeffrey Rossbach, *Ambivalent Conspirators: John Brown, The Secret Six, and a Theory of Slave Violence* [University of Pennsylvania Press] 1982, p. 206), and she was introduced to an abolitionist meeting, in the same year, as the rescuer of sixty slaves (Conrad, op. cit., p. 108). The lower estimates are more likely, and take nothing from her courage or resourcefulness.

17. This is the major theme of Jeffrey Rossbach's *Ambivalent Conspirators*.

18. Mary Thatcher Higginson, *Thomas Wentworth Higginson: The Story of His Life* (Houghton Mifflin, 1914), p. 219.

19. For Montgomery's part in the Kansas violence, see Jay Monaghan, *Civil War on the Western Border, 1854–1865* (University of Nebraska Press, 1955), pp. 81, 100–10, and Otto J. Scott, *The Secret Six: John Brown and the Abolitionist Movement* (Times Books, 1979), pp. 271–76.

20. Scott, op. cit., p. 319. Commanders of black regiments were urged to show restraint in dealing with southern civilians, lest their soldiers be accused of vengeful "savagery." Montgomery, who believed in punishing sinners, horrified the leaders of other black units—Thomas Wentworth Higginson and Robert Gould Shaw—when he torched the city of Darien, Georgia. Cf. T. W. Higginson, *Army Life in a Black Regiment* (Houghton Mifflin, 1900), p. 174 (on keeping blacks clear of atrocity); Dudley Taylor Cornish, *The Sable Arm: Black Troops in the Union Army, 1861–1865* (University Press of Kansas, 1987), pp. 148–50 (on Shaw's formal protests at the burning of Darien); and Tilden G. Edelstein, *Strange Enthusiasm: A Life of Thomas Wentworth Higginson* (Yale University Press, 1968), pp. 268, 273, 284–87 (on Higginson's view of Montgomery). One of Montgomery's earlier foraging expeditions became famous for the pigs and other movables he captured. Cf. Higginson, op. cit., p. 156, and Edelstein, op. cit., p. 273. Tubman remembers the episode with glee, noting that they called a black pig "Jeff Davis" (Bradford, *Harriet*, p. 101).

21. William H. Pease and Jane H. Pease, *The Fugitive Slave Law and Anthony Burns: A Problem in Law Enforcement* (Lippincott, 1975).

22. Higginson actually dreamed, for a moment in 1860, of recruiting James Montgomery to lead a rescue raid on the imprisoned followers of Brown. Cf. Mary Higginson, op. cit., pp. 196–98.

23. These are the words Tubman repeated to Bradford (*Harriet*, p. 122). Other accounts are less clear about her strategy, but confirm the events. Both Troy newspapers, the *Whig* and the *Arena*, reported the rescue (cf. Conrad, op. cit., p. 234), and Bradford relied on a written statement from Nalle's lawyer, Martin I. Townsend.

24. Bradford, *Harriet*, p. 127.

25. Bradford, *Harriet*, p. 85.

26. Lawrence illustrated Bradford's 1886 book, down to obscure details, some of which he later forgot or misinterpreted. The opening scene of playing children *excludes* Harriet in the book, but his caption includes her. His caption indicates that the whites in Panel 19 are studying a flyer with a reward for her capture, but he is clearly illustrating the passage in the book where whites intercept a letter sent south by a literate collaborator with Tubman. Bradford wrote: "These wiseacres therefore assembled, wiped their glasses

carefully, put them on, and proceeded to examine the suspicious document. What it meant they could not imagine" (p. 63). The Lawrence panels are in the Hampton University Museum, Hampton, Virginia. A catalogue for a traveling exhibit of them was published in 1991 by the University of Washington Press: *Jacob Lawrence: The Frederick Douglass and Harriet Tubman Series of 1938–1940*, by Ellen Harkins Wheat.

Antitype: Stephen A. Douglas

1. Murat Halstead, *Trimmers, Trucklers and Temporizers*, eds. William B. Hesseltine and Rex G. Fisher (State Historical Society of Wisconsin, 1961), p. 17.
2. Ibid., p. 19.
3. Robert W. Johannsen, *Stephen A. Douglas* (Oxford University Press, 1973), p. 591.
4. Henry David Thoreau, *Civil Disobedience*, ed. Owen Thomas (Norton, 1966), p. 228.
5. Johannsen, op. cit., p. 417.

3. REFORM LEADER: ELEANOR ROOSEVELT

1. Lorena Hickok, *Reluctant First Lady* (Dodd, Mead, 1962), pp. 120–21.
2. Joanna Schneider Zangrando and Robert L. Zangrando, "Eleanor Roosevelt and Black Civil Rights," in *Without Precedent: The Life and Career of Eleanor Roosevelt*, ed. Joan Hoff-Wilson and Marjorie Lightman (Indiana University Press, 1984), p. 103.
3. George Bernard Shaw, *The Intelligent Woman's Guide to Socialism and Capitalism* (Brentano's Publishers, 1928), pp. 61–62.
4. John D. Rosenberg, *The Darkening Glass* (Columbia University Press, 1961), p. 131.
5. Mickey Kaus, *New Republic*, February 15, 1993, p. 6: "Mrs. [Hillary Rodham] Clinton has not chosen to be independent. She has hitched herself firmly to her husband's career and used his success to promote herself. Nepotism is not feminism." By Mr. Kaus's standard, a true feminist must either not marry at all or be careful to marry a bum.
6. Elliott Roosevelt to his father, March 6, 1875, in Joseph P. Lash, *Eleanor and Franklin* (Signet Books, 1971), p. 30.
7. Eleanor Roosevelt, *This Is My Story* (Harper & Brothers, 1937), p. 6 and plate 4. This book was dedicated to her father.
8. Ibid., pp. 20–21.
9. Lash, op. cit., p. 211.

10. Geoffrey Ward, A *First-Class Temperament: The Emergence of Franklin Roosevelt* (Harper & Row, 1989), p. 109.

11. Lash, op. cit., p. 410.

12. Though she always distrusted psychiatry, her children's later troubles made her engage in informal discussions with Dr. Lawrence Kubie about what she had done to her children. To another doctor she made the heartrending confession: "My children would be much better off if I were not alive. I'm overshadowing them." Joseph P. Lash, *Eleanor: The Years Alone* (Norton, 1972), pp. 181–82.

13. Geoffrey C. Ward, *Before the Trumpet* (Harper & Row, 1985), p. 254.

14. Eleanor Roosevelt, *This Is My Story*, pp. 145–46.

15. Ibid., pp. 148–49.

16. Lash, *Eleanor and Franklin*, p. 370.

17. Ward, *A First-Class Temperament*, pp. 633, 677.

18. See, especially, Joseph P. Lash, *Love, Eleanor: Eleanor Roosevelt and Her Friends* (Doubleday, 1982).

19. Maurine H. Beasley, *Eleanor Roosevelt and the Media* (University of Illinois Press, 1987). Though she began by saying her press conferences would be nonpolitical, Eleanor schemed with reporters to "plant" questions affecting the causes she believed in (Beasley, pp. 52, 59–60).

20. Doris Faber, *The Life of Lorena Hickok, E. R.'s Friend* (Morrow, 1980), pp. 122–23.

21. Ibid., p. 176.

22. Ibid., p. 152. There is convincing evidence that Lorena Hickok was a lesbian, and Blanche Wiesen Cook is certain that Eleanor reciprocated her love physically. That may be so, though effusive letters do not prove it. Eleanor was demonstratively affectionate in ways that led others to believe she had sexual affairs with her protégé Joe Lash and with her black allies in the civil rights fight. How did the prudish woman who told her adult daughter that sex is an unpleasant duty become so guiltlessly promiscuous? The "natural" reading of the Hickok correspondence, if applied to her writings to and about her father, would lead to the conclusion that she had an incestuous affair with him. The truth seems to be that the model of a deep love for her father made her *freer* to express affection whenever she felt sex was precluded. The incest taboo was still at work. Joseph Lash and Doris Faber published the Hickok letters before Cook did, and they did not find her reading of them convincing. Cook answers that these authors are just homophobic. But neither ever expressed the homophobic revulsion Eleanor herself did on reading Gide's novel. See Cook's *Eleanor Roosevelt* (Viking, 1992), and Geoffrey Ward's review in *The New York Review of Books*, Sept. 24, 1992 (with correspondence in the issue of March 25, 1993).

23. Faber, op. cit., p. 156. It is noticeable that as Eleanor became more con-

fident and independent, her need for a protective female cocoon lessened and her closest friendships with women cooled. But her friendships with men remained strong—with Louis Howe (until his death), Franklin's bodyguard Earl Miller, Joseph Lash, Aubrey Williams (of the NYA), Adlai Stevenson, and (of course) with her husband. She once wrote Franklin, from a convention of the League of Women Voters, "I prefer doing my politics with you" (Lash, *Love, Eleanor*, p. xv).

24. Lash, *Eleanor: The Years Alone*, p. 54.
25. Ibid., p. 158.
26. Eleanor Roosevelt, *This I Remember* (Harper & Brothers, 1949), pp. 12–13. When Eleanor assigned some of her income directly to charities, Republicans in Congress claimed she was trying to avoid income tax. After that, she kept her professional accounts as meticulously as John Ruskin ever did.
27. Zangrando and Zangrando, op. cit., pp. 98–103.
28. Lash, *Eleanor: The Years Alone*, p. 185.
29. Lash, *Eleanor and Franklin*, p. 614.
30. Winifred D. Wandersee, "Eleanor Roosevelt and American Youth," in Hoff-Wilson and Lightman, op. cit., pp. 66–69.
31. Ibid., p. 77: "Some of her contemporaries felt that without her support the American Youth Congress would have faded out of existence much sooner than it did."
32. Ibid., p. 80.
33. Curt Gentry, *J. Edgar Hoover: The Man and the Secrets* (Norton, 1991), pp. 298–306. The watch over Eleanor's radical friends was such that Army Counterintelligence agents bugged Sergeant Lash's hotel room when he met Trude Pratt in Urbana, Illinois, in 1943 and Mrs. Roosevelt's hotel room when he was supposed to meet her in Chicago. Hoover later confused the two buggings and claimed that the army had tapes of Lash and Mrs. Roosevelt having sexual intercourse. A man of many obsessions, Hoover was intensely obsessed with the anti-McCarthyite Eleanor—in 1960, he told agent G. Gordon Liddy that she was "the most dangerous enemy of the Bureau" (Liddy, *Will* [St. Martin's Press, 1980], p. 83). For Lash's account of the buggings, with duplicates of the counterintelligence reports, see *Love, Eleanor*, pp. 448–93. The FBI version of the tale's ending is that Franklin, learning of Eleanor's infidelity, had Lash sent to the South Pacific to die like King David's Uriah.

Antitype: Nancy Reagan

1. Thorstein Veblen, *The Theory of the Leisure Class* (1899) (Penguin, 1979), p. 96.

4. DIPLOMATIC LEADER: ANDREW YOUNG

1. Garrett Mattingly, *Renaissance Diplomacy* (Penguin Books, 1964), p. 55. Wotton was King James I's ambassador to Venice. He had traveled incognito throughout Europe as a spy. Seen Logan Pearsall Smith, *The Life and Letters of Sir Henry Wotton* (Oxford University Press, 1987), vol. 1, pp. 8–26, 34–43.

2. Scholars I interviewed in Japan alleged that this happened to Edwin O. Reischauer, the United States ambassador to Japan in the 1960s. He tried to be more Japanese than the Japanese themselves, an effort the Japanese—proud of their otherness—did not appreciate, while Reischauer's partisanship made his advice suspect in the State Department.

3. For the overlapping of the courtier's and the diplomat's roles, see Mattingly, op. cit., p. 181.

4. Castiglione, *The Book of the Courtier*, trans. Charles S. Singleton (Anchor Books, 1959), pp. 110, 112, 147–48.

5. Andrew Young interview with Bill Moyers, cited in David J. Garrow, *Bearing the Cross: Martin Luther King, Jr., and the Southern Christian Leadership Conference.* (Morrow, 1986), pp. 656–57.

6. Young letter of April 25, 1961, cited in Taylor Branch, *Parting the Waters: America in the King Years 1954–63* (Simon & Schuster, 1988), p. 575.

7. Ibid., p. 576.

8. Garrow, op. cit., pp. 255–59.

9. Branch, op. cit., p. 781.

10. Garrow, op. cit., p. 468.

11. Castiglione, op. cit., pp. 290–91. *The Book of the Courtier* is a dialogue, and not every speaker voices the author's own views. But this speech by Signor Ottaviano Fregoso probably comes closest to Castiglione's own beliefs about the courtier's task.

12. Garrow, op. cit., p. 487.

13. Ibid., pp. 382–84.

14. Ibid., p. 384.

15. Hosea Williams claimed in later life that his own stylistic differences from Young were tactical, that they were a "Mr. Inside and Mr. Outside" team of a different sort: "I would go into a town and rile up the blacks and make whites say, 'What will these crazy niggers do next?' and then in would come nice little Andy saying 'There are some points we would like to discuss with you. . . .' But Williams admits to calling Young Uncle Tom one time too many: "He jumped on me physically, right in front of Dr. King" (author's interview with Williams, *Time*, July 16, 1990, p. 66).

16. Garrow, op. cit., p. 465.

17. He had told the Senate at his confirmation hearing that "I think one of the most valuable opportunities that the United Nations affords is the opportunity to communicate informally with a large number of the nations of the world on a moment's notice."

18. Wolf Blitzer, "Andy Young's Undoing," New Republic, Sept. 15, 1979, p. 12. I read this passage to Young and he confirmed its accuracy.

19. Time, July 16, 1990, p. 66. He added: "Last summer I took thirty small businessmen, mostly black, to Jamaica, Trinidad and Barbados, and we came back with 134 million dollars in contracts."

20. The announcement by the Olympic Committee came just weeks after Young lost the 1990 primary election for governor—had it come sooner, he might have won in the euphoria of that victory for the Georgia economy.

21. To the former criticism he said in 1990: "One of the criteria for deciding between colored, Asians, and blacks is the comb test. If the comb can get through your hair without getting interrupted, then *you colored*. But if the comb gets hung up, then *you black*. I am now 58 years old, and never have I ever been able to get a comb through my hair without getting a fractured arm." Time, July 16, 1990, p. 66.

Antitype: Clark Kerr

1. Clark Kerr, The Uses of the University (Harvard University Press, 1963), p. 86.

2. Ibid., p. 88.

3. Videotape of the final Godkin Lecture, included in the PBS documentary Berkeley in the Sixties (Kitchell Films, 1990).

4. Ibid.

5. Kerr, op. cit., pp. 53–55.

6. His one grudging reference to the students' industrial role was limited to this: "If the faculty looks on itself as a guild [union], the undergraduate students are coming to look upon themselves more as a 'class': some may even feel like a 'lumpen proletariat' " (op. cit., pp. 103–4).

7. In the Godkin Lectures, Kerr blithely dismissed the danger of federal control exerted through federal money: "Federal control as a substantive issue is, as Sidney Hook has said, a 'red herring' " (op. cit., p. 57).

8. Kerr, op. cit., p. 104.

5. MILITARY LEADER: NAPOLEON

1. Carl Von Clausewitz, On War, ed. and trans. Michael Howard and Peter Paret (Princeton University Press, 1984), pp. 75–77.

2. Ibid., p. 119.

3. Ibid., p. 120.
4. I was given this comparison by the Hall of Fame football player Raymond Berry, when he was coaching the New England Patriots. "Sally and I go to the ballet. But I've often wondered how well they would do if people were running through the orchestra grabbing their music off the stands, or wandering around the stage trying to trip up the dancers. We could look perfect if we went out and did our kicking plays, passing plays, with no opponents on a Sunday afternoon. But we have eleven very talented people out there trying to wreck our plans every time." He was making Clausewitz's point about the difference between an army's movements on the drill field and the same units' actions in battle.
5. Cf. François Furet, "Napoleon Bonaparte," in A Critical Dictionary of the French Revolution, ed. François Furet and Mona Ozouf, trans. Arthur Goldhammer (Harvard University press, 1989), pp. 273–86.
6. Cf. Patrice Gueniffey, "Carnot," in Furet and Ozouf, op. cit., pp. 197–203.
7. Cf. Denis Richet, "The Italian Campaign," in Furet-Ozouf, pp. 197–203, and David G. Chandler, The Campaigns of Napoleon (Macmillan, 1966), pp. 46ff.
8. Cf. Vincent J. Esposito and John Robert Elting, A Military History and Atlas of the Napoleonic Wars (AMS Press, 1970), text to map 3.
9. Clausewitz, op. cit., p. 518.
10. Thomas Babington Macaulay, "Frederick the Great," Edinburgh Review, April 1842. Machiavelli mocked the showpiece battles of his time, so protective of valuable mercenaries that casualties were accidental rather than intended. Cf. Niccolò Machiavelli, Florentine Histories, trans. Laura F. Banfield and Harvey C. Mansfield, Jr. (Princeton University Press, 1988), pp. 151, 227.
11. Cf. Hans Delbrück, History of the Art of War Within the Framework of Political History, vol. 4, The Dawn of Modern Warfare, trans. Walter J. Renfroe, Jr. (Greenwood Press, 1985), pp. 422, 427–28, 431. Clausewitz, op. cit., p. 248: "Battle exists for its own sake alone"—the Napoleonic concept.
12. Delbrück, op. cit., p. 409.
13. Peter Paret says that the greatest break from eighteenth-century customs of war was this principle that la guerre nourrit la guerre: "Napoleon and the Revolution in War," in Makers of Modern Strategy, ed. Peter Paret (Princeton University Press, 1985), p. 125.
14. Delbrück (op. cit.) quotes Napoleon's insistent words on numbers as the main factor in battle:

    I never believe I have enough troops; I assemble all the forces I can (p. 424).

The nature of strategy consists of always having, even with a weaker army, more forces at the point of attack than the enemy has (p. 428).

On the day before a battle, instead of having my divisions stay apart, I drew them all together at the point I wanted to overwhelm (p. 428).

Clausewitz (op. cit.) was equally emphatic on the necessity for sheer numbers in war:

The first rule, therefore, should be: Put the largest army into the field. This may sound like a platitude, but in reality it is not (p. 195).

15. Of course, Napoleon had to use occasional feints to divide opposing troops— e.g., the Austrians guarding the line of the Po River. But he did not like tricky maneuvers, which added to the inevitable mistakes in war. It is false to claim, as some do, that he always sought encirclement of the foe or flank attacks, or maneuvers to the rear of an enemy. Sean Colin said he favored flank attacks—cf. *The Transformation of War*, trans. L. H. R. Pope-Hennessey (Greenwood Press, 1912), pp. 117–22. Russell F. Wrigley thought he preferred the *manoeuvre sur les derrières*—cf. *The Age of Battles: The Quest for Decisive Warfare: From Breitenfeld to Waterloo* (Indiana University Press, 1991), p. 306. Napoleon attacked *wherever* he could seize quick advantage over a foe, and that was often not at the center; but Paret rightly says that he preferred the massive central attack whenever that was feasible ("Napoleon and the Revolution in War," p. 133).

16. Napoleon even disliked the word "plans," preferring "preparations" (Paret, "Napoleon and the Revolution in War," p. 131). He said, "No plan of operations extends with any certainty beyond the first encounter with the main enemy force" (Delbrück, op. cit., p. 425).

17. Clausewitz, p. 102.

18. Ibid., pp. 161–64.

19. Richet, op. cit., pp. 87–88.

20. Ibid., pp. 89–91.

21. Clausewitz, op. cit., pp. 159–61.

22. Clausewitz, quoted in Peter Paret, *Clausewitz and the State* (Oxford University Press, 1976), p. 224.

23. Cf. Leo Tolstoy, *War and Peace*, bk. 15, chap. 2 (Maude trans.):

Kutuzov felt and knew—not by reasoning or science but with the whole of his Russian being—what every Russian soldier felt. . . . [He was] one of those rare and solitary individuals who, discerning the will of Providence, submit their personal will to it.

24. Clausewitz, op. cit., pp. 220, 615, 477:

> The Russians showed us that one often attains one's greatest strength in the heart of one's country, when the enemy's offensive power is exhausted, and the defensive can then switch with enormous energy to the offensive. . . . The highest wisdom could never have devised a better strategy than the one the Russians followed unintentionally. . . . There can be no doubt that if the Russians, knowing what they know now, had to repeat it under the same conditions, they would do systematically what they did, mostly unintentionally, in 1812.

25. Peter Paret, "Napoleon as Enemy," in Paret, *Understanding War* (Princeton University Press, 1992), p. 83.
26. Plutarch, "Fabius," in *The Parallel Lives* (185).
27. Ibid., 187.
28. Clausewitz, op. cit., pp. 100–112.
29. Ibid., p. 87.
30. Paret, *Makers of Modern Strategy*, p. 224.
31. Furet, in Furet and Ozouf, op. cit., p. 285.

Antitype: George McClellan

1. *The Civil War Papers of George B. McClellan: Selected Correspondence, 1860–1865*, ed. Stephen W. Spears (Da Capo Press, 1992), pp. 79, 85.
2. Ibid., p. 82.
3. Carl von Clauseqitz, *On War*, ed. and trans. Michael Howard and Peter Paret (Princeton University Press, 1984), p. 117.
4. McClellan, *Civil War Papers*, pp. 87, 100.
5. Clausewitz, op. cit., p. 117.
6. For McClellan's taste for siege warfare, see *Civil War Papers*, pp. 204–5.
7. To his political advisor in New York, McClellan wrote: "Help me to dodge the nigger—we want nothing to do with him" (ibid., p. 128). McClellan was proud of his own southern family ties and liked to remember when the region's aristocrats were not harried by abolitionists or "pestiferous wooden-nutmeg-psalm-singing yankees" (ibid., p. 369). He felt that officials in Washington were subservient to "fanatics" (349) who took a "radical and inhuman" view of the South (362).
8. Ibid., p. 494, "The remedy for political error, if any are committed, is to be found only in the action of the people at the polls."
9. Ibid., pp. 482, 106, 135, 113–14, 374. Those around Lincoln were traitors (p. 235).

6. CHARISMATIC LEADER: DAVID

1. Max Weber, *Economy and Society*, ed. Guenter Roch and Claus Wittich (Bedmeinster Press, 1968). The definition of charisma is on p. 241:

   The term "charisma" will be applied to a certain quality of an individual personality by virtue of which he is considered extraordinary and treated as endowed with supernatural, superhuman, or at least specifically exceptional powers or qualities.

   Weber borrowed, for use in sociological theory, Rudolph Sohm's description of a certain kind of religious authority, laid out in Sohm's *Kirchenrecht* of 1892. Cf. Carl Friedrich, "Political Leadership and Charismatic Power," *Journal of Politics*, February 1961, p. 14. The religious charismatic is originally a miracle worker, one who wields visible supernatural power.

2. Friedrich, op. cit., p. 16.

3. See, for instance, Arthur Schweitzer, *The Age of Charisma* (University of Chicago Press, 1984). Also Ann Ruth Wilner and Dorothy Wilner on Africa ("The Rise and Role of Charismatic Leaders," *Annals of the American Academy of Political and Social Science*, March 1965, pp. 77–88), and Reinhold Bendix on Cambodia and Korea ("Reflections on Charismatic Leadership," in *Max Weber*, ed. Dennis Wrong [Prentice-Hall, 1970], pp. 166–81).

4. On Stalin, see Robert C. Tucker, *Philosophers and Kings: Studies in Leadership* (George Braziller, 1970), pp. 69–94.

5. Gandhi is admirable, and charismatic, but his effort was limited to opposition, to bringing down colonialism. He did not assume political office himself, nor oppose the indigenous legal order that replaced British rule. He was not a charismatic *ruler*, the point of Weber's structural analysis. We do not need to restrict charismatic leadership to charismatic rulers; but it helps to clarify what Weber meant before applying his thought to analogous instances.

6. For the element of charisma in Hitler, see Ian Kershaw, *The Hitler Myth* (Oxford University Press, 1987).

7. Weber, op. cit., p. 1231.

8. Weber discusses David mainly in the context of the movement of rural-military societies toward city life. Weber, *The Agrarian Sociology of Ancient Civilizations* (NLB, 1976), pp. 138–41. Cf. Reinhard Bendix, *Max Weber: An Intellectual Portrait* (University of California Press, 1977), pp. 209–11. For the mythologizing of David, see ibid., pp. 235–36.

9. Sacred kings tend to recede into legend even when records are more accessible than those for, say, the Aztec founding authorities. Charismatic figures

like Simeon Stylites, St. Francis, or the Baal Shem Tov are legendary even to their contemporaries.

10. Robin Lane Fox, *The Unauthorized Version: Truth and Fiction in the Bible* (Knopf, 1992), pp. 188–89. Fox is speaking primarily of the "throne-succession narrative" of II Samuel 9 to I Kings 2, the record isolated for study by Leonhard Rost (*Der Thronnachfolge Davids* [Kohlhammer, 1926]); but the narrative of "David's rise" has also won historians' respect. Cf. David M. Howard, Jr.'s article on David in *The Anchor Bible Dictionary* (Doubleday, 1992).

11. I Samuel 22.1–2. All citations are from the New English Bible.

12. Weber, *Agrarian Sociology*, p. 139. Weber thinks this is a later romanticization of David's role. But it is true that the Israelites were still at least partly bronze-age warriors having to cope with the iron weapons of the Philistines. See II Samuel 19.22 for Philistine control of iron. David only learns in time to use Goliath's sword.

13. I Samuel 23.22–23.

14. Ibid., 24.1–5.

15. At II Samuel 12.19, Tamar's torn robe symbolizes her rape. At II Samuel 10.4, David's emissaries are humiliated by the Ammonite king when he sends them back with half the garments torn off their buttocks.

16. I Samuel 22.7–8.

17. Ibid., 30.24–25.

18. For Adullam as a hilltop fortress rather than a cave, see P. Kyle McCarter, Jr., *I Samuel* (Doubleday, 1964), p. 357.

19. Cf. W. F. Albright, *The Biblical Period from Abraham to Ezra* (Harper & Row, 1963), p. 57.

20. I Samuel 10.25, 12.14 (italics added).

21. Ibid., 22.20, 23.6 and 9, 30.7, II Samuel 20.25.

22. Cf. Erik Erikson, *Gandhi's Truth* (Norton, 1969), pp. 402–6.

23. One of David's sons (Amnon) rapes his half-sister Tamar and is killed by his half-brother Absalom (II Samuel 13).

24. II Samuel 17.8–11.

25. Ibid., 17.14.

26. Ibid., 18.8.

27. Weber, *Economy and Society*, pp. 246–49.

28. A good late example of the type is in Raphael's *Disputà* of the Sistine *stanze*.

29. The bronze statues of Donatello (1440–42) and Verocchio (1473–75) led up to Michelangelo's great work of 1501–4.

30. The narrow oblong of marble that was partly worked by Agostino di Duccio had been left as useless in the cathedral yard for forty years. It was intended to be a bearded figure of David as one in the line of prophets who foretold Christ's coming. The "miracle" of using the botched stone made Mich-

elangelo boast, on a sketch for the statue "I [do] with my bow what David with his sling." The bow (*arco*) was the driving mechanism of the sculptor's drill. Cf. Charles Seymour, *Michelangelo's David: A Search for Identity* (University of Pittsburgh Press, 1967), pp. 7–9.

Antitype: Solomon

1. Max Weber, *The Agrarian Sociology of Ancient Civilizations*, trans. R. I. Frank (NLB, 1976), p. 140.
2. Cf. Tomoo Ishida's article, "Solomon," in *The Anchor Bible Dictionary* (Doubleday, 1992), esp. pp. 107–12.
3. Cf. John Bright, *A History of Israel*, 3rd ed. (Westminster Press, 1981), pp. 213–17.
4. *Proverbs* 25.2.
5. *Ecclesiastes* 1.2, 8–9.
6. Weber, *Economy and Society*, pp. 956–1005.

7. BUSINESS LEADER: ROSS PEROT

1. Thorstein Veblen, *The Instinct of Workmanship* (1914; Augustus M. Kelly, 1964), p. 314.
2. Peter F. Drucker, *Concept of the Corporation*, 2nd rev. ed. (1946; Mentor Books, 1983), pp. 139–48.
3. Ibid., pp. 237–58.
4. Thorstein Veblen, *The Engineer and the Price System* (1919), p. 112.
5. The authorized account of Patterson and the National Cash Register Company is Isaac F. Marcosson, *Wherever Men Trade* (Dodd, Mead, 1945). For the social significance of Patterson in American history, see Daniel J. Boorstein, "The Incorruptible Cashier," chap. 23 in *The Americans: The Democratic Experience* (Random House, 1973), pp. 200–203, 635–36.
6. Thomas J. Watson, Jr., with Peter Petre, *Father and Son & Co.* (Bantam, 1990), p. 11.
7. See the long list in Marcosson, op. cit., pp. 127–29. Besides Thomas Watson and Fred Nichol of IBM, it includes C. F. Kettering, Frank Clements, and R. H. Grant of General Motors, Alvin Macauley of Packard Motor Company, and Earl Reeder of Coca-Cola. The modern corporate world was seeded with Patterson's disciples, or with men trained by those disciples.
8. Tom Hopkins, *How to Master the Art of Selling* (Warner, 1982), pp. 83–93. The author proposes "The Champions' Formula for Rejecting Rejection."
9. For an account of the antitrust actions and trial, see William Rodgers, *Think: A Biography of the Watsons and IBM* (Weidenfeld & Nicolson,

1969), pp. 35–78; and Richard Thomas DeLamarter, *Big Blue* (Dodd, Mead, 1986), pp. 5–10.

10. Flint's autobiography, *Memories of an Active Life* (Putnam, 1923), deals with Watson and the origins of IBM on pp. 312–13. Newspapers had called Flint "the Father of Trusts" as an insult. He adopted the title as a badge of honor—just as he boasted of supplying belligerents with arms.

11. See Emerson W. Pugh, *Memories That Shaped an Industry* (MIT Press, 1984), pp. 3–6.

12. Franklin M. Fisher, James W. McKie, Richard B. Mancke, *IBM and the U.S. Data Processing Industry* (Praeger, 1983), pp. 3–13.

13. DeLamarter, op. cit., pp. 26–28.

14. Fisher, McKie, and Mancke, op. cit., pp. 3–13. By this time, Watson's son, Thomas junior, who had recognized uses for computers as a World War II pilot, was helping set policy. See Watson, *op. cit.*, pp. 203–5.

15. Perot approached his congressman through his father, denouncing the "drunken tales of moral emptiness [and] passing out penicillin pills" (AP dispatch, "Perot Sought Release from 'Godless' Navy," *Chicago Tribune*, May 24, 1992). Until this letter became known, Perot had told different stories of his reason for leaving the navy.

16. DeLamarter, *op. cit.*, p. 16.

17. House Subcommittee on Government Operations, *Hearings on Federal Health Programs*, September 30, 1971, p. 90.

18. Ibid., September 28, pp. 28, 34.

19. Ibid., June 1, 1972, p. 449.

20. Todd Mason, *Perot: An Unauthorized Biography* (Dow Jones-Irwin, 1990), 50–51.

21. IBM has always been so urgent about developing and keeping patents that it has made a cult of secrecy. It worries about employees taking information with them when they leave, so there is as much *internal* secrecy as is feasible. See James Chposky and Ted Leonsis, *Blue Magic* (Facts on File Publications, 1988), chap. 19, "The Shroud of Secrecy."

22. Arthur M. Lewis, "The Fastest, Richest Texan Ever," *Fortune*, November 16, 1968, p. 169.

23. Perot has assiduously built up a picture of his own youth that is more wishful than accurate. Remembered by teachers as a mild-mannered and unassuming fellow, the diminutive Texan has claimed that he broke wild horses at the age of eight, and was the first to deliver papers in a rough black neighborhood (where he became friendly with whores). When I went to his hometown in Texarkana, I found that Perot's classmate Hayes McClerkin remembers only that the Perots "kept some riding horses, like pets, you know" (what mother would put a tiny eight-year-old on an unbroken horse?). J. B. Rochelle, now a doctor in Texarkana, had earlier delivered

papers in the black neighborhood. (Besides, Perot in a different vein says Texarkana had no crime problems.) The shrine Perot built to his own Boy Scout days has a Scout Handbook with an evenly scooped-out middle section that is supposed to demonstrate how much he read it, though the gouge does not resemble wear in the normal sense. See Garry Wills, "The Rescuer," *New York Review of Books*, June 25, 1992, pp. 28–34.

24. Rodgers, op. cit., p. 48.
25. Ibid., p. 42.
26. Early ads for the cash register said: "It is an automatic cashier which records mechanically every cash or credit sale made in a store. It never does one thing while thinking of another, and never makes a mistake."
27. Doron P. Levin, *Irreconcilable Differences: Ross Perot versus General Motors* (Penguin Plume, 1990), pp. 39–47.
28. Veblen, *The Engineer and the Price System*, pp. 112–15.
29. C. Wright Mills, *Power, Politics, and People* (Oxford University Press, 1963), pp. 271–22.

Antitype: Roger Smith

1. Albert Lee, *Call Me Roger* (Contemporary Books, 1988), pp. 8–10. Lee was a speechwriter for General Motors who had tried to engage the CEO's eyes at speechwriting sessions, and could not, an experience others had reported to him.
2. Ibid., p. 51. Cf. Levin, op. cit., pp. 138–45.
3. Levin, op. cit., pp. 133–35.
4. Ibid., pp. 322–28.

8. TRADITIONAL LEADER: JOHN XXIII

1. Lord Acton, *Selected Writings*, ed. J. Rufus Fears (Liberty Classics, 1985), vol. 2, pp. 384–85.
2. When Verdi's wife—returned from Milan, where a friend had introduced her to Manzoni—said that Verdi could visit Manzoni, Verdi reacted in the way Giuseppina described to her Milanese friend:

> I didn't know whether I ought to open the carriage windows to give him air, or close them, fearing that in a paroxysm of surprise and joy he would jump out! He went red, he turned deadly pale, he perspired; he took off his hat and screwed it up in a way that reduced it almost to shapelessness. Furthermore (this is between ourselves) the most severe and savage Bear of Busseto had his eyes full of tears.

Cf. Frank Walker, *The Man Verdi* (Knopf, 1962), p. 270. For Verdi's early settings of Manzoni verse, see pp. 22, 142. Manzoni stirred even the Anglican Newman in 1839: "That Capuchin in the 'Promessi Sposi' has stuck in my heart like a dart." Cf. Ian Ker, *John Henry Newman* (Oxford University Press, 1988), p 181

3. Cf. Gian Piero Barricelli, *Alessandro Manzoni* (Twayne Publishers, 1976), p. 20: "No mention is made of Jesuits in *I Promessi Sposi*, we might interject, though they were at the acme of their influence and power in the seventeenth century, the time of the novel's action." This hostility to Jesuits came in part from sympathy with their historic enemies, Pascal and the Jansenists.

4. The spiritual obtuseness of the curate is underlined by the fact that he smugly reads a panegyric on St. Charles Borromeo just before shirking his duties to his parishioners (chap. 8).

5. Peter Hebblethwaite, *Pope John XXIII: Shepherd of the Modern World* (Doubleday, 1985), p. 192, quoting Roncalli's letter to the papal secretary of state: "I confess that this convoy of Jews to Palestine, aided specifically by the Holy See, looks like the reconstruction of the Hebrew Kingdom, and so arouses certain doubts in my mind. . . ." (Sept. 4, 1943).

6. Ibid., pp. 205–7.

7. Ibid., p. 219.

8. Ibid., p. 226.

9. Ibid., p. 227.

10. Ibid., p. 237.

11. Paul Hoffman, *O Vatican!* (Congdon & Weed, 1984), p. 24.

12. Ibid., pp. 25–26. Hoffman, the *New York Times* reporter at the Vatican, had been bribing the pope's incompetent physician for leaks of information. His account of the funeral is an episode from the black comedies just coming into vogue at that time, life imitating art.

13. Hebblethwaite, op. cit., p. 282.

14. Ibid., p. 274.

15. Ibid., pp. 276, 417, 422. Cf. E. E. Hales, *Pope John and His Revolution* (Doubleday, 1965), pp. 113–15.

16. Hebblethwaite, op. cit., p. 282.

17. For the history of encyclicals, see Paul Nau, *Une source doctrinale: les encycliques* (Paris, 1952), and Garry Wills, *Politics and Catholic Freedom* (Regnery, 1964), pp. 51–73.

18. Since the fact has been published, I must acknowledge suggesting the phrase to Mr. Buckley in a joking phone call.

19. On the browbeating of bishops at Vatican I, see Gertrude Himmelfarb, *Lord Acton: A Study in Conscience and Politics* (University of Chicago Press, 1952), pp. 95–117.

20. On John's temperamental conservatism in these matters, see Hales, op. cit., pp. 75, 96, 115–19; also Hebblethwaite, op. cit., pp. 350–52.

21. Ibid., p. 344.

22. Lord Acton and Ignaz von Döllinger told this story in their anonymous "Quirinus" letters in the *Allgemeine Zeitung*, forerunners of the "Xavier Rynne" letters in the *New Yorker* for Vatican II. See the English translation of "Quirinus," *Letters from Rome on the Council* (Rivingtons, 1870), pp. 62–63: "At least nine-tenths of the Prelates are condemned to silence simply from being unable to speak Latin readily and coherently through want of regular practice. And to this must be added the diversities of pronunciation. It is impossible, e.g., that Frenchmen or Italians should understand an Englishman's Latin even for a minute."

23. Hebblethwaite, op. cit., p. 1.

24. Ibid., p. 264.

25. Ibid., p. 482.

26. Alessandro Manzoni, *I Promessi Sposi* (Mursia, 1966), p. 350.

27. G. K. Chesterton, *Orthodoxy* (Image Books, 1959), p. 115.

28. See John XXIII, *Journal of a Soul*, trans. Dorothy White (Geoffrey Chapman, 1980), p. 340.

Antitype: Celestine V

1. Dante, *Inferno* 3.60. Celestine is not named, but the earliest commentators identified him here, and two later passages seem to confirm the identification. At 19.56–57, Celestine's successor (Boniface VIII) is said to have seized Mother Church by guile, and at 27.104–5, that successor mocks Celestine for not treasuring the keys of power.

2. George T. Peck, *The Fool of God: Jacopone da Todi* (University of Alabama Press, 1980), p. 115.

3. Horace K. Mann, *The Lives of the Popes in the Middle Ages* (Kegan Paul, 1931), vol. 17, pp. 247–341.

9. CONSTITUTIONAL LEADER: GEORGE WASHINGTON

1. Donald Jackson, ed., *The Diaries of George Washington* (University Press of Virginia, 1976), vol. 1, pp. 192–97.

2. Douglas Southall Freeman, *Young Washington* (Scribners, 1948), pp. 401–15.

3. William Shakespeare, *Othello* 2.3.262–264.

4. James Thomas Flexer, *George Washington: The Forge of Experience* (Little, Brown, 1965), p. 15.

5. Ibid., p. 145.

6. John C. Fitzpatrick, ed., *The Writings of George Washington* (Washington, 1931–44), vol. 13, pp. 255–56.
7. Edmund S. Morgan, *The Genius of George Washington* (Anderson House, 1980), pp. 14–23.
8. Fitzpatrick, *Writings of George Washington*, vol. 29, p. 177.
9. Pennsylvania *Gazeteer*, Nov. 6, 1787, in Merrill Jensen, ed., *The Documentary History of the Ratification of the Constitution*, vol. 2 (State Historical Society of Madison, 1976), p. 214.
10. Francesco Guicciardini, *Considerazioni intorno ai discorsi del Machiavelli* (Gius. Laterza & Figli, 1933), pp. 18–19, criticizing Machiavelli's *Discourses on Livy* 1.9 and 1.10. Guicciardini claims that Machiavelli underestimates the impact on founders of "the deliciousness of power" (*la dolcezza della potenzia*). Washington resisted the deliciousness.
11. Plutarch, *Romulus* 27–28.

Antitype: Oliver Cromwell

1. C. H. Firth, *Cromwell's Army*, 4th ed. (Methuen & Co., 1962), p. 142.
2. Ibid., p. 144.
3. Hans Delbrück, *The Dawn of Modern Warfare*, trans. Walter J. Renfroe, Jr. (University of Nebraska Press, 1985), pp. 185–92.
4. Godfrey Davies, *The Early Stuarts, 1603–1660*, 2nd ed. (Oxford University Press, 1959), p. 90.
5. Ibid., pp. 145–46. Firth, op. cit., pp. 349–52.
6. Thomas Carlyle, *On Heroes and Hero-Worship* (Ester and Laurist, n.d.), pp. 454, 447.

10. INTELLECTUAL LEADER: SOCRATES

1. John Maynard Keynes, *The General Theory of Employment, Interest, and Money* (Harbinger, 1964), p. 383: "Practical men, who believe themselves to be quite exempt from any particular influences, are usually the slaves of some defunct economist."
2. Walter Bagehot, "The Character of Sir Robert Peel," in *The Collected Works*, ed. Norman St. John-Stevas (Harvard University Press, 1968), vol. 3, p. 252.
3. Ibid., p. 256.
4. Ibid., p. 244.
5. Ibid., p. 256.
6. John B. Judis, *William F. Buckley, Jr., Patron Saint of the Conservatives* (Touchstone Books, 1990), pp. 441–42.
7. Cf. Victor Davis Hanson, *The Western Way of War: Infantry Battle in*

Classical Greece (Knopf, 1989), pp. 178–83. For the rescue of Alcibiades, see Plato, *Symposium* 220d-e.

8. Plato, *Laches*, 181a-b.

9. W. Kendrick Pritchett, *The Greek State at War*, pt. 1 (University of California Press, 1971), pp. 49–51.

10. For Socrates' study with Prodicus, see *Protagoras* 341a, *Charmides* 163d, *Cratylus* 384b, *Meno* 96d. Socrates is willing to put up money for others' instruction (*Protagoras* 311d) or even to attract listeners (*Euthyphro* 3d). As to family status, we are told that Plato's father, Sōphroniscus, was an admired friend of Lysimachus, whose own father was Aristides ("the Just") (*Laches* 181a).

11. *Laches* 180c-d.

12. When Socrates awaits his death under legal sentence because he will not desert his post (*Crito* 51b) he speaks from years of encountering death in such an assigned place.

13. For the gymnasia as places of dispute, see Plato, *Lysis* 204a. Socrates is presented in the *Lysis* as going from one palaestra (wrestling school) to a second one, before admirers divert him to a third one (whose manager he knows). Socrates does not address the lowborn, or women, or slaves—who are out of place in his normal locale. His use of a slave for demonstrative purposes in the *Meno* confirms the general rule.

14. Mogens Herman Hansen, *The Athenian Democracy in the Age of Demosthenes*, trans. J. A. Crook (Basil Blackwell, 1991), pp. 165–69. Though Hansen is describing fourth-century procedures, the trial framework for legislation was clearly a *survival* of ancient attitudes.

15. Socrates proposes a kind of spiritual *antidosis* at *Euthyphro* 5b, where his teacher must take his punishment if he has been unjust.

16. Aeschylus, *Isthmiastae*, vv. 29–38, in Lloyd-Jones ed. (appendix to Herbert Weir Smyth, *Aeschylus*, vol. 2, 1957), p. 551.

17. Modern scholars call this kind of list a *Priamel*. Sophocles' chorus in the *Antigone* says nothing is more daunting (*deinoteron*) than man, and lists the other daunting things man overcomes. Sāppho (16) puts a loved one's beauty over that of infantry and naval battalions. Cf. Garry Wills, "The Sapphic *Unwertung aller Werte*," *American Journal of Philology*, October 1967, pp. 432–42. Pindar puts water at the head of his list of good things (*Olympian* 1.1). For a traditional ranking of goods as the basis of discussion, see *Euthydemus* 279.

18. For the existence of oracles by lot at Delphi, see H. W. Parke and D. E. W. Wormell, *The Delphic Oracle* (Basil Blackwell, 1956), vol. 1, pp. 18–19. Formerly, it was thought that the Delphic priestess called Socrates the wisest man in one of her spoken responses. But no metrical pronounce-

ment is cited in the vast literature about Socrates, and the information fits the yes-no format: "Is anyone wiser?" The bean says no.

19. Plato, *Protagoras* 339e. Cheering spectators were a regular part of these exhibits (cf. *Euthydemus* 276b-c). Socrates is stunned by a verbal blow at *Euthydemus* 283d. For another "shoot out," see ibid., 274

20. The sophist Hippias confesses that his agonistic displays got no money from the "tough audience" in Sparta—a thing Plato clearly thought an indication of Spartan virtue. It is not so clear what the historical Socrates thought of Sparta. Cf. Plato, *Hippias Major* 283c–285e.

21. *Gorgias* 457 (Dodd's text).

22. Aristotle, *Sophistic Refutations* 165b.

23. See *Iliad* 23.394–97 (Eumelus rolled from his chariot), 692–98 (Euryalus blacking out in the boxing match), 775–77 (Ajax tripped in dung during the footrace).

24. Plato, *Hippias Minor* 364b. The parallel between the sacred games and Hippias's verbal fencing is expressly drawn by Socrates: "I doubt that any athlete comes here to compete (*agōnioumenos*) more boldly, or with greater confidence in his physical prowess than you come with your trained mind" (364a). A sophist skilled at all argument is compared to the games' pancratiast (multiple-event competitor) at *Euthydemus* 271c-d. For competitive intellectual activity at the games, see also Lucian, *Herodotus* 1–8. For Gorgias at the Olympics, see Philostratus, *Sophists' Lives* 49. For Diogenes at the Isthmian games, Dio Chrysostom, *Olympic Oration* 8.4–36.

25. At the palaestra, *Charmides, Lysis, Euthydemus*. At the military dueling ground, *Laches*. Other conversations are with people who have just competed at major games (*Ion, Hippias Major, Hippias Minor*). Socrates stays for the horse race at the beginning of *Republic* 328a-b. He goes off at the end of *Symposium* toward the palaestra, where he will spend his whole day, as usual.

26. Socrates engages in competitive interpretation of the poets, a recognized sophistic exercise, in *Protagoras, Ion,* and *Hippias Minor*. But Socrates sometimes quotes the poets without indulging in sophistic reworkings of them—e.g., at *Lysis* 214a, where the poets are called "the fathers of our understanding, and our guides to it."

27. *Protagoras* 331c-d.

28. *Hippias Major* 287a. In the *Charmides* (155ff.) Socrates pretends to be a doctor in order to engage a youth in dialogue.

29. *Charmides* 161b-c, *Hippias Minor* 369b-c.

30. H. I. Marrou, *The History of Education in Antiquity*, trans. George Lamb (University of Wisconsin Press, 1982), pp. 36–44.

31. Especially in *Ion* and *Apology* among the early dialogues.

32. In this they followed the example of the Ionic cosmologists who, as M. I. Finley points out, "did not hesitate to draw analogies and clues from the potter's wheel, the fulling-mill, the smith's bellows, and other objects of craft and industry." Finley, *Economy and Society in Ancient Greece* (Penguin, 1983), p. 180.

33. Herodotus, *Histories* 2.167; Xenophon, *Oeconomicus* 4.2. It is often argued that the prejudice against practical crafts arrested the development of Greek science. Cf. Finley, op. cit., pp. 179–81, and Benjamin Farrington, *Greek Science* (Pelican, 1953), pp. 130–33, 149–52. Gregory Vlastos thinks it perverted Platonic and Aristotelian thought at an even deeper level. Cf. Vlastos, "Slavery in Plato's Thought," in *Platonic Studies*, 2nd ed. (Princeton University Press, 1981), pp. 147–63.

34. Plato makes much of the fact, for instance, that the sophists were paid for their instruction and that they were foreigners. But Socrates was from a comfortable background and he had many foreign ties (to Pythagoreans, especially). He was a student of Prodicus, from the island of Ceos. Socrates was a voice of the "new education" exemplified by the sophists—stressing eristic cross-examination, criticism of accepted readings of the poets, use of craft analogies, and the allegorizing of theological myths.

35. In fact, modern students can find in the sophists some moral concerns lacking in Socrates—e.g., egalitarianism and pan-Hellenism in place of Socrates' unquestioning acceptance of slavery and the Athenian empire (for which he fought). Cf. Vlastos, "Slavery in Plato's Thought," p. 149. Those who say the sophists just equipped arguers to win, no matter whether they argued for the worse or better case, rarely reflect that Aristotle equips people similarly in his *Topics* and *Sophistic Refutations*. These people never call Aristotle a sophist. An example of the caricature view of sophists is the shock expressed by Lynn Cheney, chair of the National Endowment for the Humanities, when she could not extract from the classical scholar Bernard Knox a condemnation of the sophists as history's villains: "A Conversation with Bernard Knox," *Humanities*, May–June 1992, pp. 35–36.

36. The problem of the historical Socrates is not quite as baffling as that of the historical Jesus, but it has been teased at almost as insistently. I take my guidance from Gregory Vlastos's powerful argument that the most reliable information on Socrates is in the ten earliest authentic dialogues of Plato. He notes that none of the peculiarly Platonic doctrines is found in these works—the belief in an immortal soul, the reminiscence theory of knowledge, the need for mathematics as a purifying discipline, the ideal forms, the separation of golden men from inferior mortals. All of those later positions have political and social as well as philosophical implications, and none of them can reasonably be foisted on Socrates (for good or ill). The ten earliest diologues, listed alphabetically, are:

Apology
Charmides
Crito
Euthyphro
Gorgias
Hippias Minor
Ion
Laches
Protagoras
Republic, Book 1.

I have quoted mainly from these dialogues for the Socratic scene, and I shall quote *only* from them for Socratic teaching. For stylometric arguments identifying them as early, see Leonard Brandwood, *The Chronology of Plato's Dialogues* (Cambridge University Press, 1990). Vlastos's summary position, drawing on his many Socratic writings, is stated in *Socrates, Ironist and Moral Philosopher* (Cornell University Press, 1991).

37. *Laches* 187a–188b. The general uses military language of maneuver (*periagomenou*) and ambush (*empesei*) to a fellow general.

38. *Charmides* 165b, 166c. "Hector for the truth": *elengcho* originally meant to "brand with dishonor," from the epic language of disgraced heroes. It became a word for challenge and refutation in debate, but with its agonistic background still felt. "Hunt myself down": *di-ereunaō*, the intensifying prefix with a verb Homer used for hunting dogs (*Odyssey* 19.436).

39. Socrates makes or seems to make four different arguments against escape in *Crito*.

> 1. When he says that he implicitly agreed to obey the laws by not emigrating, this resembles Locke's "tacit consent" to the social contract; readers place Socrates in a context of modern arguments for or against civil disobedience. That is how Hume read *Crito*. In his essay "Of the Original Contract," he says: "The only passage I meet with in antiquity where the obligation of obedience is ascribed to a promise is in Plato's *Crito*, where Socrates refuses to escape from prison because he had tacitly promised to obey the laws." But Vlastos has shown that Plato did not accept the social contract as a basis for the state, and there is no sign elsewhere that Socrates did. In fact, this would not fit with the second argument.
>
> 2. While the social-contract argument is indirect, if present at all, the Laws (in their speech to Socrates) repeatedly argue from the need for superior-inferior relations in all of society. They repeatedly draw the analogy:

$$\frac{\text{Parent}}{\text{Child}} = \frac{\text{Master}}{\text{Slave}} = \frac{\text{State}}{\text{Citizen}}$$

This was Plato's view of the matter, and it may have been Socrates' as well, since it fits with the following two arguments, which are more identifiably Socratic.

3. The Laws go farther than the second argument when they say the city has a greater claim on its citizens than does a parent on a child, or a master on a slave, because the city is "holier" and has a "larger assignment" (*meizōn moira*) among the gods as well as men (51a-h). The city is the *cult* center of life, not just a secular authority (like a master over a slave). Socrates is pious to the city's gods, though he criticized what he thought unworthy myths about them. The religious claim on Athenians was greater than any other, and Socrates here recognizes that. He reminds us of a radical like Dorothy Day who submitted to Catholic Church authorities (however corrupt) because she believed in the divine origin of her church.

4. The last argument has special weight with Socrates. He has gone beyond the ordinary citizen's duty to obey the gods and the laws because he has pledged not to return evil for evil. The argument that others take to *exempt* him from obedience—the unjust sentence—he thinks is an argument in *favor* of obeying: he will not match a new injustice to that committed against him.

40. Cf. Søren Kierkegaard, *The Concept of Irony, With Continual Reference to Socrates*, trans. Howard V. Hong and Edna H. Hong (Princeton University Press, 1989), p. 326:

What doubt is to science, irony is to personal life. Just as scientists maintain that there is no true science without doubt, so it may be maintained with the same right that no genuinely human life is possible without irony. . . . Irony is a disciplinarian feared only by those who do not know it but loved by those who do. Anyone who does not understand irony at all, who has no ear for its whispering, lacks *eo ipso* what could be called the absolute beginning of personal life; he lacks what momentarily is indispensable for personal life; he lacks the bath of regeneration and rejuvenation, irony's baptism of purification that rescues the soul from having its life in finitude. . .

41. Those who think the city wronged Socrates out of some deep political plot or historical injustice have been well answered by Vlastos, by M. I. Finley—

and by Plato himself, who said in the Seventh Letter (325b-c) that it was an odd accident (*tuchē tis*) that brought Socrates to trial. Finley, sensitive to Athenian politics, endorses that judgment. Other people were regularly hauled before the tribunal on odd charges—it is a wonder Socrates avoided it so long. The verdict was close (a matter of 31 votes out of 501), and Socrates was obliged not to use the normal tactics of this *agōn* since he had denounced them so repeatedly (cf. *Gorgias* 522b). It was a messy case with no single explanation. Certainly, Socrates did not feel that the whole city had betrayed or renounced him—any more than he could hate or renounce it. Cf. M. I. Finley, "Socrates and Athens," in *Aspects of Antiquity* (Viking Press, 1968), pp. 58–72.

42. St. Augustine, *Teaching Catechumens (De Catechizandis Rudibus)* 12(17). *Corpus Christianorium*, Series Latina 46 (1969), p. 141.

Antitype: Ludwig Wittgenstein

1. The Socrates comparison is made, for instance, on pp. 263–64 of Ray Monk, *Ludwig Wittgenstein: The Duty of Genius* (Penguin, 1991), the book from which I draw the biographical material on Wittgenstein.
2. Wittgenstein himself realized that his language theories were poles apart from those of Socrates. Cf. Monk, op. cit., pp. 337–38.

11. CHURCH LEADER: MARY BAKER EDDY

1. The goal toward which Paul led followers *could* not have existed before the death of Jesus, since Paul's aim was to reap for himself and others the redemptive benefits of, precisely, that death.
2. For the elder James's "conversion" to Swedenborgism, see Howard M. Feinstein, *Becoming William James* (Cornell University Press, 1984), pp. 67–75. For an admiring treatment of Swedenborg, see Emerson's essay on him in *Ralph Waldo Emerson, 1863–1882: Essays and Lectures*, ed. Joel Porte (Library of America, 1983), pp. 655–89.
3. For James's belief in the power of positive thinking, see his letter to a friend: "I always want when I write to you to ring a trumpet blast that will wake the echoes in your will and put you in fighting tune" (Feinstein, op. cit., pp. 213–14).
4. See, for instance, J. Hillis Miller, *The Disappearance of God* (Harvard University Press, 1963).
5. William Wordsworth, "The World Is Too Much With Us," in *The Poetical Works*, ed. Ernest de Selincourt (Oxford University Press, 1964), p. 206.
6. See the collection of texts on women's incapacity for higher education in Elaine Showalter, *The Female Malady: Women, Madness, and English*

Culture, 1830–1980 (Penguin, 1987), pp. 124–27. Dr. Edward Clarke said education was destroying the nerves of American women. Dr. Henry Mandsley said it was leading to atrophy of the female breasts. Dr. George Savage forbade further studies for the teenage Virginia Woolf and set her to therapeutic gardening. Dr. T. S. Clariston said that a further unsexing of women by the schools would make men seek partners in lands where the women preserved their native vigor, creating a new "rape of the Sabines."

7. Ibid., pp. 130–31.

8. Alex Owen, *The Darkened Room: Women, Power and Spiritualism* in *Late Victorian England* (University of Pennsylvania Press, 1990), p. 4.

9. Letter to Julius Dresser, February 14, 1866, quoted in Ernest Sutherland Bates and John V. Dittemore, *Mary Baker Eddy: The Truth and the Tradition* (Knopf, 1932), p. 109.

10. Ibid., p. 95. Eddy got to know other women at Quimby's clinic during long hair-drying sessions after his treatment. Without modern electrical blowers, the women had to comb and "air" their hair in a methodical way.

11. "The mind of the female contains more of that superior substance required to receive the higher development of God's wisdom." Horatio W. Dresser, ed. *The Quimby Manuscripts* (Citadel Press, 1921), p. 393.

12. Ibid., p. 257.

13. Ibid., pp. 185, 201.

14. Ibid., p. 388.

15. Bates and Dittemore, op. cit., p. 104. Mark Twain referred to her "alleged poems."

16. Ibid., p. 9a. She also wrote: "When our Shakespeare decided that 'there are more things in the world than were dreamed of in our philosophy,' I cannot say of a verity that he had foreknowledge of P. P. Quimby" (ibid., p. 89).

17. Ibid., p. 132.

18. Commenting on Eddy's sentence "His spiritual noumenon and phenomenon silenced portraiture," Twain said (*Christian Science* [Harper & Brothers, 1899], p. 121): "You cannot silence portraiture with a noumenon; if portraiture should make a noise, a way could be found to silence it, but even then it could not be done with a noumenon."

19. Emerson, op. cit., pp. 683–84.

20. See Georgine Milmine, *The Life of Mary Baker Eddy and the History of Christian Science* (Doubleday, Page & Company, 1909), p. 330. Willa Cather edited and heavily rewrote this book—see the Bison Book Edition (1993), with an introduction by David Stauck.

21. Mary Baker Eddy, *Science and Health*, final ed. (Pasadena Press), p. 25.

22. The problem with the attempt to reach an "historical Jesus" is that the gospels are *later* than the Pauline epistles, and each is built on a core

"passion narrative" that reflects the theological concerns called Pauline.
23. St. Paul, I Corinthians 1.12.
24. Cited by Robert Peel, *Mary Baker Eddy: The Years of Trial* (Holt, Rinehart & Winston, 1991).
25. The watchers had to concentrate so hard on their mental defense work that none could serve more than two hours at a stretch, creating the need for a considerable pool of potential watchers. See Bates and Dittemore, op. cit., p. 191.
26. Ibid., p. 192.
27. There was an ugly aftermath to the Spofford trial. Eddy's husband was arrested for conspiring to kill Spofford. See Peel, op. cit., pp. 50–56, and Milmine, op. cit., pp. 247–58.
28. Bates and Dittemore, op. cit., pp. 366–67. Peel, op. cit., pp. 269–71.
29. Twain, op. cit., p. 102.
30. Sidney Ahlstrom, in *Notable American Women, 1607–1956* (Harvard University Press, 1971), pp. 551–61. This article, by the eminent historian of American religion, is the best short treatment of Eddy, and it includes a balanced assessment of the impassioned writings for and against her. It was on his recommendation that I took the Bates and Dittemore book as "a solidly documented account . . . written by an experienced and learned biographer [Bates, who wrote and edited for the *Dictionary of American Biography*] on the basis of extensive letters and other materials from church archives supplied by Dittemore, a former editor of the Mother Church." I checked each episode in the three-volume life by Eddy's ablest defender, Robert Peel.
31. Original as ever, Eddy did legally adopt one son—who was forty-one years old at the time. She was sixty-eight.

Antitype: Phineas Parkhurst Quimby

1. *The Quimby Manuscripts*, p. 28.
2. Ibid., p. 29.
3. Ibid., p. 34.
4. Ibid., p. 231. This receptivity toward another's diseased mentality is not far from Eddy's reception of Malicious Animal Magnetism. But Quimby did voluntarily, to help his patient, what Eddy suffered involuntarily.
5. Ibid., p. 230.
6. Quimby's son claimed that all Miss Ware's corrections were dictated by Quimby when she read his own writings back to him—an odd procedure. Eddy's texts were reworked, to improve her grammar, by her disciples, especially by James Henry Wiggin. Her constant rewriting of *Health and*

Science sent it into 382 distinct editions during her lifetime. See Ahlstrom, *Notable American Women*, pp. 556–57, and Milmine, *The Life of Mary Baker Eddy*, pp. 247–58.

7. For Roosevelt's effort to use Coué's autosuggestion ("Day by day, in every way, I am getting better and better") against polio, see Geoffrey Ward, *A First-Class Temperament* (Harper Perennial, 1989), p. 646. For similarities of Coué to Quimby, see C. Harry Brooks, *The Practice of Autosuggestion by the Method of Emile Coué* (Dodd, Mead, 1922), pp. 104–10. Like Quimby, Coué found a demonstration of the unconscious in children's susceptibility to suggested diseases.

8. Even the author of the introduction to Quimby's papers admits that, but for Eddy, Quimby would not be remembered today (*The Quimby Manuscripts*, p. xiv).

12. SPORTS LEADER: CARL STOTZ

1. Charles Price, *The World of Golf* (Random House, 1962), pp. 167–201. Pros even now, in an era of more flexible clubs and livelier balls, have a hard time equaling Jones's scores on established courses.

2. Charles Rice, *A Golf Story: Bobby Jones, Augusta National, and the Masters Tournament* (Atheneum, 1986).

3. Information on Walker and the Walker Cup provided by Rand Jerris, librarian of the United States Golf Association.

4. John A. Kouwenhoven, *Partners in Banking: An Historical Portrait of a Great Private Bank, Brown Brothers Harriman & Co., 1818–1968* (Doubleday, 1968), p. 187.

5. Ibid., p. 287.

6. Thorstein Veblen, *The Theory of the Leisure Class* (Penguin, 1981), pp. 254–68.

7. St. Paul, I Corinthians, 9.24–7. For the indicative, not the imperative of most translations, in verse 24 ("you are running," not "you must run"), see Victor C. Pfitzner, *Paul and the Agon Motif: Traditional Athletic Imagery in the Pauline Literature* (E. J. Brill, 1967), pp. 88–89. Paul used images from the racecourse in Galatians 2.2., Philippians 2.16; he used a wrestling-boxing metaphor in Philippians 1.30. The pseudo-Pauline letters use similar tropes—"Compete in the best competition, that of faith" (I Timothy, 6.12), and "Only the competitor who competes by the rules wears the wreath" (II Timothy, 2.5).

8. Ignatius of Antioch, Letter to Polycarp 1.2. For Ignatius as the inventor of the maxim, see William R. Schoedel, *Ignatius of Antioch* (Fortress Press, 1985), p. 261.

9. Epictetus, *Discourses* 1.24.1. At 3.10.6–8, the sage-as-athlete is asked by

God, "Did you play by the rules, keep to your diet, listen to your coach?"

10. It is typical that the Rose Bowl, sending eastern teams west in the winter, arose from a hunt cup event to which wealthy easterners were invited. See Fred Russell and George Leonard, *Big Bowl Football: The Great Postseason Classics* (Ronald Press, 1963), pp. 3–6.

11. See "The Controversy over Baseball's Origins," *Encyclopaedia Britannica*, 1973 ed., vol. 3, pp. 223–24.

12. Pollard, a star running back from Brown (the first black to win a place on the backfield of Walter Camp's All-American teams), was an all-around athlete himself, and the father of one of those African-Americans who, with Jesse Owens, won medals at Hitler's Olympic Games of 1936. John M. Carroll makes a convincing argument that Pollard, both as an athlete and a businessman, "established more 'firsts' for his team than perhaps any other African-American in this century." Carroll, *Fritz Pollard: Pioneer in Racial Advancement* (University of Illinois Press, 1992), p. 239.

13. Robert Peterson, *Only the Ball Was White* (Pentice-Hall, 1970), pp. 103–15. Foster "was far and away the most important influence in raising the [black leagues'] game to respectability."

14. Carl Stotz and Kenneth D. Loss, *A Promise Kept* (Zebrowski Historical Services, 1992), pp. 40–41.

15. Ibid., pp. 63–64.

16. There is a useful Little League chronology, charting its spectacular postwar growth, in Harvey Frommer, *Growing Up at Bat* (Pharos Books, 1989), pp. 189–200.

17. David Halberstam does not mention Little League in his giant survey *The Fifties* (Random House, 1993)—a surprising omission.

18. Stotz, op. cit., pp. 176–77.

19. An uneasiness about Stotz may explain the refusal by the League's director of communications, Dennis Sullivan, to let me see the archives in Williamsport. The writer of the League's authorized book, Harvey Frommer, who was allowed to use the archives, says only that "there were ideological and philosophical differences between McGovern and Carl Stotz" (op. cit., pp. 34–35). The differences are not specified.

20. Stotz, op. cit., p. 187.

21. A wry look at the excesses of Little League parents and coaches is provided by Bill Geist, *Little League Confidential* (Dell, 1992).

22. Daniel Coyle, *Hardball: A Season in the Projects* (Putnam, 1993).

Antitype: Kenesaw Mountain Landis

1. Harold Seymour, *Baseball: The Golden Age* (Oxford University Press, 1971), p. 368.

2. J. G. Taylor Spink, *Judge Landis and Twenty-five Years of Baseball* (Thomas Y. Crowell Co., 1947), pp. 68, 69.
3. Ibid., p. 77.
4. For a list of Landis's precipitate actions on suspicion or allegation of wrongdoing, see Seymour, op. cit., pp. 372–95.
5. David L. Porter, *Biographical Dictionary of Baseball* (Greenwood Press, 1987), p. 323.

13. ARTISTIC LEADER: MARTHA GRAHAM

1. For Morris as a leader with an artistic program, see E. P. Thompson, *William Morris: Romantic to Revolutionary*, 2nd ed. (Stanford University Press, 1988), pp. 655–67.
2. See James Sherman, *The Drama of Denishawn Dance* (Wesleyan University Press, 1979).
3. Agnes De Mille, *Martha: The Life and Work of Martha Graham* (Random House, 1991), p. 52.
4. Ibid., p. 57: "The greatest dancer in the western hemisphere had just whirled around in front of the cameras, but who knew that or gave it the slightest thought?" Agnes De Mille, Cecil B. De Mille's niece, later tried to draw her uncle's attention to Graham, but he remained uninterested (pp. 186–87).
5. Ibid., pp. 49, 65.
6. She was hired for the Eastman School by its twenty-six-year-old director of opera, Rouben Mamoulian, the "mad Armenian," born in Tiflies, who fled the Russian Revolution. Mamoulian had been trained in the Stanislavsky school of acting, and he responded to Graham's intense summoning of feeling on the stage. Mamoulian would later direct Gershwin's opera *Porgy and Bess* and a number of successful Hollywood films, including the first one in Technicolor. See Don McDonagh, *Martha Graham* (Praeger, 1973), pp. 42–46, 49–52; and Hollis Alpert, *The Life and Times of "Porgy and Bess"* (Knopf, 1990), pp. 53–61, 99–118.
7. A good summary of Horst's importance to the development of modern dance is in McDonagh, op. cit., pp. 196–98.
8. Martin Friedman, "Designs for the Theater," in *Noguchi's Imaginary Landscapes* (Design Quarterly Press, 1978), pp. 25–35. Noguchi's design for Graham's costume as Medea, presented as a sun goddess, shimmered with metal irradiating strips. At the dance's end, she stepped out of the dress, which was left standing by itself, the last rays of a sun now set.
9. De Mille, op. cit., pp. 96–102. One of her dancers called Graham's body "crotch sprung." Graham took from the student of myth Joseph Campbell (whom she came to know while teaching at Bennington) a theory of kun-

dalini yoga that finds three mystical wheels (chakras) in the pelvic area (ibid., pp. 429–30).

10. St. Ignatius of Loyola developed a form of prayer timed to deep breathing, as if all a person's need were to ache out toward God from this literal "aspiration." Cf. "Third Method of Prayer" in *Spiritual Exercises* (Newman Press, 1949), pp. 81–82.

11. Martha Graham, *Blood Memory* (Doubleday, 1991), pp. 211–12.

12. McDonagh, op. cit., p. 225. Two congressmen tried to get Graham's State Department tour canceled in 1962, after seeing her perform as Phaedra. They considered the show obscene. Ibid., pp. 266–68.

13. Paul Taylor tells how she pointed to him at the Connecticut College classes and said, "I want him." Taylor, *Private Domain* (Knopf, 1987), p. 33.

14. Paul Taylor (ibid., p. 32) and Merce Cunningham both comment on the uselessness for males of Graham's famous seated exercises. Cunningham, *The Dancer and the Dance* (Marion Bayars, 1985), p. 42. In Graham's film, *A Dancing World*, Mary Hinkson of her troupe does the famous "swastika squat" at the top of her leap.

15. One of Graham's least admirable ways of showing temperament was her tendency to strike dancers she knew could not hit her back. Louis Horst would slap her in return, but he had always held an elder mentor's role in her life. Then Hawkins began to respond in kind to her physical mistreatment. For hitting episodes in Graham's life, see De Mille, op. cit., pp. 275, 293, 301, 353. She also threw things—Horst's dachshund, telephone receivers torn from their cradles, loose pieces of furniture (ibid., pp. 63, 64, 145, 147).

16. De Mille, op. cit., p. 184. The dancers she had trained learned to duplicate this feat. Paul Taylor records his astonishment when he saw Helen McGehee do it. Taylor, op. cit., p. 116.

17. De Mille, op. cit., p. 368.

18. Ibid., p. 209.

19. The dancers for *Oklahoma!*, De Mille's most famous work of choreography, use the open mouths, and cupped hands vibrating around them, that Graham had invented to enact calls and cries. Ibid., p. 88.

20. McDonagh, op. cit., pp. 194–98. One actress, Anne Jackson, pays tribute to Graham's teaching on pp. 95–97 of *Martha Graham: The Evolution of Her Dance Theory and Training, 1926–1991*, ed. Marian Horosko (Chicago Review Press, 1991).

21. For Shawn's publicity stunts and hucksterism, see Doris Humphrey, *An Artist First* (Wesleyan University Press, 1972), pp. 54–56.

22. Taylor, op. cit., p. 41. Susan A. Manning rightly points out what modern dance in America owed to German *Ausdruckstanze*. She neglects, in fact, one of the principal channels of that influence—Louis Horst, whose year of

study in Vienna made him especially sensitive to developments in European modern dance. The film of Mary Wigman's *Witch Dance* (1930) shows how much Graham's "seated dance" was at home in the foreign repertory. But Manning may overreact to boasts of nationalism, since her subject, Wigman, carried nationalism to the extreme of Nazism. Cf. Manning, *Ecstasy and the Demon: Feminism and Nationalism in the Dances of Mary Wigman* (University of California Press, 1993).

23. De Mille, op. cit., pp. 163–64.
24. Ibid., pp. 344–48.
25. Graham initially danced in diaphanous costumes—as Agnes De Mille testifies, "Her wonderful breasts showed through" (op. cit., p. 88). See also the revealing costumes on her troupe in the photograph at p. 107 of Graham's own book *Blood Memory*.

Antitype: Madonna

1. Christopher Andersen, *Madonna Unauthorized* (Simon & Schuster, 1991), pp. 54–60.
2. E. Ann Kaplan, "Madonna Politics: Perversion, Repression, or Subversion? Or Masks and/or Master-y," in *The Madonna Connection: Representational Politics, Subcultural Identities, and Cultural Theory*, ed. Cathy Schwichtenberg (Westview Press, 1993), p. 156.
3. David Tetzloff, "Metatextural Girl: → patriarchy → postmodernism → power → money → Madonna," in Schwichtenberg, op. cit., p. 258.
4. Lisa Henderson, "Justify Our Love: Madonna and the Politics of Queer Sex," in Schwichtenberg, op. cit., p. 124: "With vigilance, her work can be articulated to our struggles."
5. Susan Bordo, " 'Material Girl': The Effacements of Postmodern Culture," in Schwichtenberg, op. cit. Prediet, Madonna "defied rather than rejected the male gaze (p. 283), but postdiet "she has self-normalized" (p. 285).
6. Andrew Greeley, "Like a Catholic: Madonna's Challenge to Her Church," in *Desperately Seeking Madonna*, ed. Adam (Delta Books, 1993), pp. 96–100. Father Greeley is an enthusiast—he had earlier urged Rome to canonize John F. Kennedy as a Doctor of the Church.
7. Marjorie Rosen, *Popcorn Venus: Women, Movies and the American Dream* (Avon, 1973), p. 161. According to Rosen, West had a "non-threatening, overextended rudeness and relish that embellished [Theda] Bara's vamp (whom she satirized)" (pp. 163–64).
8. Ibid., p. 162. The effect of the censors was serious in West's case, as Molly Haskell points out: "Mae West was forced to clean up her image and her dialogue and thereby committed professional suicide." Haskell, *From Reverence to Rape* (Penguin, 1974), p. 118.

9. Rosen, op. cit., p. 163.
10. Andersen, op. cit., pp. 42–48.
11. Parker Tyler, *The Hollywood Hallucination* (1944; Simon & Schuster, 1977), p. 99: "The scandalous sway of Miss West's hips—reminds me of nothing so much as the motion of a cradle."
12. Parker Tyler, *Screening the Sexes: Homosexuality in the Movies* (Anchor Books, 1973), p. 3.
13. Mick St. Michael, ed. *Madonna in Her Own Words* (Omnibus Press, 1990), p. 76.
14. Kevin Sessums, "White Heat," *Vanity Fair*, April 1990, p. 208.

14. RHETORICAL LEADER: MARTIN LUTHER KING, JR.

1. Roger Ailes, with Jon Kraushar, *You Are the Message: Secrets of the Master Communicators* (Dow Jones-Irwin, 1988).
2. Cicero, *On the Orator*. Marcus Antonius is the critic of special training in oratory: "What is more beside the mark than speaking about speaking? Every speech is beside the mark unless nothing else will serve" (112).
3. Mogens Herman Hansen, *The Athenian Assembly* (Basil Blackwell, 1987), pp. 14–19.
4. Ibid., pp. 50–63.
5. On the importance of enunciation, cf. Cicero, *Brutus* 210–15.
6. Peter Brown, *Power and Persuasion* (University of Wisconsin Press, 1992), pp. 35–70.
7. Cicero, *On the Orator* 17–18.
8. Clayborne Carson et al., eds., *The Papers of Martin Luther King, Jr.* (University of California Press, 1992), vol. 1, p. 107.
9. Ibid., p. 48.
10. Ibid., p. 2.
11. Ibid., p. 7.
12. Keith D. Miller, *Voice of Deliverance: The Language of Martin Luther King, Jr. and Its Sources* (Free Press, 1992).
13. This explains though it does not justify the intellectual and moral blind spot that made King plagiarize, on such a blissfully grand scale, in his academic work. He was warned from his earliest days that he did not cite sources properly (see *Papers of MLK*, vol. 1, pp. 127, 130). But he continued without a qualm, and without any real effort to disguise what he was doing. He even plagiarized himself. An editor had to point out that much of one book he submitted to a publisher was taken from another book he had already published. See David J. Garrow, *Bearing the Cross: Martin Luther King, Jr., and the Southern Christian Leadership Crisis* (Morrow, 1986), p. 544. Normal as this kind of borrowing was among preachers, it is inexcus-

able in academic terms, and I believe his doctorate should be rescinded by Boston University. (I also think John Kennedy's Pulitzer Prize, won in an even greater exercise of false pretense, should be rescinded—for one thing this would make judges of prizes and examiners of doctoral students more conscientious at their work.) We do not admire King for his scholarship. He earned greater prizes, from the Nobel award to the martyr's palm. The ideas in his college papers were not his. But, as Cyrano said of Christian, "the blood is his."

14. *Papers of MLK*, vol. 1, p. 105.

15. Ibid., p. 47.

16. Cf. G. K. Chesterton, *Varied Types* (Dodd, Mead, 1903), p. 78: "It is not song that is the narrow or artificial thing, it is conversation that is a broken and stammering attempt at song."

17. Cicero, *Brutus* 185: "*Efficiatur . . . ut afficiuntur.*"

18. For King's hesitating, groping way forward into his vocation, see Taylor Branch's superb *Parting the Waters: America in the King Years, 1954–1963* (Simon & Schuster, 1988). For the years after 1963, see David J. Garrow, op. cit.

19. Miller, op. cit., p. 146.

20. Text of the March on Washington speech from James M. Washington, ed., *A Testament of Hope: The Essential Writings and Speeches of Martin Luther King, Jr.* (Harper San Francisco, 1986), pp. 217–20. But I correct the misprint "languished" for "anguished," from the recording of the speech. For the preparation of the speech, and departures from it in delivery, see Branch, op. cit., pp. 875–83, and Garrow, op. cit., pp. 283–84.

Antitype: Robert Parris Moses

1. The best treatment of Robert Moses' tortured witness is in Taylor Branch, *Parting the Waters*.

15. OPPORTUNISTIC LEADER: CESARE BORGIA

1. James MacGregor Burns, *Leadership* (Harper & Row, 1978), p. 24, on what he imagines was medieval autocracy: "Authority was quite one-sided. Rulers had the right to command, subjects the obligation to obey."

2. David Hume, "Of the First Principles of Government": "The sultan of Egypt or the emperor of Rome might *drive* his harmless subjects, like brute beasts, against their sentiments and inclinations; but he must at least have *led* his marmadukes or praetorian bands, like men, by their opinions." Eugene F. Miller, ed., *Essays Moral, Political, and Literary*, (Liberty Classics, 1985), p. 32.

3. St. Augustine, *The City of God* 19.12.
4. Ibid.
5. William Shakespeare, *Henry IV, Part Three* 3.12.193. Richard says this, in the play's historical setting, five years before Machiavelli was even born and sixty eight years before *Il Principe* was published (1532).
6. It is often said that English has no equivalent of *virtù*, but "mastery" fits all of its uses. It is neutral toward "morality" without excluding it (as in "self-mastery"). It keeps the assertively *male* quality of the word—*vir* in Latin corresponding to master (mister) in English.
7. *Il Principe*, chap. 25. For the sense of *impetuoso*, "headlong," see Mark Phillips, *Francesco Guicciardini: The Historical Craft* (University of Toronto Press, 1977), pp. 168–73. Machiavelli could find the dialectic of *virtù* and *fortuna* running throughout his classical sources. See, for instance, the Machiavellian interplay at Cicero, *On Manilius' Law* 10:

> His early conquests have to be assigned to his valor (*virtus*), not his good fortune (*felicitas*); while his later reversals stem not from his defect (*culpa*) but his luck (*fortuna*).

See the same orator's speech *On Clemency to Marcellus* 5: "*Fortuna* lays the major claim to events and, where success is concerned, thinks it almost entirely hers."
8. The Homeric simile, often imitated, is at *Iliad* 16.384.92. Machiavelli put the same image into rhyme for his poem on Luck (vv. 151–57).

> As a swift torrent runs
> over its bounds to smash
> What it reaches; and comes
>
> Lifting and lowering lands,
> Reshaping its banks and bed,
> Shaking earth to its sands.
>
> So Fate trips along
> Turning things up-down
> Backward-forward, right-wrong.

Mario Martelli, *Niccolò Machiavelli: Tutte le opere* (Sansoni, 1971), p. 979.
9. *Discourses* 2.23. Valentino's execution of an unpopular subordinate left his subjects "approving, though dumbstruck"—*soddisfatti e stupidi* (*Il Principe*, chap. 7). Cf. *Discourses* 2.23.
10. *Discourses* 1.6, 2.23.

11. Fredi Chiapelli, *Machiavelli: Legazioni, commissarie, scritti di governo* (Giuseppe Laterza & Figli, 1984), vol. 2, pp. 114–15.
12. Ibid., p. 120.
13. Ibid., p. 121. "Altrimenti voi intenderete presto! presto!" *Presto* is the leit-motif of Valentino and those around him, according to Machiavelli's report (see pp. 122, 123, 124).
14. Ibid., p. 125.
15. *Presto* continues to be a key word—cf. Chiapelli, op. cit., pp. 198, 203.
16. For Florentine criticism of Machiavelli's independent ways as an emissary, see John M. Najemy, "The Controversy Surrounding Machiavelli's Service to the Republic," in Gisela Bock et al., *Machiavelli and Republicanism* (Cambridge University Press, 1990), pp. 101–17.
17. Ibid., pp. 274–77 (November 8, 1502).
18. Ibid., p. 203.
19. Ibid., p. 263.
20. Ibid., pp. 248–49 (October 27).
21. The truce terms are in Chiapelli, op. cit., pp. 280–82.
22. Ibid., p. 307.
23. Ibid., p. 317 (November 28).
24. Ibid., p. 324 (December 2).
25. Something of the two men's relationship can be seen in an exchange re-counted in Machiavelli's December 6 dispatch. The duke told Machiavelli he had heard of a Florentine plot against him from Paolo Orsini, who had read about it in some letters. Machiavelli asked if Orsini had shown the letter to the duke, and whether, in the past, Orsini had invariably told him the turth. The duke answered that, in fact, Orsini had told him many lies—and "laughter concluded the matter" (ibid., p. 330). Machiavelli as-sured his masters in Florence that he tried to read Valentino's gestures and facial expressions as well as his words, probing for what lay behind his abrupt switches of tactic and mood (ibid., p. 349).
26. Ibid., p. 362 (December 23).
27. Ibid., p. 365 (December 26).
28. See, for instance, Bradford, op cit., pp. 202–3.
29. Chiapelli, op. cit., p. 370 (January 1).
30. See, for instance, Allan Gilbert, *Machiavelli: The Chief Works* (Duke University Press, 1965), vol. 1, p. 163.
31. Chiapelli, op. cit., p. 240 (October 23).
32. Ibid., p. 261 (November 1).
33. Ibid., p. 274 (November 8).
34. Even Gennaro Sasso, in his fine monograph on Machiavelli's attitude to-ward Valentino, accepts the idea of inconsistencies between the dispatches

and the "Description": *Machiavelli e Cesare Borgia: Storia di un giudizio* (Ateneo, 1966), pp. 87–88, 183.

35. Francesco Guicciardini, *The History of Italy*, trans. Sidney Alexander (Princeton University Press, 1969), pp. 165–66.
36. Sasso makes a convincing case for this view (op. cit., pp. 101–4). And see Najemy, op. cit., p. 107.
37. Machiavelli had predicted that Julius, famous for *keeping* his word, would soon *break* it with Valentino. By November 26 he was able to write of a prophecy fulfilled: "It is seen how the Pope, ever so honorably, writes paid to his debts—with a sponge for his pen!" Chiapelli, op. cit., 3.194.
38. Guicciardini, op. cit., pp. 168–69. Guicciardini did not agree with all of Machiavelli's judgments on Valentino. But on this they were in accord. Cf. *Il Principe*, chap. 7: "This point I do not want to lose in the background, since it deserves study and imitation by others: the Duke found, when he conquered the Romagna, that it had been governed feebly by men who did more to rob than to rule their subjects, and divided them rather than united, so that the province teemed with bandits, marauders and all kinds of violence. He decided that *the only way to reduce it to order, to acquiescence in the ruling power, was to give it proper government* (buon governo)."
39. Chiapelli, op. cit., p. 108 (November 4, 1503).
40. Ibid, p. 201 (November 28).
41. Martelli, op. cit., pp. 948–49, *Decennale Primo*, vv. 463–65, 472–74; Gilbert, op. cit., vol. 3, p. 1455.
42. Guicciardini, op. cit., p. 166;

> Valentino, gravely ill in the [Vatican] palace, gathered all his men around him, and although he had always previously thought, partly by the terror of his arms and partly by the favor of the new Spanish cardinals, of whom there were eleven, to elect a pontiff of his own choosing after his father's death, now, because of his very dangerous illness, he had much more difficulty than he had earlier imagined in carrying out this or any other of his schemes. For this reason, he complained with the greatest indignation that although he had formerly often anticipated all the difficulties that might result from his father's death, it had never occurred to him that he also might happen to be impeded by a dangerous illness at the same time. Therefore, having to frame his counsels not to plans previously made but to *unexpected necessity*. . . .

43. *Il Principe*, chap. 7.

44. I do not translate the title of *Il Principe* because it is a technical term not covered by the word "prince." We tend to think of a prince as a legitimate heir in some kingly line. *Principato* was "one-man rule" for Machiavelli, legitimate or illegitimate, kingly or priestly or military, it did not matter. For his purposes, the only important distinction was between old (established) and new forms of one-man rule. The latter was the more difficult kind, but one made necessary by the shifting conditions of Machiavelli's day.

45. Bacon, in his essay "Of Honor and Reputation," distinguished the most honorable roles by their degrees of glory and importance. For superiors, the offices of honor are:

   1. *Conditores imperiorum.* Founders of states.
   2. *Legislatores.* Lawgivers, who are second founders.
   3. *Liberatores.* Saviors of endangered or captive states.
   4. *Propugnatores imperii.* Soldiers who defend the state.
   5. *Patres patriae.* Good rulers.

   For subjects, here are the offices of honor.

   1. *Participes curarum.* Advisors to the ruler.
   2. *Duces belli.* Subordinate military officers.
   3. *Gratiosi.* Friends of the ruler.
   4. *Negotiis pares.* Diplomats.

   Machiavelli, in this scheme, began at the fourth grade of a subject's honor, moved up to the third rank as Piero Soderini's friend, and held the first rank when he advised Soderini officially.

46. Machiavelli follows Plutarch in praising the classical founders who first set up a state and then absented themselves to prevent a cult of one man (*Discourses* 1.9). But Guicciardini says that such self-abnegation is unlikely in one who has tasted the deliciousness of power (*la dolcezza della potenzia*). Besides, good rulers are so rare that one who does occur should be encouraged to stay in power, for fear of a worse one following. Cf. Francesco Guicciardini, *Scritti politici e recordi*, ed. Roberto Palmarocchi (Giuseppe Laterza & Figli, 1933), p. 18.

47. This satirizing interpretation began in the sixteenth century with Cardinal Reginald Pole, who believed "that Machiavelli had written the book with the secret intention of ruining the house of Medici," and continued into the time of Leopold von Ranke, who thought that "Machiavelli, recognizing the desperate disease of Italy, had the courage to prescribe poison." (Cf. L. Arthur Burd, *"Il Principe" by Niccolò Machiavelli* (Oxford University Press, 1891), pp. 36–37.

48. *Discourses* 1.10.

49. Garrett Mattingly, "Machiavelli," in *The Renaissance* (American Heritage, 1961), pp. 57–64, esp. p. 60 on Valentino as "a ruthless gangster and an expert confidence man" mistaken by Machiavelli for "a great prince, subtle, inscrutable, dangerous." See also Mattingly, *Renaissance Diplomacy* (1955; Penguin, 1964), pp. 101, 113, for "Machiavelli's praise of the Borgian blunderer."

50. J. G. A. Pocock is perceptive in his treatment of Machiavelli's horrified-intrigued attitude toward innovation, though I believe he goes too far when he says Machiavelli thought of *virtù* as "an innovative force." *Virtù* is many-sided; it can even be a mastery of the ancestral arts of preserving good government. *The Machiavellian Moment: Florentine Political Thought and the Atlantic Republic Tradition* (Princeton University Press, 1975), pp. 156–67, esp. p. 166. For the association of harshness with the new, see *Il Principe*, chap. 17, which quotes Dido's lament in Vergil (*Aeneid* 2.563):

> Brute need and my reign's newness drive me . . .
> *Res dura et regni novitas me talia cogunt . . .*

51. Phillips, op. cit., p. 88.
52. Guicciardini, *Scritti*, p. 51 (*Considerazioni*, chap. 12, dealing with Machiavelli's *Discourses* 2.12).
53. In his poem on Luck, Machiavelli replaces the single "Wheel of Fortune" of normal iconography with a clockwork of interconnected (but *not* mechanically determined) wheels:

> In her house wheels are whirling,
> As many as man's yearnings,
> The goals he holds as sterling. . .
>
> The man of fixed desire
> Must leap from wheel to wheel
> To keep on mounting higher.

I Capitali: Di Fortuna, vv. 61–63, 115–117 (Martelli, op. cit., pp. 977–78; Gilbert op. cit., vol. 2, pp. 746–47).

54. *Il Principe*, chap. 12.
55. Ibid., chap. 20.
56. Ibid., chap. 10.
57. Ibid.
58. *Discourses* 2.24 (Martelli, op. cit., p. 181; Gilbert, op. cit., vol. 1, pp. 192–93). Guicciardini mocked this argument, saying that *any* physical equipment of war would have to be surrendered if trust in the subjects'

feelings were the only firm resource for rulers (*Scritti*, p. 58). For Machi-avelli's entire doctrine on fortifications—which did not prevent him from serving on the Florentine commission for the upkeep of the city walls—see J. R. Hale, "To Fortify or Not to Fortify? Machiavelli's Contribution to a Renaissance Debate," in Hale, *Renaissance War Studies* (Hambledon Press, 1983), pp. 189–210.

59. *Il Principe*, chap. 3.
60. Ibid., chap. 21.

> That *principe* is respected who is a true friend or an open foe—the kind who joins one side or the other without reserve.

For fraud as preferable to force in dealing with a foe, see *Discourses* 2.13. It should be remembered that Valentino was dealing with enemies at Sini-gaglia—a category to which he had relegated them ever since the formation of their conspiracy at Magione.

61. *Il Principe*, chap. 17 (Burd, p. 293). Cf. *Discourses* 2.26.
62. The ratio of conquest to control is spelled out in passages like *Il Principe*, chap. 4 (Burd, pp. 201–2):

> One would have great trouble acquiring the Turkish realm; but great ease in holding it, once conquered. . . . The contrary is true of re-gions governed like that of France, to which one could gain access by buying off some local baron (since there are plenty of discontented ones, or ones disposed to change). Those types, I say, can afford you entry and an easy victory; but then holding on will involve you in endless difficulty, both with these helpers and with those you have conquered.

63. Michelangelo created idealized portrait statues of both the dedicatees of *Il Principe*. Machiavelli first dedicated the book to Giuliano di Medici; but when Giuliano died (1516), he changed the dedication, now naming his brother, Lorenzo. Since Lorenzo, too, died shortly after (1519), the broth-ers were included in Michelangelo's vast project for the Medici chapel in the New Sacristy of San Lorenzo. Giuliano was made a figure of action and Lorenzo of contemplation. Giuliano's torso has the torque to his left of Michelangelo's figures dealing with an evil world—the David, the judging Christ of the Sistine wall, the Moses, the bust of Brutus. Machiavelli and Michelangelo both idealize Giuliano, and in the same direction, toward a heroism that must grapple with fate. Cf. Erwin Panofsky, "The Neoplatonic Movement and Michelangelo," in *Studies in Iconology: Humanistic Themes in the Art of the Renaissance* (Harper & Row, 1972), pp. 199–212.

64. *Il Principe*, chap. 18:

> You must recognize that there are two ways of doing battle—one by way of law, the other by way of force. The first one is proper to man, the second to beasts, but since the first one is often unavailing, seeking aid from the second is appropriate. Therefore a *principe* must know how to deploy both the beast and the man. This aspect of the *principe* was subtly indicated by the ancient writers who wrote how Achilles and many other ancient *principi* were turned over to be raised by Chiron the centaur, who kept them under his tutelage. Having a teacher who was half beast and half man had no other point than to show this need for a *principe* to understand how to employ, now one, now the other, since one *without* the other cannot survive. And since deploying the beast is necessary for a *principe*, the best ones for him to take are the lion and the fox, since the lion cannot escape snares on his own, any more than a fox can escape wolves.

Machiavelli's source was Cicero *On Duties* 1.11:

> Since there are two ways of settling conflict, either by discussion or by violence, and since the former is proper to man, the latter to beasts, one must seek shelter in the latter if use of the former is not feasible.

The use of animal qualities was a constant concern of classical antiquity—in Homer's similes, in Aesop's fables, and in war images like this from Pindar (*Isthmian Odes* 4.45–48, Snell, 2nd ed.):

> Dashing in fray as the wildest lion,
> but tricky as a fox feigning death
> when the eagle whirs down on him—
> whatever it takes to kill a foe.

65. For the Titian allegory in London's National Gallery, cf. Erwin Panofsky, "Titian's Allegory of Prudence: A Postscript," in *Meaning in the Visual Arts* (University of Chicago, 1955), pp. 146–68. The portraits are of Titian (the old man), his own son Orazio (the mature man), and his nephew Mario Vecelli (the boy). The triple beast-face comes from Egyptian representations of Serapis as reinterpreted in the Renaissance. The allegory of Prudence is derived from Piero Valeriano's *Hieroglyphica* (1555).

Antitype: Piero Soderini

1. Roslyn Pesman Cooper, "Piero Soderini: Aspiring Prince or Civic Leader?" in *Studies in Mediaeval and Renaissance History*, New Series, vol. 1 (University of British Columbia Press, 1978), pp. 69–126. Her thesis is stated on p. 74: "Rather than as an aspiring prince, Soderini might be regarded as a model of an anti-*Principe*." Guicciardini, speaking for the aristocrats who considered Soderini "a traitor to his class," claimed that he was a schemer, and many historians have followed his lead. But see the support given Cooper (and Machiavelli) by Robert Black, "Machiavelli, Servant of the Florentine Republic," in *Machiavelli and Republicanism*, ed. Gisela Block et al. (Cambridge University Press, 1990), pp. 92–94.
2. Black, op. cit., p. 87.
3. Cf. H. C. Butters, *Governors and Government in Early Sixteenth-Century Florence, 1502–1579* (Oxford University Press, 1985), pp. 308–10.
4. Niccolò Machiavelli, *Discourses on the First Ten Books of Titus Livius* 3.3.
5. *Il Principe*, chap. 6. Cf. "Machiavelli and Savonarola" in Burd's edition of *Il Principe* (Oxford University Press, 1891), pp. 373–78.

16. SAINTLY LEADER: DOROTHY DAY

1. William James, *The Varieties of Religious Experience* (1902; Library of America, 1987), p. 330.
2. Ibid., p. 316. Cf. James's description of the adolescent Jesuit saint, Aloysius Gonzaga (p. 322):

> When the intellect, as in this Louis, is originally no larger than a pin's head, and cherishes ideas of God of corresponding smallness, the result, notwithstanding the heroism put forth, is on the whole repulsive.

3. Ibid., p. 335.
4. John Ruskin, *Roadside Songs of Tuscany* (Library Edition; George Allen, 1907), vol. 32, p. 72.
5. James, op. cit., p. 325.
6. William D. Miller, *Dorothy Day: A Biography* (Harper & Row, 1982), p. 311.
7. Dorothy Day, *The Long Loneliness* (Harper & Brothers, 1952), p. 22.
8. Ibid., p. 34.
9. Ibid., p. 83. The suffragists were not allowed to bathe, in those days of segregation, since black women had been in their communal tubs.

10. Ibid., p. 83: "I had seen myself too weak to stand alone, too weak to face the darkness of that punishment cell without crying out, and I was ashamed and again rejected religion."

11. Day never told this story in her writings, but an account of it was given by her roommate of the period, Agnes Boulton, who had been drinking with the company before Holladay's death, and went back with Day while the body was being examined by the police (Miller, op. cit., pp. 113–15).

12. In one of her long interviews with the psychiatrist Robert Coles, Day described walking along the East River with one death-shadowed youth in "a sort of sexual silence." Coles, *Dorothy Day* (Addison-Wesley, 1987), p. 151.

13. Miller, op. cit., pp. 128–29.

14. See June O'Connor, *The Moral Vision of Dorothy Day: A Feminist Perspective* (Crossroad Publishing Co., 1991), p. 18: "At novel's end, June [the Day character], an adult working woman, remained a willing participant in a stirring adolescent fantasy." Years later, in her Catholic retreat notes, Day herself wrote, "All day in a state of unrest, feeling how M. [Moise] 'had women hypnotized' " (Miller, op. cit., p. 399).

15. We have no direct evidence of the way she "weighed" her sins, since she was normally reticent about the whole period unless prodded by others or correcting accounts written by her earlier companions. Her first autobiography, *From Union Square to Rome* (1938), gave few details of her "godless" days. Her second, *The Long Loneliness* (1952), was more forthcoming, since other people's memories of her had been published in the interval.

16. Day, op. cit., p. 148.

17. James, op. cit., pp. 213–18.

18. Maurin, from a large and pious family, spent years as a Christian Brother and seven years in a lay activist group (Le Sillon) before leaving France for Canada, where he tried to manage a farm. After some vagrant years in America during which he lapsed from his Catholicism, he began steady work as a French teacher in 1917, first in St. Louis, then in the Woodstock area of New York. He underwent a conversion experience there, and began teaching without pay, earning his food by manual labor. His teaching had turned to a continual seminar on the Gospels by the time he went to New York City in the early thirties, where he read in the public library, buttonholed people in Union Square, and haunted Catholic journalists' offices. Cf. Marc Ellis, *Peter Maurin: Prophet in the Twentieth Century* (Paulist Press, 1981).

19. Day's work received widespread recognition outside her church after Dwight Macdonald published a sympathetic *New Yorker* profile of her in two parts (October 4 and 11, 1952).

20. "Oh, far-off day of American freedom, when Karl Marx could write for the

morning *Tribune* in New York" (Day, *Loaves and Fishes* [Harper & Row, 1963], p. 13).

21. Ibid., p. 176.
22. Miller, op. cit., pp. 487–90.

Antitype: Ammon Hennacy

1. On Hennacy's wooing of Day, see Miller, op. cit., pp. 423–26. On Hennacy's relish for pretty girls, see Day's wry comment that he admired the Mormons for their polygamy (*Loaves and Fishes*, pp. 114–15).
2. Patrick G. Coy, "The One-Person Revolution of Ammon Hennacy," in *A Revolution of the Heart: Essays on the Catholic Worker* (Temple University Press, 1988), p. 147.
3. Day, *Loaves*, p. 106.
4. Edward M. Still, Introduction to *The Correspondence of Mother Jones* (University of Pittsburgh Press, 1985), p. xxiii.
5. Day, *Loaves*, p. 112.
6. Ibid., p. 109.
7. Coy, op. cit., p. 153.
8. Ibid., pp. 167–68.
9. James, op. cit., p. 340.

Acknowledgments

—•—

F riends and students helped me, over the years, in the intellectual game of choosing and criticizing exemplars of leadership. It is a subject that has intrigued me in my work on various presidents and political figures; but I have felt with increasing urgency that we unduly limit ourselves when we look mainly to elected officials to give us leadership. There are many important forms of guidance—spiritual, intellectual, artistic. The search for different types of leaders made me consult people expert in different areas of social interaction. I thank all those who read parts of the book and gave me their valuable criticism—especially Taylor Branch, W. Robert Connor, Marc Giordano, Delbert Hillers, Bernard Knox, Robert Lerner, Martin Marty, William McFeely, Edward Muir, Alex Owen, Edward Renehan, William Safire, Geoffrey Ward, and Rudolph Weingartner. None, of course, is responsible for advice *not* taken. I translated all passages not expressly assigned to another translator.

My editor, Alice Mayhew, helped shape the book. Her associate, Eric Steel, was continually supportive—Natalie Goldstein and Garry L. Wills helped with the illustrations. My conscientious typists were Katie Melody and Joan Stahl. Natalie Wills, as always, did a bit of everything.

Index